Motorcycle Journeys Through

New England

Fourth Edition

Ken Aiken

Whitehorse Press
Center Conway, New Hampshire

Whitehorse Press books are also available at discounts in bulk quantity for sales and promotional use. For details about special sales or for a catalog of motorcycling books, videos, and gear write to the publisher:

Whitehorse Press
107 East Conway Road
Center Conway, New Hampshire 03813
Phone: 603-356-6556 or 800-531-1133
E-mail: CustomerService@WhitehorsePress.com
Internet: www.WhitehorsePress.com

ISBN 978-1-884313-27-1

5 4 3 2 1

Printed in China

Acknowledgments

There are numerous people who have befriended me in my travels, many whose names I don't even know, but I thank them for their acts of kindness.

Mike Manning and Dunlop for the thousands of miles of rubber that was necessary to ride these roads and Andy Goldfine, whose gear has kept me safe despite myself.

Alex Fauver and Lucas Brown for their cheerfulness and attention to detail as they cross-checked data to create the maps for this book. With or without two wheels, they'll be going far.

Jim LeClair of the Maine Coast Welcome Center for organizing my exploration of coastal Maine and providing superb advice about areas I was unfamiliar with. Debbie Mossman of the Berkshires Visitors Bureau for her efforts on my behalf and Andrea McHugh of the Newport Convention & Visitors Bureau for her assistance in arranging the itinerary of my visit to that fascinating city.

Ralph and Donna Aiken whose unwavering support and assistance made this project feasible and Ewa Spoczynska for putting up with my absences while I'm on the road.

Finally, I wish to acknowledge Dan and Judy Kennedy of Whitehorse Press, whose support has always been far greater than simply being publishers, and to this book's editor, Lisa Dionne, whose passion for excellence has improved every page. Thank you for your friendship over the years.

Stop for a wicked good cup o' joe with Jim and Patti LeClair at the Maine Coast Welcome Center in Belfast, an information oasis where you can fine-tune your travel plans.

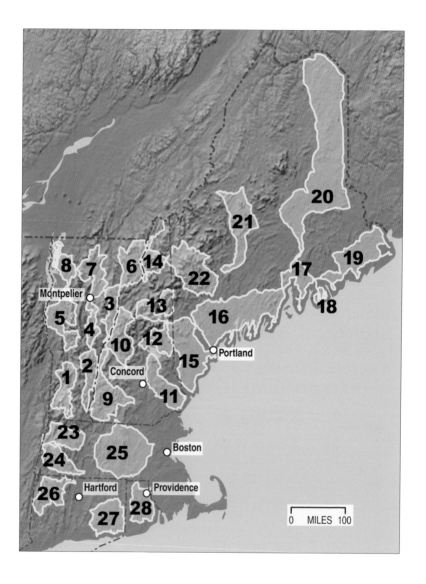

Contents

Introduction

On weekend car rides as a child, my father would point out different land-marks, ponder about what people did for a living in various villages, and tell stories about the places we rode through. We traveled the backroads and watched the interstate highways being built, witnesses to history past and future. Travel thus became something other than covering distance, more than just focusing on the boundaries of pavement, and spurred an avid interest in how the here-and-now came to be.

The pace and the immediacy of touring on two wheels is especially well suited to pondering and appreciating the land and the ongoing forces—both natural and man-made—that continue to shape New England. Roads often follow paths whose origins can be traced to cart roads, which evolved from native and pre-colonial trade routes, which may have begun as game trails. Back then, geographic obstacles were typically circumnavigated or accommodated, leaving routes which rise, fall, and sweep with contours that

A photo op at the Albany Covered Bridge near Conway, New Hampshire.

During colonial times, most New England towns had a public "green" much like this one in Craftsbury Commons, Vermont.

are natural to their traditionally wild settings, instead of the more sedate expectations of modern transportation.

Much of what we have all come to internalize as distinctly "American" had its roots in the upper right-hand corner of what would eventually become the United States, to slowly seep westward with its human tide. By appreciating how these foundational influences eventually may have come to underpin our broader image of ourselves, New England can be a unique destination, one in which connections can appear everywhere—if you know where and how to look. That's where I come in. There are many threads to chase—history, philosophy, architecture, industry—but I've tried to keep a few going that you can appreciate both in local detail and with a wider lens, some meant to add color and context to the extrasensory movie on your visor, others to offer a leg-stretcher worthy of deploying the sidestand. And others because they are just too quirky, unique, or fascinating *not* to mention. To experience such things is why we travel, no?

Lastly, we ride—and you and I know what that means. I've tried to include the sort of information that is important to us, and often overlooked in other guidebooks and travel media. And, if I understand us right, we also enjoy the kind of unexpected discoveries that you can make wholly on your own, the result of your own curiosity or serendipity. To that end, I encourage you to explore beyond these pages, both on the roads themselves and in chasing down some of the forgotten stories and curious details that are bound to catch your fancy along the way.

A BIT OF GEOLOGY

Much more of New England remains rural or undeveloped than one might imagine if the conclusion were formed on an outsized impression of its most notable cities against a backdrop that seems awfully small to folks from larger, more rectangular states. Long, exposed vistas of terrain both tortured and serene, however, make it hard not to think in terms that are bigger than our own short span of recorded history.

A lot of what you can see today was formed or shaped by a continental sheet of ice that existed a mere 12,000 years ago. Picture a wall of ice a mile and a half high advancing southward like a giant bulldozer blade, scouring giant trenches, tearing at even the toughest mountains, and plowing rock, sand, and dirt ahead of itself. When the front edge of the glacier stopped advancing, it left titanic piles of detritus to form what we now call Long Island, Block Island, Cape Cod, Martha's Vineyard, and Nantucket. As the ice retreated (melted backward), huge whales of compacted material were randomly left behind, as were miles-long serpentine walls of sand and gravel formed by great rivers that ran beneath the melting ice. Boulders were left perched in highly unlikely places, and scooped-out depressions filled with water. The mountains, which had been pushed from the northwest during the advance, were left moderately sloping in that direction, with crumbling, craggy cliffs on their southeastern faces.

This was, of course, accomplished at a truly glacial pace of about 245 feet a year. Estimates posit that it took 4,300 years for the glacial edge to retreat

The frequency of yard sales along the highways—especially on Saturday mornings—means you must be ready for unpredictable stops by drivers.

from the coast of Connecticut to St. Johnsbury, Vermont. As we traverse the political, cultural, and geographic diversity that is New England, I've tried to keep a running commentary of some of the more interesting local evidence of its pre-history. Its legacy might take the form of a productive commercial sand or gravel pit, a small quarry or mineral site, or one of the

Whee!

innumerable stone walls so commonly found at the edges of an old, cleared field.

To this arcana, let me add some common everyday terminology that you may not have heard in your neck of the woods: a "gap" is a low point in a mountain range, what would be called a "pass" somewhere else. "Notches" are longer than gaps and were carved by glacial ice during the last ice age; elsewhere they might be classified as canyons. "Gulfs" have nothing to do with the ocean; they were the outlets of vast post-glacial lakes carved by water rushing between mountains.

Bear, deer, moose—you never know what might cross your path in New England.

A BIT OF HISTORY

Most scholars have come to agree that present-day New England was far from empty territory when the first European settlers arrived, with complex political and trade networks between Native American tribes. Most of their history, however, has been recorded as raids and uprisings against the inexorable encroachment on their land and way of life, and what little remained after that onslaught was typically absorbed or pushed further into the wilderness to the north and west.

Except for the very first intrepid Europeans to risk journeying into the unknown, this portion of the New World was settled by means of the imperial nations bequeathing vast grants of land for colonies, with subsequent grants to colonial governors for surveyed townships. Although the names of many new towns invariably paid homage to a place of origin, British royalty, or a relevant person of the time, many monikers harken back to indigenous heroes or traditional descriptions. "Massachusetts" was the name of a regional tribe, while "Connecticut" is the English interpretation of a Mohegan word meaning, "upon the long river."

Vermont and Maine were not part of the original thirteen colonies, and their names derive from French. The former was a part of New Hampshire, and then the independent Republic of Vermont from 1777 to 1791, before becoming the 14th state. Maine was originally part of Massachusetts and entered the Union as the 23rd state in 1820. The northern border between New England and Canada was not established until 1843.

Mount Desert Island, as seen from the Schoodic Peninsula.

In addition to the role it played in our collective independence from Great Britain, New England remained at the fore of our country's initial transition from a strictly agrarian to a more industralized economy. The rivers that had provided transport for raw materials were harnessed to power the mills, factories, and furnaces that would invite a new wave of future citizens to our shores, seeking opportunities for improving their lives alongside the individual freedoms to speak, worship, and participate in governing the world they lived in.

Today, when enough time has passed to cushion and transform an economic "failure," you'll often find that what remains is a richly-layered portrait of a region's resilience. And, quite often, someone has taken pains to rescue, restore, and preserve the formative history and artifacts that detail its links to the past and its connections to the present and future. Abandoned 19th-century mills and brick factories are being repurposed into this next phase, as condominiums, galleries, stores, and museums to serve the vibrant communities that are slowly rebounding around them.

The Small House, at the living history museum of Old Sturbridge Village, wouldn't seem out of place in many parts of Vermont or New Hampshire.

TOWNS & VILLAGES

That many traditional New England towns share a similar layout and feel is something so obvious that it often goes without remark, a ubiquity so accepted that it conjures no curiosity as to its origin—unless it happens to differ from your own norms. There are lots of misconceptions about the origin of the town common typically found at the center of an old community, and each story is very, very different, but there is, in fact, a pattern at the core.

An All-American lobstah boat.

The first settlements in the New World were often enclosed in palisades behind which people and livestock could be protected from outside threats. As some of these concerns became less pressing, stockades were less imperative, but holders of land grant charters would often plan nucleated communities of home lots, with farm plots and common grazing and logging lots arranged around the larger periphery. Included among the former would be an allocation of land for ecclesiastical use, upon which a meeting house would be erected, whose purpose would unquestioningly include more secular functions.

Church services of the times were mandatory, all-day affairs, broken only by a short "nooning." Sheds and warming houses were erected nearby to provide some comfort in cold and nasty weather, though very few have survived. Taverns came to offer similar services, while other important community resources, such as the blacksmith shop, would invariably gravitate toward this center of public activity. Paths cutting between buildings on what would largely be an open (and even unsightly) lot often became the main thoroughfares through a village and, with a little imagination, you can

Roadside treasures.

start to picture how it all might have looked before it was carved into pieces and meted out according to the whims and needs of its citizenry.

Before you head off to explore New England, I had best explain the difference between a city, town, village, and gore. Townships are much like cities, but governed by an elected town manager and selectmen. As the *only* true democracies in North America, their citizens vote on everything from school budgets to purchasing new fire trucks. Villages within townships are either incorporated (with their own government) or unincorporated (managed by the town). Gores are unincorporated areas without any local government and extremely sparse to non-existent populations. In Maine, a "plantation" is a sparsely populated area with a limited form of local government, sort of halfway between a gore and an unincorporated village. In this book, I use the word town, village, settlement, and hamlet to denote a populated area, but when appropriate I will clarify a place as being the Town of Rockingham or Rockingham village (note that sometimes the proper name includes a capitalized form of the word "village"—as in Manchester Village). In this context, the word "city" does not denote size, but a form of government: Bennington, Vermont (pop. 15,737), is a town; Vergennes, Vermont (pop. 2,741), is a city.

The population figures for New England towns can be confusing or misleading, since residents are concentrated in some areas and dispersed in others. And seasonal tourism can skew the impression even further. Some towns and villages have a small population of residents, but tourism makes the place seem much larger. Freeport, Maine, only has 1,880 *residents,* but more than 10,000 visitors a day! Brookfield, Vermont, has 1,222 residents, but there isn't a single settlement in the township that exceeds 100 people.

HITTING THE ROAD

Obviously, the maps in this book are for reference purposes only, and you will probably want to supplement your information with more detailed resources. In turn-by-turn directions, please note that any data enclosed in [square brackets] denotes supplemental information—including sites of interest, turns for side trips, etc.—that may deviate from the main route in the text.

The trips outlined in this book tend to avoid some of the busiest stretches of traffic, but even when a popular destination is courting tourism, you can usually find a way around it with a little planning and timing. For

A sugar shack at the bottom of an incandescent stand of maples near Woodstock, Vermont.

Thousands of years ago, gulfs, like this one in Williamson, served as outlets for water in the post-glacial Champlain Sea.

example, if you can swing it, the stretch between Labor Day and Columbus Day can be an especially great time to visit: midweek traffic may be reduced to a trickle after the kids go back to school; the weather can be gorgeous, with leaves beginning to turn; and even the most seasonal of far-flung resort amenities will still be open and likely, quite welcoming.

Some of the older roads I point out, especially ones that are gated in winter, could have been constructed on a roadbed that, to understate the case, might not be up to modern specs, with maintenance standards as varied as the towns overseeing them. Ride within the limits of what you can see. A local out to enjoy a lunchtime loop might be well aware that the slight rise and fall of the pavement obscures a hazard—perhaps a gaping, parallel crack or a frost heave the size and consistency of a sunken bowling ball—requiring one to deliberately drift left or right from the "classic" line.

In the more mountainous and less populated regions of New England, it

Innovations in manufacturing introduced at the Springfield Armory would revolutionize American industry. Today, the handsome old brick building is home to the world's largest collection of historic firearms.

is common to find loose gravel on the pavement where dirt roads enter secondary roads, especially after heavy rainstorms. And, be careful about the deep sand on the shoulders of the roads in southern New Hampshire, yet another remnant of the glacial retreat. Oh, and one more thing: when you ask a Yankee for an estimate of how far it might be to a particular town, the answer will invariably be in time, not miles.

Expect to encounter road-crossing wildlife, even in urban areas. Deer whistles are ineffective except as lucky charms; as to the nature of the luck they will bring you, you'll have to evaluate that after the fact. Moose are simply to be avoided. They are not easily intimidated, even by the blasting air horn of a logging truck, so you will make little impression. Typically weighing more than a half a ton as adults, a moose can move surprisingly quickly on those tall, spindly legs. If you happen to get in a lucky swerve as one emerges from the woods, resist the urge to rubberneck, lest you have a closer call with the second one he or she was traveling with.

Helmets are required for all motorcyclists in Vermont and Massachusetts, in Connecticut, Maine, and New Hampshire for all riders younger than 18, and in Rhode Island for riders under the age of 20.

Lane-splitting is not permitted in any New England state; riding abreast is not permitted in Vermont.

Safety glasses are required in Rhode Island, and in Vermont, New Hampshire, and Connecticut, unless the motorcycle is fitted with a windscreen.

Sound emission limits are in effect within New Hampshire (106 dBA at 20 inches from the muffler), Massachusetts (82 dBA at 50 feet at 45 mph or less), Rhode Island (86 dBA at 50 feet at 35 mph), and Connecticut (complicated, but essentially 84 dBA at 50 feet at 35 mph).

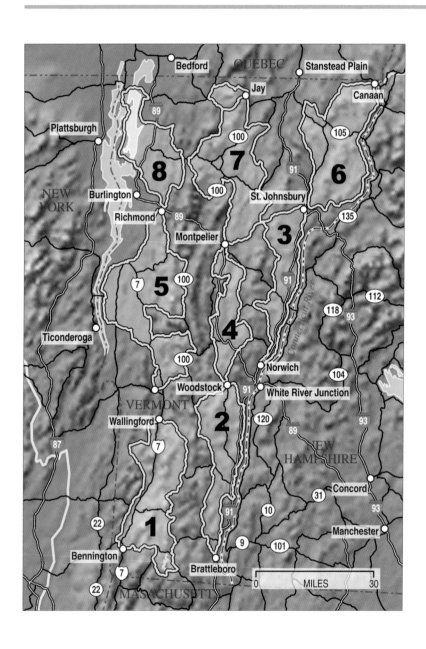

Vermont

When people ask me if I'm from the United States I say, "No, I'm from Vermont." Citizens of the Green Mountain State often tend to have a different perspective than those living in other parts of the country, perhaps due, in part, to the state's relative isolation until the creation of the interstate highways during the 1960s. Or, it just might be that Vermont *is* different.

Geologically, Vermont differs from New Hampshire, since the Connecticut River is actually an ancient fault line that precisely divides the very dissimilar bedrock of the two states. The Champlain Valley in Vermont ends fairly abruptly at New York's Adirondack Mountains and the Taconic Mountains clearly define Vermont's southwestern boundary from that of New York's Hudson Valley morphology. Fossil imprints of dinosaur tracks in northern Massachusetts (Greenfield) clearly show an age difference of 150 million years from the rocks just a few miles north in Gilford, Vermont. Only with the slight intrusion of the Green Mountains into Québec and northwestern Massachusetts do the political boundaries fail to coincide with geological reality.

Vermont was the frontier during the early 18th century and it wasn't until the conclusion of the French and Indian War in 1763 that it was even safe to settle here. A land grab ensued, with consequent arguments over posses-

What fun to have stumbled upon someone's collection of vintage tractors along Route 12 in Barnard!

It's against the law to post advertising signs along Vermont's highways, but there aren't any such rules about the parking of old trucks.

sion, as the New York and New Hampshire colonies issued conflicting land titles to a region known simply as The Grants. Land speculators, farmers, and pioneers got caught in the middle of this political squabble until one group organized a grassroots entity, called the Council of Safety, to support the New Hampshire claims, and backed it up with a local militia known as the Green Mountain Boys.

Despite having a bounty on his head of 20,000 silver dollars, the leader of the Green Mountain Boys, Ethan Allen, walked about freely and openly in The Grants. When the American colonies declared independence from Great Britain, Allen and his men captured the British fort of Ticonderoga on Lake Champlain, and the Council of Safety declared its independence from both the United States and Great Britain, establishing the region as the Republic of Vermont. When fallout from the conflicting land claims caused Congress to decline to recognize the new state, Allen made overtures to British Canada before being invited to join America as its 14th state.

Vermont does have graffiti, but you're more apt to find the restoration of advertising originally painted on buildings during the late 19th and early 20th centuries.

Most parts of Vermont were never known to have promising agricultural land, but there were resources like iron, copper, lime, timber and, most importantly, rushing rivers and streams for both transportation and motive power. Until the introduction of stationary steam engines in the mid-19th century and the advent of electricity at the be-

The gold-domed Vermont State House in Montpelier is a popular stop for visitors.

ginning of the 20th, falling water was virtually the only alternative to muscle power. Industry was firmly established when the Champlain Canal was opened in 1826 connecting Lake Champlain to the Hudson River and Erie Canal, allowing heavier goods to be even more easily transported to market. The railroads arrived in the 1850s, opening up routes from Boston to Chicago. Towns grew wealthy. Then came the devastating flood of 1927 that destroyed industry, infrastructure, and homes.

They were rebuilt, but the double whammy of the Great Depression and the Flood of 1932 spun Vermont into an economic crash from which it is still recovering. The state remained virtually in suspended animation until the intrusion of the Interstate Highway System provided the means for jaded folks from points south to "discover" its unpaved and unbulldozed ambience and charming lack of modernization. Cheap property assured the preservation of Vermont's surviving architectural heritage.

So, as with much of New England, the land you will be riding through will have been shaped by geology, political history, and economics—all of which will be apparent from the seat of your bike as you jig and sway to the rhythm of roads that were often born in the 19th century from necessity, convenience, and tradition—and which will have remained virtually unchanged for nearly two centuries.

Ride 1 **The Marble Belt**

Distance: *These 161 miles won't be covered in three hours or even four. Plan on six hours or more.*

Highlights: *Twisting mountain roads, stunning landscapes, especially during foliage season. Mount Equinox, Old Bennington, Hemmings Auto Oasis, the American Museum of Fly Fishing, Hildene, the Farrar-Mansur House, Skyline Drive, and much more.*

From downtown Bennington (pop. 9,168) Route 9, the Molly Stark Trail, heads east and within a mile begins the climb to Woodford, the highest village in the state at an elevation of 2,215 feet. The wild ridgeline dominating the north and eastern views from town make up some of the more than 22,000 acres of mature Green Mountain habitat around the now-unincorporated township of Glastenbury. In Searsburg, turn right onto Route 8 for the sheer joy of cruising along the remote and quiet edges of the George D. Aiken Wilderness, an untracked, marshy plateau of ponds and scrubby meadows.

A view of Mount Equinox from the south. The private toll road to the summit has some of the tightest, most steeply banked corners of any paved road east of the Rockies.

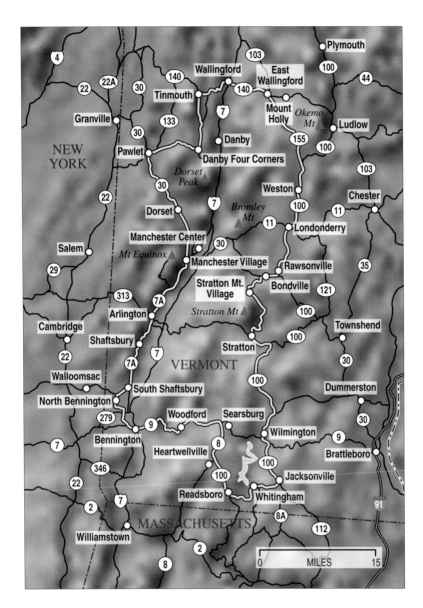

Route 100 begins in the hamlet of Heartwellville and descends leisurely to the village of Readsboro (pop. 809), beyond which it becomes a trucker's worst nightmare and a motorcyclist's dream. (A secret connection to the Mohawk Trail in Massachusetts is Tunnel Street in Readsboro, to River Road in Massachusetts, to Zoar Road, to Route 2, the Mohawk Trail.) Just past the southern shore of Harriman Reservoir, Route 100 twists and undu-

FROM BENNINGTON, VERMONT

0	From US Rte 7 in Bennington, head east on Rte 9 (Molly Stark Trail)
13.8	Right onto Rte 8
19.0	Left onto Rte 100
23.9	[Pass by Tunnel St. in Readsboro]
32.5	[Pass through Jacksonville]
38.1	Continue on Rte 100 north and Rte 9 west
39.2	Right at the traffic light in downtown Wilmington to continue north on Rte 100
53.1	Left onto the Arlington-Stratton Rd.
56.5	Right onto West Jamaica Rd.
58.7	Left (the 4th left) onto Mountain Rd.
63.1	Left onto Stratton Mountain Access Rd.
64.1	[Pass through Stratton Mtn. Village]
67.8	Right onto Rte 30 south
69.5	Left onto Rte 100 north
76.3	Brief merging with Rte 11 in Londonderry
85.1	Straight onto Rte 155
95.1	Left onto Rte 140
101.3	Straight into Wallingford
104.3	From Wallingford, continue west on Rte 140
106.4	Left (south) onto Mountain View Rd.
109.9	Right at the T-junction
113.2	Right onto Danby-Pawlet Rd.
119.1	Straight onto Rte 133 (W. Tinmouth Rd.)
120.4	Left onto Rte 30 south in Pawlet
132.0	Right onto West Rd.
135.4	Bear right onto Rte 7A
137.4	[The turn to Hildene is on the left]
139.6	[Mt. Equinox Skyline Dr. is on the right; round-trip to the summit is 10.6 miles]
143.7	Arlington
153.1	Bear right onto Rte 67 in S. Shaftsbury
155.4	Straight onto Rte 67A (Main St.) in N. Bennington
157.6	Right onto Silk Rd.
159.1	Left onto Fairview St.
159.6	Left onto Walloomsac Rd.
159.8	Leave traffic circle via Monument Ave.
160.1	Left onto Rte 9 east in Old Bennington
161.1	End at US Rte 7 in Bennington ■

lates through the small village of Whitingham, the birthplace of Brigham Young. Just turn right and follow the shore of Sadawga Lake to find the marble marker that indicates the historic site and proclaims him to have been, "a man of much courage and superb equipment." Slow down going through Jacksonville and then climb through the forest to Wilmington, a winter resort town with the Haystack and Mount Snow ski areas located just off Route 100 north of the village. (East Dover Road, a fantastic short-cut to Route 30 on Ride 2, will be found by the golf course 3.6 miles from the traffic light in downtown Wilmington.)

This ride departs from Route 100 for a more interesting trip, starting at the Stratton-Arlington Road, eight miles beyond West Dover. In about three miles, turn north onto West Jamaica Road and then, a couple of miles later, take a left onto Mountain Road, following this wooded byway to its terminus at the Stratton Mountain Access Road. A jaunt through Stratton Mountain Village will put you at the intersection with Route 30 in Bondville.

Dual Sport Detour

If you are on a dual sport bike (I once managed this segment on a K75 Beemer) the stretch of Stratton-Arlington Road over the mountains to East Arlington could become one of your favorite rides. If you are on a heavy machine, have a fat rear tire, don't know what a corduroy road is, or are riding alone, you'd best make the right turn by the town clerk's office and fire station to continue on pavement. ■

North of Rawsonville, Route 100 goes through South Londonderry and Londonderry—which are winter resort towns for the Bromley Ski Area—to the village of Weston (pop. 630). There are more than a few reasons to park and explore the town, including a number of excellent art galleries, the oldest professional theater in the state, and the original Vermont Country Store, famed for its mail-order catalog of practical and hard-to-find traditional and nostalgic items. And for an even more authentic trip into the past, take note of the Farrar-Mansur House Museum (802-824-5294) on the green, a 18th-century tavern filled with period furnishings, heirlooms, and housewares. From the lower level of the adjacent water-powered grist-mill—one of the few still in existence—you can observe how the many belts and gears transfer power from the turbine to the grindstones; the second story of the mill houses a fine collection of early trade tools and machinery.

North of Weston, ride straight onto Route 155, skirting the west side of Okemo Mountain and Mount Holly to Route 140 in East Wallingford. The highway forms the northern border of the Green Mountain National Forest and is filled with tight corners, quick rises, and dips—it's not a stretch of pavement to be taken lightly. It crosses US Route 7 in Wallingford, home of Paul Harris (founder of True Temper Hardware and the Rotary Club) before climbing into the Taconic Mountains. (Going north on US Route 7 leads to Rutland and Ride 5. Going south on US Route 7 is a quicker, shorter ride to Manchester to pick up the last portion of this trip.)

About 300 million years ago, at the same time the Appalachians were forming, a cataclysmic event sheared off the tops of the southern Green Mountains and pushed the peaks westward. Only the very narrow Valley of Vermont separates the Taconics from the Green Mountains, but the movement of these peaks just these few miles generated enough heat to transform the sedimentary limestone bedrock into metamorphic marble. From Brandon south to Dorset, Vermont's famous marble lies beneath the Taconic Mountains.

The roads south from Tinmouth to Danby Four Corners and west to Pawlet are a pleasure to ride. Don't look for road signs; just follow my directions. There are a couple of unanticipated 90-degree corners waiting at the

The Jacksonville General Store at the junction of Route 112 and Route 100 is a place to sit and watch motorcycles roll by.

Dorset can claim the first commercial marble quarry in Vermont.

bottom of Tinmouth Mountain; otherwise these are sedate, scenic country roads. Danby-Pawlet Road will merge with Route 133 to take you into Pawlet.

From Pawlet, Route 30 travels southeast along the beautiful Mettawee Valley and through the village of Dorset. The first marble quarry in the U.S. was established in 1785 and its historic marker can be seen alongside Route 30, but the famous Premier Mine—the source of most of the world's pure white marble—lies deep beneath Dorset Mountain. For the next 130 years, more than two dozen local quarries harvested stone for lintels, hearths, headstones, monuments, and many notable buildings, such as the New York Public Library. The Dorset Inn has been in continuous operation since 1796, but the Mt. Aeolus Inn (1852) in East Dorset garners more contemporary attention; in 1895, a room behind the bar served as the birthplace of Bill W., future co-founder of Alcoholics Anonymous. Today, the place operates as a hotel and retreat for recovering alcoholics who come by the thousands every year to pay their respects at Wilson's gravesite.

After riding through South Dorset, bear right on West Road to avoid the traffic pandemonium of "Malfunction Junction" and the upscale factory outlets in Manchester Center. After passing the Southern Vermont Arts Center you'll arrive at Route 7A next to the American Museum of Fly Fishing (802-362-3300; www.amff.com) in Manchester Village. Its famous Equinox House started life as Marsh Tavern in 1769 and it soon became a hotbed of militants who called themselves the Green Mountain Boys. It expanded over the years until it became a luxury resort built by Franklin Orvis in the 1850s—the north wing was actually the Orvis homestead (800-362-4747; www.equinoxresort.com). Not coincidentally, the trees off to your left (east) border the Batten Kill, one of the world's great trout streams. At this four-diamond resort hotel you can attend the Land Rover Off-Road Driving School, the British School of Falconry, the Orvis Fly-Fishing School, or the Orvis Shooting School (shotguns).

I call this part of Route 7A "Mansion Mile," and the greatest edifice of them all is Hildene, the Georgian Revival-style mansion of Robert Todd Lincoln, son of President Lincoln and chairman of the Pullman Company (802-362-1788; www.hildene.org), which built and operated railroad sleeping cars. Hildene stayed in the Lincoln family until 1975, when it was taken over by a local foundation. It's completely furnished with the Lincoln family's possessions. A recent addition is the 1903 Pullman Palace car, *Sunbeam*.

Skyline Drive toll road climbs 3,248 vertical feet to the summit of Mount Equinox, from which you get a fantastic panoramic view that can, on a clear day, stretch all the way to Mount Royal in Montréal. These 5.3 miles (10.6-mile round trip) have the tightest, most steeply banked corners of any paved road east of the Rocky Mountains; be *extremely* cautious of the oncoming traffic on the blind corners and hairpins. Both the mountain and the road are owned by the only chartered order of Carthusian monks in the country; a scenic pull-out near the top affords a view of the monastery,

The greatest edifice on Mansion Mile is Hildene, the Georgian Revival-style home of Robert Todd Lincoln, son of President Lincoln and chairman of the Pullman Company.

Robert Frost wrote some of his most famous poems while living on his farm in South Shaftsbury.

which maintains a strict separation from the secular world, per its doctrines. With the exception of some worship, brothers live, study, and perform manual labor in near-complete solitude and silence, within the walls of their cells, praying for the benefit of all humankind.

Arlington (pop. 1,199) was a revolutionary hotbed in the 1770s and much of Vermont's early political history was centered here. The house built by Ethan Allen and his brother Ira Allen is now a B&B inn (877-362-2284; iraallenhouse.com) and state historic site. It was here that Ethan Allen wrote his agnostic *Oracles of Reason* and where Ira, then secretary of the Council of Safety, drafted many of Vermont's early documents. The home of Thomas Chittenden, the first governor of the Republic of Vermont and the first governor of the State of Vermont, can be found opposite the Arlington green. History is tangible in southern Vermont.

Arlington was also one of the homes of Norman Rockwell and where he painted most of his famous *Main Street America* series. Between 1939 and 1953, more than 200 local residents were used as his models, and many of these paintings can be viewed in the Arlington Gallery. If you are a fan of the artist, consider spending a night in Rockwell's studio (Inn on Covered Bridge Green, 3587 River Rd.; 800-726-9480; www.coveredbridgegreen. com). Another resident of Arlington was Dorothy Canfield Fisher, the noted author who brought the Montessori method of teaching to the United States and presided over the first adult education system. She founded the Book of the Month Club, sat on its board from 1926 to 1951, and was the official chronicler of the town, so it is no surprise to find the local library named for her. Rockwell Kent, whose dramatic black-and-white illustrations in a 1930s edition of Herman Melville's *Moby-Dick* helped to spur its popular recognition as an American classic, was also born in Arlington.

Between 1920 and 1929, just down the road in South Shaftsbury is where Robert Frost penned some of his most noted poems, including "New Hampshire," and "Stopping by Woods on a Snowy Evening," the latter of which has been a memory staple of New England schoolchildren ever since. The house, which was built in 1769, remains virtually unchanged since Frost lived there, and is now open to the public (802-447-6200; www. frostfriends.org).

In South Shaftsbury, Route 67 goes to North Bennington, site of Bennington College, one of the most highly regarded colleges in the nation.

The tallest structure in Vermont honors the local militias who turned the tide of the American Revolution by defeating General Burgoyne's Hessians at the Battle of Bennington in nearby Walloomsac, New York.

In true nostalgic fashion, the gas station attendants at the Hemmings Auto Oasis and Museum will not only pump fuel, but also clean a car's windshield and check the oil.

Taking scenic local roads that lead past the Silk Covered Bridge, you'll arrive at the Bennington Monument (802-447-0550; historicsites.vermont.gov/bennington/index.html). At 306 feet, it is the highest structure in Vermont; an elevator will take you to the top for a bird's-eye view of three states. Built on the site of a warehouse stockpiled with supplies that were sought by British troops advancing on Saratoga, the monolith honors the local militias under John Stark and Seth Warner who fought General "Gentleman Johnny" Burgoyne's Hessians at the Battle of Bennington in nearby Walloomsac, New York—considered to be the turning point in the Revolutionary War.

One of the highest concentrations of 18th-century buildings in Vermont will be found in Old Bennington. The Old First Church (c. 1805)—considered to be one of the finest Federal-style churches in all of New England—faces the highway across a narrow strip of the old green. In the Old Burying Ground (802-447-1223; www.oldfirstchurchbenn.org) behind the church are the resting places of Robert Frost and other notable Vermonters. The Walloomsac Inn was built in 1766, but this sprawling derelict is now a private residence.

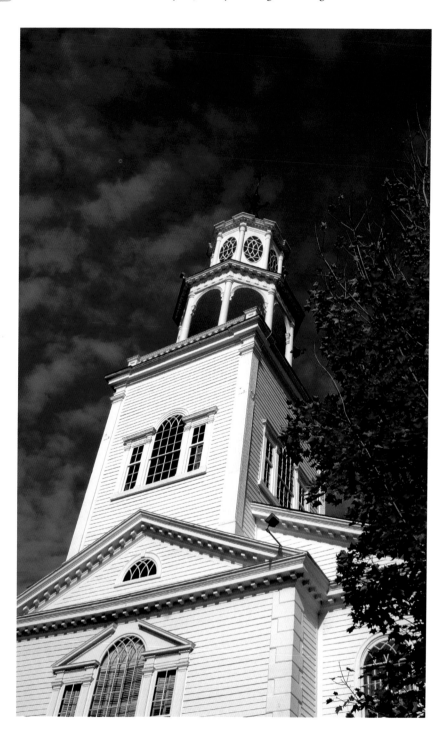

*Built in 1805, the Old First Church in Bennington is a superb
example of Federal-style architecture, which sought to associate the
newly independent country with the republican ideals of the
classical world.*

Route 9 goes down the hill, passing the Bennington Museum (802-447-1571; www.benningtonmuseum.org). Inside those stone walls are the world's largest collections of Bennington pottery and Grandma Moses paintings. The only surviving example of the Wasp luxury car resides in this museum, but just a couple hundred yards down the street is the Hemmings Auto Oasis gas station and adjoining auto museum (216 Main St.; www.hemmings.com), with numerous examples of collectible cars, trucks, and motorcycles in states of restoration. And in true nostalgic fashion, the gas station attendants will not only pump fuel, but also clean a car's windshield and check the oil. During the summer, every other Thursday evening is Cruise-In Night, and the parking lot behind the station fills with classic cars.

Bennington has a number of affordable hotels. The Kirkside Motor Lodge (250 W. Main St.; 802-447-7596; www.kirksidemotorlodge.com) and Bennington Motor Inn (143 W. Main St.; 800-359-9900; www.coolcruisers.net) are conveniently located, but there are numerous others. This town also has quite a few good places to eat, including the Blue Benn Diner (314 North St.; 802-442-5140); Lil' Britain (116 North St./Rte 7; 802-442-2447); and Madison's Brewing Company Pub and Restaurant (428 Main St.; 802-442-7397; madisonbrewingco.com).

Ride 2   The Piedmont

Distance: *Just over 140 miles and about 3-1/2 hours of riding time; with stops, this easily stretches to five or six hours.*
Highlights: *Valley roads with river views, quintessential Vermont villages, American Precision Museum, two very long covered bridges, and the birthplace and burial site of Calvin Coolidge.*

Like its Route 7 counterpart on the western side of the state, Route 5 is a natural north-south passage. It follows Vermont's first major highway, the Connecticut River, and runs through towns and villages that were prosperous decades before the railways arrived in the mid-1800s. In the late 1960s, Interstate 91 supplanted Route 5 as a transportation corridor, leaving this scenic highway to local traffic and appreciative motorcyclists.

The Piedmont (literally, "foothills") lies between the Green Mountains and the Connecticut River. The hardwood forests here bear more resemblance to those of southern New England, replete with white, red, and chestnut oaks, along with beech, maple, yellow birch, and white birch. Tucked into this irregular, hilly landscape can be found the traditional Vermont that's portrayed in countless magazines and books. There are few places in the United States where a person can motorcycle on 200-year-old highways, but many of the roads in this region follow the same paths trod-

An early morning view from Route 5 in Bellows Falls, mirrored in the Connecticut River.

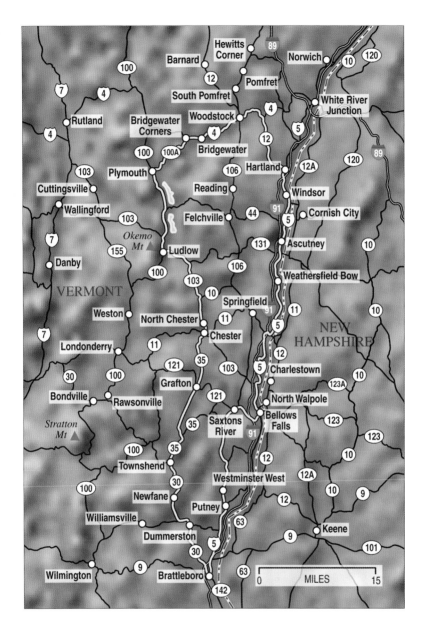

den by men and beasts at the beginning of the 19th century, routes traced with an eye to accommodating both geography and necessity. Stone walls, covered bridges, historic buildings, and ancient maple trees stand as immobile testament to the layout of the original roads.

Ride 2 links directly to Ride 4 in Woodstock, and indirectly via a few short miles of connector roads to Rides 3 and 5. This allows you to build a much longer route or, by riding only certain portions of each, to traverse the state from one end to the other.

Brattleboro (pop. 8,289) is the southeastern gateway to Vermont and always has been, dating back to the region's first white settlement, Fort

FROM BRATTLEBORO, VERMONT

0	From Main St. in Brattleboro, head north on US Rte 5/Rte 9 (Putney Rd.)
2.0	Second right on roundabout to continue north on US Rte 5 (Putney Rd.)
4.6	[Pass by Hidden Acres Campgrounds]
5.6	[Pass by Brattleboro North KOA]
8.9	Left onto Kimball Hill Rd. in center of Putney village
21.6	Right onto Rte 121 in Saxtons River village
26.0	Straight through traffic light onto Westminster St.
26.5	The Square in Bellows Falls is L-shaped
26.8	Bridge to Rte 12 in North Walpole, New Hampshire
29.8	Right to join US Rte 5; Exit 6 of I-91 is directly ahead
37.0	Right to continue on US Rte 5/Rte 11
37.8	Hard left by the RR tracks and bridge to Charlestown, New Hampshire
53.9	American Precision Museum in Windsor
59.0	Bear left, turn left to continue on Rte 12
66.7	Left as Rte 12 merges with US Rte 4 (Woodstock Rd.)
70.4	Bear left onto US Rte 4 (Central St.)
70.7	From Woodstock, continue west on Rte 4
78.8	Left onto Rte 100A at Bridgewater Corners by the general store
84.5	Bear right into Plymouth Village
84.9	Right onto Rte 100A and down through Plymouth Notch
85.8	Left onto Rte 100 south
91.0	[Echo Lake Inn, Tyson-Reading Rd. on the right]
94.5	Left onto Rte 100/Rte 103
96.4	Straight to continue on Rte 103 in downtown Ludlow
108.4	In N. Chester, bear right onto Depot St.
109.3	Bear left onto Rte 35 (Grafton Rd.)
116.4	Hard right over the Saxtons River into Grafton village
116.6	Left at the Grafton Inn onto Townshend Rd.
123.3	Straight onto Rte 35
126.7	Left onto Rte 30 south at the Townshend green
143.4	End in Brattleboro ■

Dummer (1724), a 17-square-foot British stockade established to defend the frontier of the Massachusetts Bay colony. The original site of the fort is now underwater, however, having been flooded at the turn of the 20th century with the construction of the Vernon Dam downriver. Although railroads came to replace rivers in importance—and were in turn supplanted by highways—Brattleboro has remained a crossroad of east-west and north-south transportation to this day.

Located at the confluence of two rivers, Brattleboro had an industrial advantage when it came to powering mills and factories; the hilly geography, however, worked to both concentrate the development and contain some of the inevitable sprawl, which gives it the feel of a semi-urban island in the middle of a rural sea. Known today for its vibrant community of artists, Brattleboro's staid brick downtown houses an eclectic mix of restaurants, boutiques, and galleries with an alternative-lifestyle, country-urban chic. The splendid Art Deco (c. 1938) Latchis Theater and Hotel (50 Main St.; 800-798-6301; www.latchis.com) houses four lovingly restored and renovated theaters, including a grand old movie palace adorned with Greek sculpture and classically themed murals.

This trip begins at the common, a park at the head of Main Street in Brattleboro, and goes north on US Route 5/Route 9. After crossing the West River you enter a couple of miles of strip development with an abun-

Brattleboro's roots as a prosperous 19th-century mill town are reflected in the historic brick buildings along Main Street.

dance of motels, restaurants, stores, and services. From the roundabout at Exit 3 of I-91, Route 9 continues east, crossing New Hampshire to the city of Dover, while US Route 5 (Putney Road) continues north. C&S, the largest wholesale grocery supplier in New England, is located just north of the roundabout and you can expect a considerable amount of traffic. However, the highway quickly takes on a distinctly local feeling as it leaves Brattleboro, where there are two nice campgrounds—Hidden Acres (802-254-2098; hiddenacresvt.net) and Brattleboro North KOA (802-254-5908; brattleborokoa.com)—just a couple of miles farther.

Hippie culture has flourished in Putney since the late 1960s, but the seeds of "free love" and communal property ownership were planted as early as 1838 by Humphrey Noyes, a Yale theology student who underwent a religious crisis that left him believing it was possible to be free from sin in this lifetime, obviating any need to abide by moral strictures and conventions. When Noyes and his followers were eventually driven out of town, they went west to found the Oneida Community in New York, but you can see their rambling clapboard house as you ride out of the village on Kimball Hill Road.

This local road will take you through Westminster West to Saxtons River (pop. 519) and give you a first taste of "old" Vermont. It's sort of a roundabout way to reach Bellows Falls (Route 5 is quicker), but the Westminster West Road is one of my favorites, and I'm sure you will soon understand why.

Located at the great falls where the Connecticut River is constricted by a narrow gorge, the village of Bellows Falls (pop. 3,165) was a transportation center from the early days of river commerce. The first lock canal in the U.S. was built (1791–1802) to circumvent the impassable torrent, and the first bridge to cross the 410-mile-long river spanned the gorge in 1785. When the railroads arrived, all New England trains heading to Montréal or Chicago had to go through the topographic bottleneck of this narrow valley. The vast flow of water powered mills for industry for over a century before being harnessed for electricity. Even today the brick buildings on the L-shaped square hint at the rich history that can be found here. The interstate highway bypassed Bellows Falls in the late 1960s; the paper mills closed down, the truck terminals went out of business, Steamtown USA moved to Pennsylvania, and now the village waits to be "discovered." If Victorian homes interest you, cruise down Atkinson Street or any number of other streets.

US Route 5 makes a sharp right turn at the junctions of Route 103 and Exit 6 of I-91, winds down the hill, and follows the Connecticut River to

Not all who wander in Westminster West are lost . . .

When I captured this view of Bellows Falls in the mid-1960s, it was still an active mill town.

Unlike the adjoining county jail, the Woodstock Inn is known for its five-star comfort and amenities.

Windsor. Along the way you pass by Springfield, through Weathersfield Bow and Ascutney. Just past the traffic light in Ascutney (the first one encountered since leaving BF) you'll note a brick B&B inn with a Vermont historic sign marker out front commemorating William Jarvis's contribution to his home state. In 1811, as Thomas Jefferson's consul to Portugal, Jarvis was ideally placed to take advantage of Napoleon's conquest of Spain, which broke its exclusive hold on its herds of merino sheep, whose wool was prized for its quality and long fibers. Jarvis's enthusiasm for the breed launched the Vermont wool industry, whose initial and lucrative boom during the embargos of the War of 1812 eventually went bust in the face of inconsistent tariff laws and competition from farmers out West. The many beautiful 19th-century Georgian-style brick houses found throughout the Piedmont stand as witness to the wealth accrued from merino sheep.

The speed limit is posted for 40 mph but slow down anyway: you're entering Windsor (pop. 3,756), the former capitol of the Republic of Vermont and the state capitol until 1805. This is where delegates from the various towns gathered in Elijah West's Tavern and declared independence from both the United States and England on July 8, 1777, even as British troops were recapturing Fort Ticonderoga (Ethan Allen and the Green Mountain Boys had taken it from the British on May 10, 1775).

Windsor is also the birthplace of the machine-tool industry. On your left just before the first traffic light is the American Precision Museum (196 Main St.; 802-674-5781; www.americanprecision.org), housing North America's premier collection of machine tools. This brick building is the original Robbins & Lawrence Armory where the American System of machine production was invented and the first precision mechanism with interchangeable parts was created in 1847. Folding rules, the bandsaw, the hydraulic water pump, Sharps rifles, and a very long list of other humble inventions that quietly changed the world were conceived in this brick village.

The Cornish-Windsor Bridge is one of the longest covered bridges in the United States and it is located at the end of Bridge Street (at the traffic light by the museum at the junction of Route 44). Since the state line officially lies at the high-water mark on the western side of the Connecticut River, riding onto it would put you immediately in New Hampshire.

Take note of the Old South Congregationalist Church on Route 5 (Main Street) in Windsor; even in this village of wonderful 18th- and 19th-century architecture, it stands out. The many detailed pattern books published by its designer, Asher Benjamin, the first of their kind in America, distilled architectural history and aesthetics into practical, detailed plans for builders in the field. Among the thousands of public and private buildings that bear the stamp of Benjamin's influence, however, the Federal-style church in Windsor, with its elaborate, classically inspired details, is a rare original.

Route 5 continues through White River Junction to the beginning of Ride 3 in Norwich, but take a left onto Route 12 in the village of Hartland and then continue on Route 4 to Woodstock.

Woodstock (pop. 977) is not, and never has been, a typical Vermont village. Many of its residents have played pivotal roles in the history of the United States. Numbered among this distinguished list are George Perkins Marsh, a champion of the creation of the Smithsonian Institution and the author of *Man and Nature*, a groundbreaking work which unflinchingly de-

Sheep have enjoyed a historic association with Vermont agriculture.

tailed the devastating multi-tiered effect of unthinking human development on the land. Using meticulous scientific documentation, his unprecedented positions helped to shape the contemporary ideals of conservation and environmental management that would hold sway over America in the next century.

Frederick Billings, whose many accomplishments included supervising the construction of the Transcontinental Railroad, would eventually return to his native Woodstock and purchase the Marsh farm to advance his own ideas regarding scientific and sustainable farming and land use, which included not only building an enviable dairy of Jersey cows, but also planting more than 10,000 trees to reforest the well-harvested landscape.

Laurence Rockefeller (son of John D.) later married Billings's granddaughter, purchased the Woodstock Inn, and settled on the estate. Today the Marsh-Billings-Rockefeller National Historic Park (802-457-3368; www.nps.gov/mabi/index.htm), which includes the popular farm, is the only such park in the country dedicated to the history and evolution of land

The Old South Congregational Church in Windsor was built by colonial "house wright" Asher Benjamin, whose popular and accessible handbooks of building plans would have a great influence on New England architecture before the Civil War.

F.H. Gillingham & Sons store has been owned and operated by the Gillingham family since 1886.

stewardship. It also offers the system's first self-guided Civil War Home Front walking tour, facilitated by a GPS-enabled iPhone app, that frames the conflict within the context of local history and culminates at the gravesites of eleven African-American veterans of the 54th Massachusetts who are buried adjacent to the park.

In keeping with the close-to-the-land ethic described above—but not uncommon to most of Vermont—Mountain Creamery (33 Central St.; 508-457-1715; www.mountaincreameryvt.com) locally sources or makes nearly everything it serves from scratch. The downstairs offers take-out fare, including their hand-carved sammies, small-batch ice cream, and infamous mile-high apple pies, which are expected to be enjoyed Vermont-style, with a slice of cheddar cheese. Check out the numerous art galleries in the village, tour the Dana House museum, browse interesting boutiques, and make sure to stop at F.H. Gillingham & Sons General Store (16 Elm St.; 802-457-2100; www.gillinghams.com), a local institution owned and operated by the same family since 1886. Bentley's Restaurant (3 Elm St.; www.bentleysrestaurant.com), one of the few places open for dinner after 9:00 p.m., also corners the market on entertainment, with dancing on the weekends.

Ride 4 begins in the heart of the village and goes north on Route 12 past Billing's Farm. However, this route continues to follow Route 4 west to Bridgewater along the Ottauquechee River. Along the way you'll discover the popular White Cottage Snack Bar (802-457-3455) and the Lincoln Covered Bridge, which is a very unusual modified Pratt tied-arch construction built in 1877, a design which is more commonly seen in all-metal railroad bridges.

Before making the left turn onto Route 100A at Bridgewater Corners, consider going a few yards farther and taking a self-guided tour of the Long Trail Brewing Company (www.longtrail.com). Way back in '89, Andy Pherson began microbrewing his alternative to European ales in the basement of the old woolen mill, and named it after the hiking trail that runs the length of the Green Mountain state, and which passes nearby. The restaurant has vegetarian and healthy choice items on the menu, along with a few creative dishes that include beer as one of the ingredients.

Indelibly tied to the town of Plymouth, the story of the rise of Calvin Coolidge reads like an American myth about a farm boy who grew up to become president of Harvard University and the vice president of the United States. While vacationing at the family home, word arrived by messenger in the middle of the night—there were no phones or telegraph in the tiny village—that President Polk had been assassinated. By the light of a kerosene lamp in the parlor of the family home, Calvin Coolidge was sworn in as the 30th President of the United States by his father, a notary public. Located in Plymouth Notch, the tiny village hasn't changed much since the 1920s, except for installation of electricity and a single gas pump. Coolidge's boyhood home, still attached to the general store, and the meeting room/dance hall above it, became the Summer White House during his presidency. He is buried in the Notch Cemetery.

Many of Windsor county's distinctive stone buildings were constructed of locally quarried gneiss, granite, and schist using an old Scottish masonry technique.

The village of Plymouth has changed very little since the day native son Calvin Coolidge was sworn in as President of the United States.

Heading south on Route 100 from Plymouth Union to Ludlow, you'll pass Lake Amherst and Echo Lake. Try to imagine this landscape completely denuded of trees to create charcoal for the great blast furnace that once existed in Tyson. The last of the extremely rich deposits of ore in these hills was forged into the massive iron plates that clad the USS *Monitor* during the Civil War. Gold was discovered in 1859 and while a few prospectors became rich, the rush was pretty much over by 1870. I've panned in these hills, but even at today's high prices it's difficult to find enough gold to make it more than a hobby.

The Tyson-Reading Road begins across from the Echo Lake Inn—one of the oldest inns in the state—and travels over the Alps to Cuttingsville. Portions of this road date to the 1760s and the "new" part was built prior to 1830. It's now paved, but otherwise unaltered, with corners made for horse and oxen, no shoulders, and almost no guardrails . . . so, if you opt for this short excursion to Felchville, watch your speed.

The economy of Ludlow (pop. 958) is dependent upon the Okemo Mountain Ski Area, but somehow it doesn't feel like a resort village. Route 100 continues to Ride 1 north of Weston, but bear left to stay on Route 103. The highway descends through Proctorsville Gulf and winds along the Williams River to the Old Stone Village.

Although Windsor county has more than 55 unique stone buildings, the concentration in North Chester is especially high. Many of these were constructed by the Clark brothers between 1835 and 1845, using a Scottish

Many a noted American has passed a pleasant summer evening on the spacious veranda of the Grafton Inn.

masonry technique they had learned while building the Welland Canal in Ontario. Known as "sneckled ashlar" construction, rows of loosely squared slabs of locally quarried gneiss, granite, and schist were interlaced with blocks of stone that rose vertically between the levels, producing structures that were both strong and handsome. As a Congregationalist community of staunch abolitionists, many of these old buildings have hidden cellar rooms that sheltered escaped slaves as part of the Underground Railroad.

Religious conflicts had split the region's Congregationalists and Baptists into two separate parishes in 1785, with the former establishing themselves near Route 103 in North Chester; the Baptists settled around the green on Route 11. When the railroad arrived in 1850, the depot was deliberately built on neutral ground between the two parishes. Today, an inn and a few interesting boutiques face the green.

Route 35 is part of the old Boston-Montréal stagecoach route and, except for the application of asphalt, some culverts, and being widened a bit, it is the same road that existed in the late 1700s.

Grafton (pop. 649) is a village that grew rich from the wool industry and was a major stop of the original Boston-to-Montréal stage route. Nearly deserted by the mid-20th century, this archetypal Vermont village was carefully restored by a private trust in the 1960s. The Grafton Inn dates to 1801, with the third floor and long verandas added by owner Harlan Phelps after making his fortune in the California gold fields. Rudyard Kipling, Ralph Waldo Emerson, Henry David Thoreau, Theodore Roosevelt, and Woodrow Wilson were frequent guests at this inn and you can easily visualize them on a warm summer evening sitting in rocking chairs and rattan furniture on the spacious ground-floor porch.

Grafton Road will take you to Townshend. This green is a fine example of a traditional New England common around which New England settlers built their villages. Another is found in the next town. The Newfane green has appeared in countless postcards and magazines published around the world. Except for electrical lines and parked cars taking the place of horse and buggies, this village looks pretty much the same as it did 150 years ago.

Route 30 follows the West River. The shortcut from Williamsville to Route 100 in Ride 1 begins as either Grimes Hill Road or, if you miss it, the Williamsville Road. Take note of the covered bridge in West Dummerston; at 280 feet, it is the longest within Vermont's state borders—and certainly warrants a drive-through and a photo or two. Entering Brattleboro you'll ride through the extensive grounds of the Brattleboro Retreat. Founded in 1834 for the treatment of the mentally ill, this pioneering institution remains a mental heath and addiction treatment center. The retreat's property ends, as does this ride, at the common.

When religious conflicts rent the parish asunder, the Baptists settled around the green in North Chester and the Congregationalists established the Stone Village; the railroad depot was built on neutral ground between the two.

Lush summer greenery spills from the trees along the banks of the Connecticut River.

Ride 3 Eastern Vermont

Distance: *Only 141 miles, but don't expect to be able to cover it in less than four hours. If you spend any time in Saint J, four hours will become six, and before you know it the day will be gone.*
Highlights: *Along river valleys and through the hills, scenic views and winding roads. The Athenaeum and Fairbanks Museum in St. Johnsbury.*

As I've noted before, Vermont differs geologically from New Hampshire. About 228 million years ago, the low mountains on the New Hampshire side of the Connecticut River were a chain of volcanic islands located off the coast of North America (Laurentia). Africa, as part of the super-continent Gondwana, drifted toward Euramerica, engaging the archipelago like a colossal bulldozer blade that scraped ocean sediment, volcanic debris, and continental bedrock onto the primordial tectonic plate, creating the Green Mountains and Piedmont.

If the very earthly foundation of Vermont is one thing that causes the state to feel different from New Hampshire, another would be its 6 percent general sales tax; New Hampshire has no sales tax, so most major stores and service businesses (including motorcycle dealerships) are located in towns

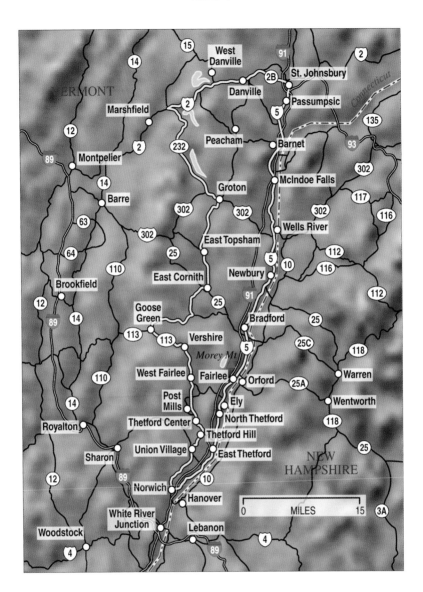

on the eastern side of the Connecticut River, especially in Hanover and Lebanon.

This trip begins in the pretty little town of Norwich, where the head-quarters for King Arthur Flour and the Montshire Museum of Science (802-649-2200; www.montshire.org) are established. Two-tenths of a mile from the village green on Main Street is Dan & Whit's general store (www.danandwhits.com), the de facto community center of the village. Their motto is, "If we don't have it, you don't need it." Next door is the Norwich Inn (802-649-1143; www.norwichinn.com), which has been in operation since 1797. Out back in the old livery stable, brewmaster Patrick Dakin creates his international award-winning Jasper Murdock Ales (English stouts, porters, ales, and a bitter) in 125-gallon batches, which are piped underground and into the pub room at the inn—truly "on tap."

Heading north, US Route 5 follows the Connecticut River through East Thetford and North Thetford. There are five times as many cows as people in this township, but you probably won't see many of either.

The old railroad depot in Ely is worth a photograph or two. The architect who lives there has restored it with authentic details, which include placing the semaphore next to the tracks and the caboose close to the baggage shed. The depot (c. 1848) in the next village is the oldest railroad

FROM NORWICH, VERMONT

0	From Norwich, head north on US Rte 5 at Main St.
57.1	Left onto Main St. in St. Johnsbury
57.6	Left onto US Rte 2
58.2	Left onto Rte 2B
61.6	Left onto US Rte 2 and proceed west
67.3	Bear left onto US Rte 2 in West Danville
75.5	Left onto Rte 232 (New Discovery Rd.)
89.0	Left onto Rte 302 east
90.8	Right onto Powder Spring Rd. in Groton village by the church
98.4	Bear right to continue on Powder Spring Rd.
98.9	Right onto Topsham-Corinth Rd. in E. Topsham
103.3	Right onto Rte 25 by the E. Corinth General Store
104.1	Left (next left) onto Brook Rd.
108.3	Bear right onto Chelsea-Goose Green Rd. in the hamlet of Goose Green
113.7	[Caution: 90-degree left corner!]
115.5	Left onto Rte 113 east
126.0	Post Mills and junction of Rte 244
130.0	Thetford village
131.5	Right onto Academy Rd. in Thetford Hill at the green
134.1	Bear left to continue on Academy Rd.
134.7	Straight onto Rte 132
135.2	Bear right (next right) onto Union Village Rd.
140.5	Jasper Murdock's Alehouse at the Norwich Inn in Norwich
140.6	End at US Rte 5 and the green in Norwich ∎

building in the Connecticut River Valley, but unless you are an avid railway buff it isn't worth seeking out.

The craggy palisades of Morey Mountain overshadow the village of Fairlee (pop. 967) and hide Lake Morey from view. Samuel Morey grew up on the New Hampshire side of the Connecticut River in Orford, but both towns claim him as a native son. His long list of accomplishments include inventing the rotary steam engine (1793), building the first car (wagon) with an internal combustion engine (1829), and having the world's second automobile accident. Although the steamship is credited to Robert Fulton, Morey perfected one eleven years earlier but failed to garner sufficient financial backing for his project. He is rumored to have deliberately sunk his prototype in the cold, dark waters of Lake Morey.

The highway becomes squeezed between high cliffs and the river before arriving in Bradford. The tawdry commercialism at the junction of Route 25 will be in marked contrast to the old village just a mile farther. (It was in this village that James Wilson made the first terrestrial and celestial globes in America and began manufacturing them in 1813.) The valley broadens as the river makes sinuous bends and ox-bows north of Bradford. White picket fences and beautiful 19th-century homes line the road as it winds through the village of Newbury. You may have thought places like this existed only in a mythic America.

Before the arrival of the railroads, Wells River (pop. 325) was as far up the river as boats could navigate. Located at the intersection of US Routes 302 and 5, the village still sees plenty of traffic. Route 302 leads to the beginning of Route 112 and into the White Mountains of New Hampshire. If you're in need of fuel for man and machine, however, it's worth a short de-

The architect who lives at the old Ely RR depot has restored it with authentic details, such as the semaphore next to the tracks and the caboose near the baggage shed.

tour to experience the hearty, plentiful and homemade fare at the P&H Truck Stop (802-429-2141; just 2.9 miles west of Wells River on Rte 302 at I-91 Exit 17). Unflappable waitresses will be topping off joe and delivering mammoth breakfasts and ginormous wedges of pie to cash-strapped students, hungry bikers, culinary pilgrims, and long-haulers keeping a schedule to and from Quebec.

Barnet, Vermont, has not one but *two* Buddhist retreats. Chögyam Trungpa Rinpoche brought the practice to North America in the 1970s, establishing Tail of the Tiger, now renamed Karmê Chöling. With practical instruction in deep meditation, the center offers a spiritual path on secular terms and a place for people to "connect with their basic goodness and the basic goodness of others." While you may not have time for the full three-month residential program, consider stopping in the village by the waterfall and taking a few minutes to meditate on your travels.

As US Route 5 leaves the Connecticut River Valley you might catch a glimpse of the (Frank D.) Comerford Dam in the distance. In the time before the glaciers, running water in the erstwhile Connecticut River had carved a gently graded gorge that dropped 320 feet over the span of fifteen miles. Begun in 1928 in the aftermath of the Great Flood, this 169-foot-high, 2,253-foot-long concrete structure tamed the Fifteen Miles Falls on

The Connecticut River, which divides Vermont from New Hampshire, was the region's main highway until the arrival of the railroads in the 1850s.

the upper river in 1930. It was the largest dam of its kind when it was built and now, 80 years later, it still supplies five percent of New England's electrical power.

St. Johnsbury is the Gateway to the Northeast Kingdom and the starting point for Ride 6, which details many of the worthy ways to spend a few hours in this unique little town. Saint J owes much of its historical prosperity to Thaddeus Fairbanks, who became the largest manufacturer of precision scales in the world; his brother and partner Erastus was twice Governor of Vermont (21st and 26th) and Erastus' son Horace was the 36th governor.

Your route ultimately turns left onto US Route 2 west by St. Johnsbury Academy, but you would be well rewarded if you continued just a bit farther on Main Street to check out two of the popular attractions gifted to the town by the Fairbanks family. The town library, the Athenaeum (802-748-8291; www.stjathenaeum.org) is the oldest unaltered art gallery in the United States, with more than 100 works of American and European artists of the late 18th and early 19th centuries. And just up the street is the Fairbanks Natural Science Museum & Planetarium (1302 Main St.; 802-748-2372; www.fairbanksmuseum.org), a magnificent red sandstone edifice built to house Franklin Fairbank's natural history collection, an extensive, eclectic, and edifying assortment of the sorts of curiosities collected by worldly Victorian-era gentlemen.

The second half of this ride returns to Norwich on some great motorcycling roads that are typically overlooked by the average tourist without an inside scoop. It will be important to fill your gas tank in either Saint J or at the general store in West Danville, since services will be scarce on this leg of the journey.

Staying on US Route 2 would be the fastest way to Danville, but the old highway has plenty of curves and much less traffic. This fair town is home to the American Society of Dowsers, practitioners of the arcane art of "water witching" by means of forked willow branches and other simple, if more modern, instruments of divination. Making a left onto Peacham Road at the green in Danville would be an alternate way to reach the village of Groton. You don't need any directions other than to stay on the pavement and turn right upon reaching US Route 302.

The local nomenclature gives a nod to Joe, an Indian scout who fought with the Green Mountain Boys against General Burgoyne at Hubbarton and the Battle of Bennington. He led the expeditions of Generals Bayley and Hazen and was highly regarded by General George Washington. A marble memorial stands in the Newbury cemetery, but his lasting legacy is

Except for paved roads and electrical lines, Thetford Hill still looks very much like it did in this hundred-year-old photograph.

Joe's Pond in West Danville. The next body of water, Molly's Pond, was named for his wife.

The junction of Route 232 is less than a mile east of the village of Marshfield and the connection with Ride 7. It also has a gas station and the Rainbow Sweets Café (802-426-3531), which may be the last option for a decent lunch until you return to Norwich.

Route 232 is one of the more popular motorcycling roads in central Vermont, but note that this narrow twisting road has some unmarked severe corners in the boulder-strewn forest, and the extremely popular Groton Lake/Forest/State Park ensures that there will be traffic on the highway. In addition, this area is noted for having the largest bear population in the state as well as an abundance of moose and deer.

From Groton you'll head into the back hills through East Topsham and East Corinth to briefly join Route 25 before turning onto local roads through Goose Green to Vershire. These superb byways are so far off the beaten track as to get little attention from non-local riders.

The copper mines in Vershire were established in 1793, and by the mid-1830s sixty percent of the copper mined in the U.S. came from these hills. The mines closed in the wake of labor unrest in 1884 but sadly, the tailings and leaching beds have contaminated the environment and fish still can't survive in the upper reaches of the Ompompanoosuc River. The road is a joy to ride, however, as it descends through Vershire, West Fairlee, and Post Mills to Thetford Center.

Henry Wells grew up in Thetford Center and then went west to Buffalo, New York, where he co-founded Wells Fargo, while Grace Paley, the internationally known poet, spent her last years in this village. You might note the small public library, a gift from the philanthropist George Peabody, who

The one-lane Union Village Bridge was built in 1867, during the Civil War.

also grew up here, but moved away to make his fortune. Vermont seems to be especially distinguished in the number of well-known people who have left the state.

US Route 5 is only 2.3 miles down the hill, but turn right onto Academy Road at the green in Thetford Hill. Established in 1819, Thetford Academy is Vermont's second-oldest secondary school and local kids attend this private institution instead of a public school.

The last six miles of this trip offer the finest touring to be found in this part of the state. You'll have to slow down to pass through the covered bridge in Union Village; the design of this structure, a multiple kingpost with a kingpost arch, is unlike the lattice style prevalent in the area. The simplest version of this kind of truss, a vertical center post supported by two angled posts, was first described in 1570 by Andrea Palladio in his influential multi-volume treatise on architecture.

Follow Route 132 only until the next right turn. Union Village Road becomes Main Street in Norwich. By now I suspect you'll be ready to settle down at the inn and enjoy a pint of Jasper Murdock Ale.

Ride 4 The Central Piedmont

Distance: *128 miles and four to six hours depending on stops*
Highlights: *Hills, forests, rural farmland, and winding valley roads; small rural villages and the state capitol, Montpelier. 19th-century architecture, the Justin Morrill homestead, the granite quarries in Barre, the floating bridge on Sunset Lake.*

Barre is the Granite Capitol of the World, and the architecture of the Twin Cities—Barre and Montpelier—is copiously adorned with this local building material. Covered bridges are also featured on this route, and the floating bridge across Sunset Lake has become rather popular with riders. In spite of numerous places of special interest—one of the world's best collection of music boxes, the sculpture of Hope Cemetery in Barre, the Rock of Ages granite quarry and, of course, the Vermont State House—this ride is really about the roads.

Departing Woodstock (pop. 977) on Route 12 north, cross the iron bridge and pass between the former Rockefeller estate (802-457-3368; www.nps.gov/mabi/index.htm) and Billings Farm (802-457-2355; www.

Before it was part of Vermont's only national park, Frederick Billings used his farm in Woodstock to advance his own ideas regarding scientific and sustainable farming and land use.

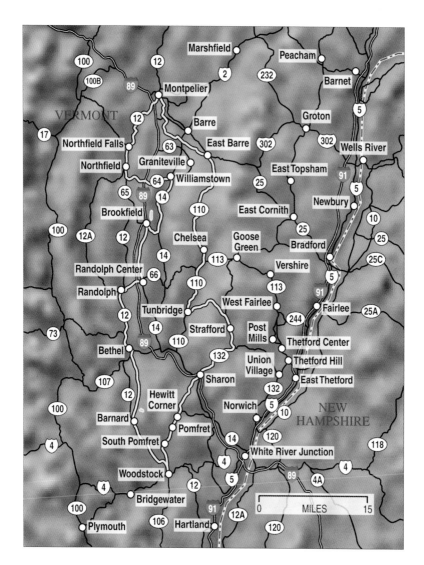

billingsfarm.org), both of which are now part of the Marsh-Billings-Rockefeller National Historic Park described in Ride 2. Bear right at the Y to South Pomfret and climb into the Piedmont. The sign on the town clerk's office and town hall will be the only clues that you've come to the village of Pomfret. On the maps it looks like the road continues straight to Sharon, and Hewitt Corner is nothing more than a place name, so the left turn onto Howe Hill Road could come as a surprise.

Since what goes up must come down, you must descend on Howe Hill

Road into the White River Valley. Slow down when you see the warning sign for the narrow underpass; there's room for only one vehicle at a time and often there's sand and gravel on the steep pavement.

Leaving the village of Sharon (pop. 1,411) you'll once again climb into the mountains. After making a left at the bottom of the hill in front of the church, simply follow the pavement to reach Tunbridge. The tiny village of Strafford is as quaint as a person could ask for and the road over the next mountain is a thoroughly enjoyable cruise. The fancy raspberry-colored Greek Revival gingerbread-style house on your right is the Justin Morrill homestead (802-765-4288; www.morrillhomestead.org). Among his many accomplishments, Justin Morrill championed the establishment of the Library of Congress, the Washington Monument, and the Land Grant colleges.

The Tunbridge World's Fair was never a "world's fair," but an annual mid-September event sponsored by the Union Agricultural Society since 1867. Until the last decade, it was regarded as one of the rowdiest country fairs in New England, but it's since been gentrified. The Mill Bridge—150 yards west of the hard right turn onto Route 110—is just one of seven covered bridges that cross the First Branch of the White River between Tunbridge and Chelsea. Turn right and follow Route 110 north.

Chelsea (pop. 1,250) is a shire town—a county seat—and is unusual in that the village has two greens. The architectural gems in this village are just

Will's Store in Chelsea is located in a unique double Georgian brick building.

FROM WOODSTOCK, VERMONT

0	From Woodstock, ride north on Rte 12 (Elm St.) at US Rte 4
1.1	Bear right onto Pomfret Rd.
3.2	Bear right onto Pomfret Rd. in S. Pomfret
7.9	In N. Pomfret, turn left onto Howe Hill Rd.
12.4	Right onto River Rd.
12.9	Left across the bridge
13.0	Right onto Rte 14 east
13.3	Left onto Rte 132 in Sharon village
19.7	Left onto Justin Morrill Memorial Hwy
22.1	Bear right to stay on J.M.M. Hwy
30.2	In Tunbridge, hard right to cross the bridge onto Rte 110 north
38.7	Continue on Rte 110 in Chelsea
51.7	In E. Barre, continue straight onto Websterville Rd.
52.8	Right to continue on Websterville Rd.
54.1	Straight onto Sterling Hill Rd. (name changes from Websterville Rd.)
55.0	Straight crossing Rte 14 onto Bridge Rd. in S. Barre
56.4	Left at the T-intersection onto Miller Rd. at the top of the hill
56.7	Right onto Airport Rd.
60.2	Straight at the traffic light and Rte 62 onto Fisher Rd.
60.7	Right onto Paine Turnpike
62.9	In Montpelier, straight onto US Rte 2 at the traffic light at the bottom of the hill
63.4	Left (west) onto Rte 12 at the traffic light
71.5	[Northfield Falls at Cox Brook Rd. by the general store]
74.2	Continue straight on Rte 12
75.3	Left onto Rte 64 up the hill
82.1	Right (south) on Rte 14 in Williamstown
84.6	The height of land between Cutter and Staples Ponds on Rte 14
85.0	Entering the Williamstown Gulf
89.7	Right onto Rte 65 and up the hill
91.6	Hard left onto Ridge Rd. by the church
98.7	Right onto Rte 66 in Randolph Center
102.0	Straight onto Rte 12 in Randolph
102.2	Bear left through downtown Randolph
109.8	Continue through Bethel on Rte 12
110.2	Right onto Rte 12/Rte 107 through the underpass and over the bridge
110.6	Left onto North Rd. appears "straight" at a right corner
117.5	Straight onto Rte 12 in Barnard by Silver Lake and the general store
127.6	End Rte 12 (Elm St.) at US Rte 4 in Woodstock ■

Look closely and you'll note the immense scale of this active granite quarry on Mill Hill.

Rock of Ages Quarry

Barre's famous granite quarries are actually located on Mill Hill in East Barre. There are more than 80 old quarries in this small area and it seems that streets and roads are built around either small hills of discarded granite or large holes in the bedrock. Small signs direct tourists to the Rock of Ages Visitor's Center (www.rockofages.com) in Graniteville, where they offer tours of the factory and an active quarry. Instead of continuing straight onto Sterling Hill Road (where Websterville Road becomes Sterling Hill Road), turn left onto Graniteville Road by the cemetery. The factory and visitor's center will be on your left, Middle Road and Holden Road on your right. After your visit, return to Sterling Hill Road and continue west. In less than a mile you'll come to Route 14 at the traffic light. The Hollow Inn & Motel (802-479-9313; www.hollowinn.com) is just a couple hundred yards north on Route 14. Less than a mile south on Route 14 is Wilkins Harley-Davidson—Vermont's largest H-D dealership—(802-476-6104; www.wilkinsharley.com). Continue the trip from the intersection of Route 14 and Sterling Hill Road by heading west on Bridge Street. ◼

local buildings, not tourist sites as they would be in southern New England. The Orange County Courthouse (c. 1847), Will's Store (c. 1818), the Shire Inn (c. 1832), the United Church of Chelsea (c. 1813), and the Orange County Jail (c. 1863) would be a big deal if located somewhere else. Route 113 goes up Heartbreak Hill to connect with Ride 3 in Vershire.

Route 110 winds north to the head of the valley on its way to the height-of-land, the dividing point between watersheds. The rivers and streams you've crossed and traveled along today have all flowed south to Long Island Sound; everything to the north and west from this point flows into the Gulf of St. Lawrence in Canada. Ahead is a flat plain that hides one of Vermont's treasures: granite.

The quickest and shortest way to reach Montpelier is from Barre (pop. 9,291). Route 110 joins at US Route 302 in East Barre and Route 14 merges with it briefly in downtown Barre. If you happen to be interested in architecture, sculpture, or learning more about granite, Barre would be the place you should visit. The even texture and coloring of the local stone makes it ideal for monument work, which attracted large numbers of immigrant craftsmen, especially during the Victorian era when ornate family memorials were popular. You'll find the product of the local quarries used in buildings throughout the historic district, and the Vermont Granite Museum (www.stoneartsschool.org) is located in a converted "stone shed" on the Barre-Montpelier Road. Hope Cemetery on Route 14 just north of the city is world famous for the variety, individuality, and craftsmanship of its monuments, which feature unique and personalized three-dimensional renderings of memories, hobbies, and lives lived, many of which were personally sculpted by family members.

Instead of heading into Barre, however, my routing directions for this

Around Graniteville, heaps of discarded stone are features of the landscape.

trip will take you into Montpelier by the most scenic route, one used exclusively by local residents. Montpelier is the smallest state capitol in the nation. It's also a gastronomic destination for hungry riders. The New England Culinary Institute (www.necidining.com) has three downtown training properties: the Main Street Grill and Bar (118 Main St.), the Chef's Table (118 Main St.), and La Brioche Bakery & Café (89 Main St.). In addition, The Coffee Corner (83 Main St.; www.coffeecorner.com) and Sarducci's (3 Main St.; www.sarduccis.com) are just two of several popular lunch destinations in the capitol city. Businesses on Main and State Streets are not chain stores, but locally owned and operated. Historic buildings, including the gold-domed State House, line State Street.

Montpelier (pop. 8,035) is the starting point for Ride 7 through the northern Green Mountains, but this trip returns to Woodstock by taking Route 12 (Northfield Street) south.

Just up Cox Brook Road by the general store in Northfield Falls are three covered bridges that were built in 1872. This is the only place in Vermont where one covered bridge can be seen from another, making for some unique photo opportunities. The first, Station Bridge, is of a lattice construction that became quite popular in this region because it did not require the heavy timbers and skilled joinery of earlier designs. You can compare it to the Newell (Second) and Upper Cox Brook (Third) bridges, which utilize a queenpost construction, one of Palladio's bridge designs that dates to 1570. Similar to the kingpost construction described in Ride 3, the two

A foliage view from the height of land in Washington.

The Hope Cemetery is virtually an open-air museum of memorial sculpture dedicated to the individual passions of its eternal residents.

slanting supports of a queenpost truss angle toward a stabilizing horizontal beam.

Norwich University was established in1819 in the village of Norwich, but it moved to Northfield in 1868. It was the first private military college in the United States. The Kreitzberg Library and Norwich University Museum are a little-known treasure trove of American history.

Route 12 continues south to Randolph (pop. 4,853) and while it's an exceptionally nice motorcycle touring road—especially through the Brookfield Gulf—this route turns onto Route 63 and goes over the mountain to Williamstown. The Rock of Ages factory and quarry in Graniteville are readily visible on Mill Hill in East Barre as you begin your descent on the east side of the mountain.

On your way by, take note of the plaque fixed to the boulder on the front lawn of the Williamstown library that commemorates the birth of Thomas Davenport, inventor of the first DC electric motor in America, and holder of U.S. Patent No. 132, issued in 1837, for the first electric machine, which utilized a battery and what we would now recognize as a brush and commutator.

The Floating Bridge across Sunset Lake is a plank-type pontoon bridge. Watch out!
Those boards are very slippery.

Wilkins Harley-Davidson is less than 3 miles north of the village on
Route 14. Just to the south you'll ride down through the Williamstown
Gulf. "Gulfs" are very narrow channels that were cut through the moun-
tains as outlets for the vast post-glacial Lake Vermont of 10,000 years ago.

Soon after exiting the gulf, you'll come to Route 65 heading up Bear
Mountain to the hamlet of Brookfield. The Floating Bridge on Sunset Lake
has, for some inexplicable reason, become a motorcycle destination. The
structure is supported by sealed barrels, since the lake was too deep for traditional piling. If the planking is underwater, expect it to be covered by algae
and quite slippery. If you just have to do it—it's definitely fun on a hot summer day—stay on the raised runners, *avoid* the center of the bridge, keep a
slow constant speed, and good luck. Most of Route 65 from the lake to
Route 12 is gravel, so you'll probably need to make a return crossing.

At the church on Route 65, just east of the Floating Bridge, take the
Ridge Road (it's the one that's paved) for an enjoyable cruise to Randolph
Center, home of Vermont Technical College, one of the top technical
schools in the country. In Randolf Center, you'll pick up Route 66, but not
the one of song and legend. Vermont Pure Spring Water comes from a deep
artesian well that's located just off the highway before reaching Interstate
89. At the bottom of the long descent down Route 66 is the Porter Music

The modern era of downhill skiing was born on this steep hill, where a simple rope tow was powered by a modified Ford Model T engine.

Box Museum (800-811-7087; www.portermusicbox.com). They restore antique music boxes for collectors and museums around the world and their own collection is one of the best to be found anywhere.

Route 66 ends at Route 12 in Randolph. Continuing south on Route 12 you'll arrive at the village of Bethel (pop. 1,968). This village on the White River is home to Vermont Castings, the largest wood stove and gas stove manufacturer in the world, but they also make professional-grade barbeques.

After going through the underpass and over the bridge you'll take another detour by *cautiously* continuing straight at the Queen Anne-style Greenhurst Inn onto North Road. This one follows the ridge while Route 12 stays in the valley. It drops down to Silver Lake by the general store in Barnard where you rejoin Route 12.

Just shy of eight miles south of Barnard, at the Vermont Historical Site marker, you'll see what during the summer looks like a green pasture bordered by a line of telephone poles on the side of a steep hill, but this is where a simple rope tow powered by a modified Ford Model T engine heralded in the modern era of downhill skiing.

Enjoying the mountainous vista from a turn-off along Route 4.

Ride 5 Green Mountain Gaps

Distance: *202 miles and four hours without stops or side trips; likely longer.*
Highlights: *Hairpin turns over mountain passes, deep valleys, and undulating roads across the broad Champlain Valley. Route 17 through the Appalachian Gap, the Old Round Church in Richmond, Vermont Marble Museum.*

The gap roads are the premier motorcycle destinations in the Green Mountains. Some come simply to ride them from one side of the mountains to the other; some make detours to include the Appalachian Gap as part of their extended New England tour. In contrast, the long, straight undulating

The signature yellow clapboard buildings mark the Bread Loaf campus of Middlebury College, site of the famous summer writers' conferences.

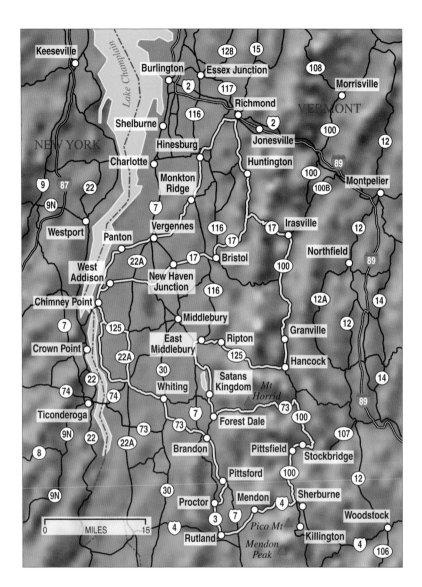

north-south roads of the Champlain Valley rolling beneath a big sky will be a delight of a different sort.

You've left Rutland behind and Maple Sugar & Spice (about 3.7 miles east on Route 4) is definitely the place to have breakfast or meet for a group ride. During the spring, the sugar shack shows just how they come by all the delicious syrup that accompanies their pumpkin pancakes. The property was once owned by Brigadier General Edward H. Ripley, who served as

FROM RUTLAND, VERMONT

0	From Rutland, ride east on US Rte 4 at US Rte 7
10.7	Bear left onto Rte 100 north
21.3	Bear left to stay on Rte 100
29.1	Left onto Rte 73 (Brandon Mt Rd.)
33.0	Caution: Left to stay on Rte 107
43.2	Hard right onto Rte 53 in Forest Dale
46.9	Through Satan's Kingdom
52.6	Right onto US Rte 7 north
55.5	Right onto Rte 116 (Ossie Rd.)
56.0	Bear right onto Rte 125 in E. Middlebury
71.5	Left on Rte 100 north in Hancock
85.9	[Lincoln Gap Rd on the left; Warren on the right]
91.5	In Irasville, turn left onto Rte 17 (McCullough Hwy)
97.6	[Top of Appalachian Gap and parking area]
100.5	Caution: Hard right onto Gore Rd.
108.2	Huntington Center
114.9	Hard left onto Hinesburg Rd.
116.4	Caution: Turn left to stay on Hinesburg Rd. (becomes Richmond Rd)
120.9	Right to stay on Richmond Rd.
122.3	Bear left onto Mechanicsville Rd.
123.2	Left on Rte 116 (Silver St.) in Hinesburg
123.5	Stay straight to remain on Silver St.
128.6	Road name changes to Monkton Rd.
128.9	Bear right to stay on Monkton Rd.
138.0	Straight through intersection with US Rte 7
138.5	Left onto Rte 22A (Main St.) in Vergennes
(continued)	

commander of the first brigade of Rutland's Light Guards during the Civil War. A large rock out back marks the grave of Old John, the gallant horse upon which Ripley led the troops into Richmond.

As Route 4 climbs Mendon Mountain you'll pass several inns and then the Pico Mountain Ski Area. The Inn at Long Trail (800-325-2540; www.innatlongtrail.com) is at the crest of the Sherburne Pass, where the Appalachian Trail (Maine to Georgia) merges with the Long Trail (running the length of Vermont) in the ski town of Killington. Hikers, mountain bikers, and others attracted to the area's recreational possibilities have long enjoyed the Irish Pub at the inn and its rustic Adirondack-style charms—so much so that reservations would be recommended if you'd like to join their ranks.

CONTINUING FROM VERGENNES, VERMONT

139.0 [Falls on the Otter Creek]
139.3 Right onto Panton Rd.
143.5 In Panton, bear left onto Jersey St.
144.1 Right (next right) on Pease Rd.
144.9 Left onto Lake Rd.
150.8 Straight onto Rte 17 by the W. Addison General Store
151.6 D.A.R. State Park
152.9 In Chimney Point, bear left, turn left onto Rte 125 heading east
160.0 Right onto Rte 125/Rte 22A
160.4 Straight onto Rte 22A
166.6 Rte 22A briefly merges with Rte 74
167.1 Rte 74 leads to the Ticonderoga Ferry to New York
167.5 Left (next left) onto Richville Rd.
173.6 Right onto Rte 30 in Whiting
176.3 Left onto Rte 73
182.2 Straight onto Rte 73/US Rte 7 in Brandon
182.6 Bear right to continue on US Rte 7 in Brandon
190.1 Right onto Elm St. in Pittsford by the green
192.1 Left onto Gorham Bridge Rd.
192.6 Right onto Rte 3
194.3 Right into Proctor village on Main St.
194.6 Left onto North St.
194.8 Right (2nd right) onto School St. (becomes West St.)
198.2 Wilson Castle on the right
199.4 Left onto US Rte 4
201.4 [Downtown Rutland]
202.2 End at US 4/US 7   ■

For even more rustic accommodations, Gifford Woods State Park (802-775-5354; www.vtstateparks.com/htm/gifford.htm) offers 22 great campsites, 20 lean-tos, and four cabins on the edge of a virgin forest. The section of Route 100 from Killington to Pittsfield is where I've always tested my cars and motorcycles. Traffic is generally light, and if you catch it right this is a fantastic motorcycling road.

Brandon Gap is the next mountain pass on the agenda. Route 73 follows a narrow valley, makes a 90-degree left turn, and immediately begins the climb. At the turn-off beneath the Great Cliff on Mount Horrid, look for moose in the beaver meadows below and peregrine falcons in the sky above. Crossing the Long Trail, the highway drops 400 feet per mile and abruptly levels out just where you *cautiously* make a right turn onto Route 53 in Forest Dale.

This is where an impoverished blacksmith by the name of Thomas Davenport invented the electric motor in 1834. His application for a patent was initially rejected, since the officials had never patented an electric device, but numerous letters and recommendations from scientists and academics of the day convinced them to reconsider. Correctly divining the eventual end of steam power, Davenport went on to create a model electric train, an electric cart, and an electric printing press on which he published the first journal on electromagnetism in 1844. His prototype electric signaler was further developed by Samuel Morse into the telegraph. In the end, however, Davenport was just too far ahead of his time, and he died impoverished in 1851, leaving others to profit from his work.

You'll get a nice view of the Great Cliff just before cresting Brandon Gap.

The road follows the clearly defined base of the Green Mountains through boulder-strewn Satan's Kingdom and along the shore of Lake Dunmore. Branbury State Park (802-247-5925; www.vtstateparks.com/htm/branbury.htm) has a popular beach and 37 tent sites, some of which are on the shore.

Middlebury Gap is next on the list and Route 125 first climbs along Ripton Gorge before leveling out on a broad upland plateau. During the summer, the famous Bread Loaf Writers' Conferences take place at the yellow clapboard campus of Middlebury College. The highway then curves around the Middlebury Snow Bowl ski area, through the gap, and down into Hancock. Texas Falls (31 feet) is just a mile up the road of the same name. The Old Hancock Hotel houses the Vermont Home Bakery (802-767-4976; www.oldhancockhotel.com) and this eatery at the junction of Route 125 and Route 100 is a popular meeting place for touring riders. They don't take plastic, but for a sawbuck or so, you can partake in the all-you-can-eat Sunday brunch that runs 'til 2.

ALTERNATE ROUTE FROM CHIMNEY POINT

0	Head east on Rte 125
3.1	Right onto Lake St.
5.4	Bear right to continue on Lake St.
7.1	Crown Point Road
12.1	Road turns away from the lake (becomes Watchpoint Rd.)
14.7	Straight onto Main St. (Rte 74) in Shoreham
15.1	Rejoin the main route by turning right onto Rte 22A in Shoreham
15.6	Left (next left) onto Richville Rd. and continue the main route from mile 167.5

ALTERNATE ROUTE FROM APPALACHIAN GAP TO CHIMNEY POINT

0	From the intersection of Rte 17 and Gore Road at the west end of The Gap, continue westward on Rte 17
6.9	Rte 17 merges with Rte 116
8.6	[Lincoln Rd. on the left takes you to New Haven Falls; about 0.5 miles round-trip]
10.2	Continue west on Rte 17 through Bristol
15.6	Cross Rte 7 (through a short jog to the right)
23.1	[Pass through Addison]
31.1	Arrive at Chimney Point ■

The Granville Reservation is unquestionably my favorite section of Route 100. The highway twists through the mountains past the fantastic 64-foot Moss Glen Falls on Deer Hollow Brook before reaching the upper beaver meadows. Deer, moose, bear, coyotes, and other animals abound in this wilderness and some of my most memorable wildlife encounters have taken place on this stretch of road.

The McCullough Highway (Route 17) through the Appalachian Gap is the most popular motorcycling road in the state. It's also shared by logging trucks that *require both lanes* to negotiate some corners and also by tourists who just freak and drive down the centerline. More than half of the 53 turns will occur between here and the top, and the combinations of grade and tight radii make these twisties quite technical. Particular corners always seem to come as a surprise, even to those of us who know the road well. After the big right-hand sweeper around the parking lot for the Mad River Glen Ski Area, you'll begin the next grade and probably make the first tight corner without a problem, but the *steeply banked blind hairpin* on the top half of this S-curve is where I inevitably scrape a peg, floorboard, or bag. Once through this corner, you can relax, it'll be a piece of cake to the parking pull-off/trailhead/overlook at the top.

There are four hairpin corners on the west side of Appalachian Gap. From the overlook you can see the first one, as well as the rocks and trees

Texas Falls is located at the end of Texas Falls Road, just off Route 125 west of Hancock.

that would cushion your fall should you fail to make it. What you *can't* see is the drainage culvert beneath the road which, depending upon the season, can create a linear dip or a raised ridge across the pavement at the point where you should make a quick transition from a hard right lean to a left one. Contrary to popular belief, this road wasn't designed for motorcyclists and it can hold some surprises.

For example, don't accelerate when exiting the fourth hairpin; you'll be making a hard, reverse-right turn on sloped pavement that might have gravel strewn across it. If you plan to take the alternate shortcut by following Route 17 all the way to Lake Champlain, you'll have more leeway there to twist the throttle.

This is an upland valley, and Main Road—a clear enough name—takes you through a couple of hamlets and the small village of Huntington before descending to the Winooski River Valley in Richmond.

Extreme caution is required for the hard left turn near Richmond. It's a blind, reverse Y on a downgrade at the bottom of a hill. The slightest amount of gravel on this turn or a bit too much speed could have you lowsiding your bike. I'd suggest continuing past it and turning around.

Or, instead of attempting this nasty turn, you could deviate a bit from the route and continue straight. Another half mile farther is the Old Round Church (c. 1812–14), originally built as a meeting house for five separate Protestant denominations, as well as the town itself (802-434-3654; www.

As the highest mountain pass in Vermont with a road, Lincoln Gap—narrow at best, with sections of gravel—comes the closest to resembling a mountain road in Europe.

oldroundchurch.com). A local carpenter and blacksmith, William Rhodes, may have been inspired to build this 16-sided structure by an octagonal one in his parents' hometown of Claremont, New Hampshire. The box pews, with their original latched doors and the two-foot-wide floor planking are just a few of the many authentic details that speak of its early origins. It is being restored by the Richmond Historical Society, who keep it open to the public and available for private events.

Turning left you'll cross the Winooski River to US Route 2 in the center of the village of Richmond. This is the beginning of Ride 8, which also offers a shortcut to Essex Junction. Alternately, you can continue straight onto Cochran Road at the intersection by the Old Round Church and find US Route 2 in Jonesville. Harbor Vintage Motors (802-434-4040; www.harborvintage.com), which specializes in VL Harley parts and antique restoration, will be just a tenth of a mile north up Route 2, on your left. From Jonesville you'll have the option to follow US Route 2 west to continue this ride from Richmond, or begin Ride 8; follow Route 2 east to go to Montpelier.

The relentless and technical twisties over Appalachian Gap will require your full attention.

The owner of Harbor Vintage Motors, David Scherk, knows more about antique and vintage Harleys than just about anyone alive.

Returning to the nasty Y corner, proceed on Hinesburg Road and head up the hill for the second half of this ride. At the top there'll be another tricky turn: a 90-degree left at an intersection where gravel is normally strewn across the pavement from the other roads, so be careful.

In Hinesburg you have more options. Route 116 north offers relatively easy access into Burlington or by way of Pond Road (the next left after the junction of Route 2A) to Shelburne. Or, in the village of Hinesburg, a right onto Charlotte Road would take you directly to the Charlotte-Essex Ferry, which crosses Lake Champlain to New York.

Continuing on our route, from Hinesburg ride south on Silver Street (do not make the left turn to follow Route 116 south) and continue straight on Silver Street to Monkton Ridge.

In Monkton Ridge bear right onto Monkton Road. You won't encounter much traffic so enjoy the ride. When you reach US Route 7 just continue straight across it into Vergennes, the smallest, and third-oldest city in the United States.

As strange as it seems, the first two American naval fleets were built and launched a long way from the Atlantic Ocean, from the basin at the foot of the falls on Otter Creek, eight miles from Lake Champlain. The first fleet, commanded by Benedict Arnold in 1776, delayed the British for a critical year; in 1814, the fleet of Commodore Thomas McDonough was victorious against the British at the Battle of Plattsburgh, which helped to bring the War of 1812 to a close.

After crossing the bridge over the falls in Vergennes, turn right onto Panton Road. If you wish to learn more about the rich maritime history of this strategic military and commercial waterway, I recommend visiting the Lake Champlain Maritime Museum (www.lcmm.org), which is located at the

Addison County has the most productive farmland in Vermont. Most people don't envision the broad expanse of the Lower Champlain Valley when they think of the Green Mountain State.

end of Basin Harbor Road—you'll see the signs. Otherwise continue across the richest agricultural land in the state, crossing Dead Creek into Panton, then following Lake Street to Route 17 in West Addison.

The new Lake Champlain Bridge spans the narrows from Chimney Point, Vermont, to Crown Point, New York. At the foot of the bridge on the Vermont side is the Chimney Point State Historic Site (802-759-2412; www.historicvermont.org/chimneypoint/). People have lived at this strategic site for 7,500 years and the history of the three cultures—Native American, French, and English—who have occupied this area is presented in the old tavern (c. 1760).

Detour Along Lake Champlain

Lake Street is a pretty road and easy to follow (simply keep the lake on your right) so don't worry about the absence of highway signs. This is a local shortcut between the Champlain Bridge and the Ticonderoga Ferry. You'll pass Crown Point Road, the very end of the military road that was built across the state from the Connecticut River at Springfield to this point on Lake Champlain in 1759. Major General Jeffery Amherst used it for his successful assault on Montréal in 1760 and it opened up the interior of the region for settlement at the conclusion of the French and Indian Wars in 1763. Lake Street becomes Watch Point Road when it turns away from the lake. Continue straight to Shoreham. The first right on Watch Point Road will be Smith Street, which will take you to the Ticonderoga Ferry if you want to detour even farther and spend some time exploring historic Fort Ticonderoga on the New York side of the lake. ∎

The section of Vermont west of Route 7 to Lake Champlain is the largest expanse of flat land in the state. As you travel across the Champlain Valley it sometimes seems that the most prominent sights are farm silos rising to the sky. This agricultural landscape is one of the richest wildlife habitats in Vermont, with extensive wetlands stretching from Middlebury south to Brandon. Route 73 actually cuts through Long Swamp.

The town of Brandon marks the northern tip of Vermont's Marble Belt, a long narrow area beneath the Taconic Mountains where the sedimentary limestone bedrock of the Champlain Valley was transformed into metamorphic marble. The heart of this industry has been centered on the small town of Proctor, which is home to the Vermont Marble Museum (802-459-2300; www.vermont-marble.com). Examples of distinctive stones from around the world, including the locally quarried Danby white and deep green verde antique are on display, and self-guided tours shed light on the history, geology, and use of marble in art, architecture, and industry.

Turning off Route 3 into Proctor, you'll cross the all-marble Fletcher D. Proctor Memorial Bridge (c. 1915) into a village where even the cutting sheds are made of stone. Like all mill towns, this one is a maze. Continue on Main Street and make a left onto North Street and then the second right onto School Street, which becomes West Street. Now you'll be riding south along a valley that's parallel to Route 3. One interesting site along the way is Wilson Castle (802-773-3284; www.wilsoncastle.com). This 32-room mansion (c. 1867–75) was built of English brick and furnished with European and Oriental antiques by a Vermont doctor who hoped to entice his aristocratic English wife to live in his native state. It didn't work, but the property has nevertheless survived intact under the stewardship of the Wilson family.

Even the stone sheds where the marble was cut and polished were built from this semi-precious material.

Riders often regroup and recap at the trailhead parking area at the top of Appalachian Gap.

Route 4A east will take you back into Rutland, a city where the architectural use of marble is as ubiquitous as granite in Barre. Rutland is a good place to have your bike serviced. You'll have no difficulty finding Central Vermont Motorcycles (360 West St.; 802-773-4533; www.centralvermont motorcycles.com), a dealer for CanAm, Honda, and Kawasaki; Dan Turco & Sons (Rte 7 in N. Clarendon; 802-773-8650; turcosyamaha.com); Outdoors in Motion (1236 Rte 4E; 802-773-4334; www.outdoors-in-motion. com); and Victory Pro Cycle (236 N. Shrewsbury Rd., N. Clarendon; 802-773-2014; procycle.net).

Alternate: Route 17 to West Addison

From the Appalachian Gap you'll follow Route 17 all the way to Chimney Point and the bridge crossing Lake Champlain to Crown Point, New York.

When Route 17 merges with Route 116, you'll be riding along the top of the Monkton Fault, and it'll be visually apparent that this is the western boundary of the Green Mountains. Just before the bridge, turn left onto the Lincoln Road for two-tenths of a mile and park on the side of the road. This is the site of New Haven Falls and an excellent swimming hole. You can actually walk behind the waterfalls, but only after crossing the river.

Route 17/Route 116 curves around the Lord's Prayer Boulder. In 1891 Dr. Joseph Green had the Lord's Prayer inscribed on this boulder because it was near one of the infamous mud holes that plagued wagon drivers. Allegedly, the cursing he heard on this road while still a child left an indelible impression on the good doctor's memory.

If downtown Bristol looks unusually familiar, it might be that you watched the film *The Wizard of Loneliness,* set in fictional Stebbensville, Vermont. The village is built on the sand-and-gravel delta of the post-glacial New Haven River. Ten millennia ago this, and everything you can see from Bristol to the distant Adirondack Mountains in New York, was beneath the waves of the Champlain Sea. You'll ride across this rolling plain for eleven miles before reaching the shore of Lake Champlain.

The highway undulates across the Champlain Valley to New Haven Junction, then twists around Snake Mountain before cutting through wetlands and cropland to reach the shore of Lake Champlain. Chimney Point Tavern, at the Vermont end of the Crown Point bridge, is the original 18th-century structure built as a ferry point and

Until the sun warms the landscape, early morning fog can linger in the valleys.

Ride 6 **The Northeast Kingdom**

Distance: *148 miles and three to four hours*
Highlights: *Narrow river valleys, pristine lakes, and small towns, St. Johnsbury (again), Lake Willoughby.*

The remote rural region in the northeastern corner of the state is mythically portrayed as being the last bastion for true Vermonters. The Northeast Kingdom, a term coined by Governor George Aiken in a 1949 speech, refers to the 1.3 million acres that comprise Orleans, Caledonia, and Essex counties. St. Johnsbury ("Saint J") is a town with treasures one wouldn't expect in northern Vermont, and time spent there will be well rewarded. In addition, Route 5A along the very edge of Lake Willoughby is one of the top scenic rides in the state, while Route 102 is simply fun to ride.

The beginning of this ride is the brief merging of US Route 2 and Main Street in Saint J (pop. 6,319). Note that the cast-iron E. Howard & Company street clock on the corner of Main Street and Eastern Avenue once resided in Grand Central Station in New York City; on the opposite corner in the green stands the marble Civil War monument designed by Larkin

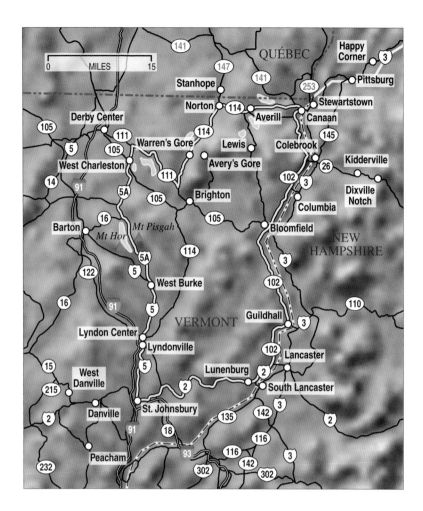

Mead. The windows of the South Congregational Church (next to the green) were made by Louis Comfort Tiffany. The church and its windows, as well as many of the other unique attractions in St. Johnsbury, were gifted to the town by the Fairbanks family, who made their fortune with the invention of the platform scale, which revolutionized the weighing of heavy and unwieldy objects.

Next to the fire station is the famed town library, the Athenaeum, home to more than 100 works of art, a great many of them representative of the Hudson River School, the first identifiable movement in American art, in which painters celebrated the uncorrupted potential of a landscape open to both settlement and exploration. *The View from South Mountain in the Catskills* (a personal favorite of mine), by Sanford Gifford, is an especially

The classically Victorian Estabrook House in Saint J recently has opened its doors as a B&B.

good example of luminism, which is characterized by the tranquil interplay of light and atmosphere. The many other pieces of note, however, are usually eclipsed by Albert Bierstadt's oversized painting, *The Domes of Yosemite,* which is featured in the main gallery. If you can, view it from the perspective intended by the artist, by climbing up to the little balcony at the rear of the rotunda (one person at a time!).

The craftsmanship that went into the curved banisters and decorative moldings of the Athenaeum is also reflected in the interior details of the Fairbanks Natural Science Museum & Planetarium (802-748-2372; www.fairbanksmuseum.org). The imposing white bulk of a taxidermied polar bear famously greets you in the lower gallery, which also displays stuffed specimens of local and exotic fauna, often arranged in animal group dioramas. The upstairs, however, is a true Victorian curiosity cabinet, the walls lined with carrels of similarly categorized objects, from minerals and gemstones, to samurai armor and Civil War artifacts. But

The cast-iron E. Howard & Sons clock at the corner of Main and Eastern Streets once stood in Grand Central Station in New York City.

whatever you do, do not miss the "Bug Art"—nine truly unique mosaics painstakingly pieced together from thousands of common beetles and moths to create portraits of American generals and intricate patterns inspired by prize-winning quilt blocks.

For three generations, the versatile salve known as Bag Balm has been manufactured in Lyndonville, Vermont. Originally developed to soothe irritated cows' udders, the iconic green cans with the red clovers have accompanied Admiral Byrd to the North Pole, kept rust off of rifles in WW II, and protected the paws of cadaver-sniffing dogs in the rubble of Ground Zero in New York City.

One of the better touring roads in New England is a short—much too short—stretch of Route 5A. Lake Willoughby is one of Vermont's most dramatic landscapes, a narrow watery finger squeezed between the towering cliffs of Mount Pisgah and Mount Hor. Arctic plants grow on the mountain tops, peregrine falcons nest on the cliffs, and giant trout cruise the cold water of Vermont's deepest lake. The road is notched into the side of Mount Pisgah and winds along the eastern shore of the lake for five miles. It reminds me of riding in Italy's Lake Region, but without castles perched on the cliffs.

FROM ST. JOHNSBURY, VERMONT

0	From Main St. at US Rte 2 in St. Johnsbury, go north on Main St.
0.4	Bear left onto Mt. Pleasant St.
0.5	Bear right onto Hasting St.
0.8	Bear left (straight) onto US Rte 5 north
8.9	[Pass through Lyndonville]
17.1	Bear right onto Rte 5A in West Burke
23.4	[South shore of Lake Willoughby]
28.4	[Junction of Rte 16]
29.6	[Junction of Rte 58]
36.5	Rte 105 merges with Rte 5A; continue north
37.3	Right onto Durgin Rd. in W. Charleston
39.4	Right on Rte 111 east
42.7	[Morgan]
44.2	[Along Seymour Lake]
49.7	Left onto Rte 114 north
57.3	[Along Norton Pond]
63.2	[Norton village on the U.S.-Canadian border]
72.3	[Wallace Pond]
76.8	Right onto Rte 102 south in Canaan
88.9	[Columbia Covered Bridge]
97.9	[Bloomfield]
113.4	[Guildhall]
120.5	Straight onto US Rte 2 west
124.2	[Highway leaves the river]
126.0	[Lunenburg]
145.3	[Enter St. Johnsbury]
147.4	Left onto US Rte 2/US Rte 5 (Railroad St.)
147.5	Right on US Rte 2 (Eastern Ave.)
147.8	Arrive at the Athenaeum ∎

Route 5A bears left as it merges with Route 105. Slow down and immediately pull into the turn-off area. The Great Falls of the Clyde River has

Approaching Lake Willoughby from the south, the glacially gouged trough between Mount Pisgah and Mount Hor is readily visible.

been tamed by dams, but the gorge would still be a major tourist attraction in many regions of the United States. Here it doesn't even rate a sign.

You have barely enough distance to shift up through the gears before taking the first right turn past Charleston Pond onto Durgin Road, which makes a sweeping left turn around the cemetery. Follow it to Route 111. If you're getting nervous about the level of gas in your tank it would be advisable to continue on Route 5A/105 into Derby Center and then pick up Route 111.

As you skirt the shore of Seymour Lake and then head north on Route 114, it might seem like you're the only person for miles around. It's not your imagination: Warren's Gore has a population of ten; adjoining Avery's Gore has a population of zero; the town of Lewis also doesn't have a single person while the town of Averill has but eight souls. If you want to get away from it all, this is the place. The village of Norton sits on the Canadian border and by comparison it's a metropolis in which most of the township's 214 people reside.

The Canadian border is only a couple thousand feet north of Route 114, a fact that apparently keeps officials at the Department of Homeland Security awake at night. You've reached the 45th Parallel, the halfway point between the equator and the North Pole.

Route 102 plays tag with the serpentine course of the Connecticut River and is a fun stretch of pavement to ride. There's very little traffic and few settlements. Do watch out for moose, though. The Columbia Covered Bridge provides a lovely photo op along the way. The downstream side of the bridge is completely sheathed in vertical planks, while the north side is open for light, so the bridge looks totally different depending upon the point from which it is viewed.

As you are returning to Saint J, it's hard to miss the turn to Dog Mountain (www.dogmt.com/local-area.html), marked as it is by the unmistakable canine sculptures of its late owner, the whimsical artist and author Stephen Huneck. Anyone who has ever been owned by a dog will enjoy the pilgrimage to the verdant hillside with the little chapel that proclaims, WELCOME ALL BREEDS, ALL CREEDS, NO DOGMAS AL-

Known as the Athenaeum, Saint J's town library is home to more than 100 works of art, including Albert Bierstadt's oversized masterpiece, The Domes of Yosemite.

LOWED. Much of the interior is papered in notes and tributes to canines loved and lost, but any sadness is nicely balanced by the irreverent joy in Huneck's artwork, which adorns the stained glass windows and "altarpiece," a winged and leaping Lab.

Beyond Lancaster, the traffic on Route 2 will bring you back to reality as you make progress west, but you can sweeten the end of the journey by stopping at Maple Grove Farms Maple Museum & Factory (1006 Portland St./Rte 2; 802-748-5141; www.maplegrove.com/museum.asp), about a mile and a half before entering St. Johnsbury. Maple Grove Farms has been the world's largest producer of maple sugar candy since 1916. There are other maple museums, but this one is actually part of the history of Vermont's most famous product.

Comfort Inn & Suites (703 Rte 5 at Exit 20 I-91; 802-748-1500; www.vermontvactionland.com), Fairbanks Inn (401 Western Ave./Rte 2; 802-748-5666; www.stjay.com), Yankee Traveler Motel (342 Portland St.; 802-748-3156), and Holiday Motel (222 Hasting St., 802-748-8192; holidaymotelvt.com) are all good places to stay.

Ride 7   The Northern Green Mountains

Distance: *170 to 210 miles; plan on six hours*
Highlights: *Mountains, river valleys, rolling hills. The resort town of Stowe, Route 108 through Smugglers' Notch, the Toll Road to the top of Mount Mansfield, Willey's Store in Greensboro, Cabot Cheese factory in Cabot, and downtown Montpelier.*

This ride offers some choice motorcycling pavement, but be on the lookout for moose. Stowe is the Ski Capitol of the East and the road through Smugglers' Notch is considered to be the most dramatic stretch of highway in the state. Route 109 is a twisty road with a concentration of 19th-century covered bridges. With pavement that snakes along the lower slopes of Jay Peak, it is the highway of choice for sportbike riders. The roads on the eastern side of the Green Mountains are rarely heard about—let's consider them to be a local secret.

With a 2010 census population of less than 8,000 citizens, Montpelier can lay claim to the title of smallest state capitol in the country—and since

The Coffee Corner and La Brioche (in the more modern brick building) are two excellent, but quite different, places to have breakfast in Montpelier.

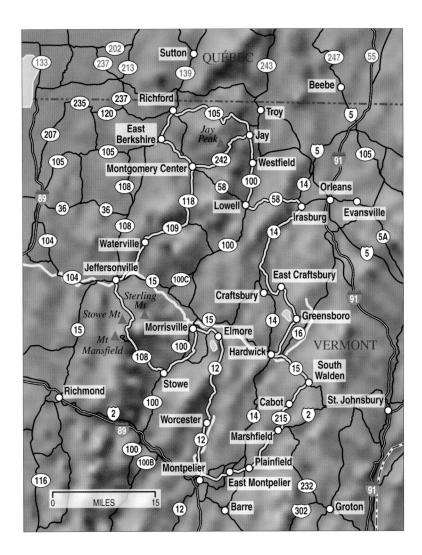

its establishment in the late 1800s, the local economy has been sustained by the business of Vermont's government, with support (in the past) from an iron foundry and water-powered mills, and (today) from higher education and a thriving insurance industry. The Coffee Corner (at Main and State Streets) is the place for breakfast and directly across the street is La Brioche, owned and operated by the Culinary Institute of New England. It would be a good idea to have breakfast in the capitol city unless it's Sunday and you can wait to have brunch in Stowe. I'd also recommend starting out with a full tank of gas.

FROM MONTPELIER, VERMONT

0	From US Rte 2 in Montpelier, proceed east on the bridge over the Winooski River, Rte 12 (Main St.)
0.5	Circling the roundabout, take the second right, following Rte 12
0.5	Right to continue on Rte 12 (Elm St.)
25.0	Left onto Lower Elmore Mtn. Rd.
25.0	Immediate right on Washington Hwy
26.5	Hard left onto Randolph Rd.
29.8	[Caution: Dog-leg corners]
32.8	Bear left (straight) onto Rte 100 south
35.9	Right onto Rte 108 (Mountain Rd.) in Stowe
41.8	[Toll Road to the summit of Mt. Mansfield]
43.3	[Stowe ski area]
45.1	[Caution: steep grade; very tight, blind corners; first gear highly recommended]
53.5	Right onto Rte 15
53.9	Left onto Rte 108
54.3	Right onto Rte 109
69.0	Left onto Rte 118
77.0	[Caution: the junction of Rte 58 (Hazen Military Rd.)]
77.0	Right onto Rte 242 in Montgomery Center
84.9	[Jay Peak ski area]
88.6	[Intersection of Cross Rd. in Jay]

From downtown Montpelier (pop. 8,035) head north on Route 12. This rural valley is isolated from Stowe Valley by the rugged Worcester Range of mountains.

Believe it or not, there's gold in those mountains and following the Civil War, when traces of placer ore were discovered in many of the brooks draining the eastern Green Mountains, it sparked an authentic, if very minor rush that fizzled in the wake of its own yellow flash. Recreational prospectors still find it worth a go, however, and I've panned flakes of this precious metal from Minister Brook in the town of Worcester.

Note that gold is not all that you'll find in them thar hills: this area has one of the highest moose populations in Vermont. I've seen more moose along this highway than anywhere else in the state.

Elmore (pop. 849) has proclaimed itself the Beauty Spot of Vermont and, while the singularity of that title is open to debate, Elmore State Park—on the shores of the lake and at the foot of the mountain bearing the same name—is a beautiful place to camp. I suggest making reservations for one of the 15 lean-tos (802-888-2982; www.vtstateparks/htm/elmore.htm).

Descending into Morrisville, take a left and then an immediate right turn onto Washington Highway (it's a residential street) and go past the cemetery and hospital (an ironic combination). Once in town, take a left onto South Randolph Road, continue straight through the four-way intersection, and then turn right at the T. Bear left (south) onto Route 100. Signs will be scarce but it's hard to get lost in such a clearly defined valley.

Moss Glen Falls is one of the prettiest (and tallest) waterfalls in the state, with a 125-foot combination of cascades dropping into one another within a narrow gorge. The only catch is that you have to park your bike and follow a half-mile path to see the last waterfall. From Randolph Road, Moss Glen Falls Road is on the left, about a quarter-mile before the intersection of Route 100. Ride a half-mile on the well-maintained gravel to a small parking area on the left. Simply follow the trail to the glen.

In the middle of Stowe village, make a right onto Route 108 (Mountain Road). This world-famous ski resort is known for its fine dining. In New England only Boston and Providence have more award-winning restaurants than Stowe (pop. 4,339). It's difficult to

LOOP DETOUR AROUND JAY PEAK

0	From intersection of Rte 242 in Jay, north onto Cross Rd.
1.6	Left onto Rte 105 west
16.0	Left to continue on Rte 105 in Richford village
20.6	Left onto Rte 118 south
27.8	Left onto Rte 242 in Hutchins
39.3	Arrive at Cross Rd. in Jay

CONTINUING FROM JAY, VERMONT

88.6	South on Cross Rd. at Rte 242 in Jay (becomes N. Hill Rd.)
92.8	Bear right (straight) onto Rte 100 south in Westfield
99.3	Left onto Rte 58 in Lowell
107.6	Right onto Rte 58/Rte 14
108.8	Straight on Rte 14 in Irasburg
119.9	Left onto North Craftsbury Rd.
122.3	[Craftsbury Common and Sterling College]
123.5	[Craftsbury]
124.3	Left onto East Craftsbury Rd.
126.1	Bear right (next right) onto Town Hwy 1 (Craftsbury Rd.)
131.6	Right onto Breezy Ave. in the village of Greensboro
138.0	Left onto N. Main St. in Hardwick
138.2	Left onto Rte 15
145.4	Right onto Rte 215 in S. Walden
150.4	Cabot village and Cabot Cheese
154.4	Right onto US Rte 2 in Marshfield
161.3	In Plainfield, stay on US Rte 2
164.6	Bear left onto US Rte 2/Rte 14 in East Montpelier at the blinking traffic light
164.8	Straight on US Rte 2
165.6	Right onto Towne Hill Rd. to take the scenic back way to downtown Montpelier
168.9	Left onto Main St. in Montpelier
169.7	Arrive at Rte 12 in Montpelier ∎

make a choice. For wood-fired, custom-made pizza it's Pie In The Sky (492 Mountain Rd.; 802-253-5100) or try the Cactus Café (2160 Mountain Rd.; 802-253-7770) for Tex-Mex. The Trapp Family Lodge of *Sound of Music* fame (802-253-8511; www.trappfamily.com) is worth a short detour up Trapp Hill Road where Johannes von Trapp—youngest son of the Baron and Maria—now brews a tasty selection of Austrian-inspired lagers. Trattoria La Festa (4080 Mountain Rd.; 802-253-8480; trattoriastowe.com) is one of my favorite dinner spots. These are just suggestions, as the number of pubs, restaurants, and lodging options are far too extensive to list in this book.

You may hear tell of a private toll road that winds from the Stowe Mountain Resort to the summit of Vermont's highest peak, Mount Mansfield, but unfortunately, motorcycles are prohibited.

The Mount Mansfield State Forest begins just beyond the entrance to the famous ski resort. Route 108 remains closed each year until the snow clears, and how early one can make it through Smugglers' Notch has become an annual game for me. One year I managed it on April 3rd and on another I was turned back on May 31st. This rugged, glacially carved pass between Mount Mansfield and Sterling Mountain has been used as a conduit for illicit exchange since the early 19th century, when Thomas Jefferson's 1807 embargo on trade with British Canada levied a disproportionate hardship on the citizens of the north country. (Jeffersonville, the center of the illegal activity, bears his name in jest.) Later, the route was also used by fugitive slaves and Prohibition-era rumrunners.

These days, Route 108 is considered to be an important summer shortcut between Stowe and Burlington, as well as one of the most dramatic roads in Vermont. Although closed to truck and trailer traffic, it's not uncommon for an RV driver to decide it doesn't apply to him—but it does. Extraction is not only time consuming and frightfully expensive, it completely blocks traffic for hours. Even for motorcyclists, the last severely banked corner should be taken in first gear. Downshift when the road begins to snake around giant boulders and *immediately* get into first gear when you see the exposed right hairpin. Stall here and you are going to take a spill. At the top you'll squeeze between boulders into an area where pedestrians will be busy looking up at the cliffs, especially if climbers are present. Keep your eyes on the road and pull into the parking lot if you wish to sightsee.

In the village of Jeffersonville (pop. 568), you can either make a right turn or continue onward; both will bring you to Route 15, but going straight will allow you to tank up with gas and grab a cup of coffee and delicious pastry or deli lunch at the Cupboard Deli & Bakery (802-644-2069).

A unique and historic road squeezes between the cliffs of Smugglers' Notch.

Riders twisting through the Head of the Snake—a narrow passage between boulders—at the top of Smugglers' Notch.

At the end of the village, Route 108 crosses Route 15 and there's a nice picnic area just before the bridge.

Route 108 continues straight after it crosses the Lamoille River, but turn right onto Route 109 and follow that through Waterville. There are five covered bridges between Waterville and Route 118. The first is a tenth of a mile off the highway on a street behind the town hall in Waterville; the second is a half-mile beyond the post office. Both were built in 1877 in the queenpost style. The third is exactly a half-mile farther and one-tenth of a mile off Route 109 on your right. Mill Bridge is a half-mile from the highway and will be found by taking your first left after crossing the concrete bridge. The Morgan is nine-tenths of a mile past this concrete bridge and can be seen on your left. If you're not sated by these, there are five more to be found along Route 118, one before you reach Montgomery Center and four in or after the village of Montgomery.

Leaving Montgomery Center you'll have two choices: one is a paved road and one is gravel. The latter, Route 58, is the Hazen Notch Road, the end of the Bayley-Hazen Military Road built between 1776 and 1779 from the Connecticut River to the top of this lesser-known notch. This is an authentic 18th-century road and the scenery is fantastic. I'd suggest that you first

Tallman's in Belvidere, which has yet to become "touristified," is typical of the sort of general store that was found throughout Vermont in the 1950s and 60s.

check with the folks at Sylvester's Market, however, to find out when it was last graded; you do *not* want to suddenly find yourself on a freshly fluffed, loose surface if you were expecting a less technical ride.

Your paved option would be Route 242, a wondrous motorcycle road with lots of corners that climbs over the eastern shoulder of Jay Peak. It too is scenic, and when the road crests the ridge by the Jay Peak Ski Resort you'll be granted a view that stretches into Canada. One of the most popular sportbike circuits in the state is Route 242 to Jay, Route 105 west to East Berkshire, and Route 118 south back to Montgomery Center. It also scores high as a fall foliage tour, because this area displays exceptional reds and oranges, and "peak" color can be as much as two weeks earlier than in southern Vermont. If you decide not to do this particular loop, turn right at the intersection in Jay and ride south on North Hill Road to reach Route 100.

Heading south on Route 100, you'll pick up Route 58 in Lowell. Staying on Route 58 through Orleans and Evansville would be the scenic way to reach Route 5A and Ride 6 through the Northeast Kingdom. Otherwise, turn south on Route 14 in Irasburg, one of three towns named after state founder Ira Allen, brother of Ethan.

If compared to most highways in the United States, Route 14 would be classified as a scenic byway and a top motorcycle touring road. Here, it barely stands out enough to attract attention. If you want to explore a bit, you could follow Route 14 south and pick up this ride in Hardwick (pop. 3,174), or ride for another 30 minutes to rejoin it in East Montpelier. I encourage you to follow the directions in this book, but also to explore some roads that you might miss if traveling without a native guide.

To follow the outlined route, turn left off Route 14 to ride through Craftsbury Common and Craftsbury before taking a left to East Craftsbury. Sterling College in Craftsbury Common is an environmental institution that puts theory to practice as its 100 or so students learn practical techniques such as farming, logging, and wilderness survival. Fans of Alfred Hitchcock might recognize Craftsbury as the setting for *The Trouble with Harry*. Follow pavement and the road will take you along Caspian Lake into the village of Greensboro (pop. 770).

Willey's (802-533-2554) is a true general store that's the center—physically, socially, and psychologically—of Greensboro village. It has to be experienced. Forget about going to the mall, it's all right here! This might look like a quaint Vermont town in the middle of nowhere, but it's not; you never know which famous person you might run into while shopping at Willey's. Ride straight up the hill, stay on Center Road and you'll arrive in Hardwick. Turn right to follow Route 14 to East Montpelier; turn left onto Route 15 to explore a bit more. Route 15 continues east as a shortcut to Ride 3, but I suggest that you follow Route 215 to Cabot.

The Cabot Co-operative Creamery (800-837-4261; www.cabotcheese. coop) is better known to the outside world as Cabot Cheese, one of Ver-

Route 242 over the shoulder of Jay Peak, a fantastic fall foliage ride, is one of the premier motorcycle roads in northern Vermont.

The northern Green Mountains and Jay Peak viewed from Route 100.

mont's most notable quality food producers. Their English-style cheddar won Best of Class in the 2010 World Championship Cheese Contest, but their Vintage Choice grade—the stuff with the purple wax coating—is the very essence of a real cheddar. Keep an eye out for their 5-Year Old School Cheddar (only sold at the creamery); it really is good enough to be worth its price.

Route 215 ends at US Route 2 in Marshfield village (pop. 267). If you turned left onto Route 2 and rode to the top of the hill, you could join Ride 3 going to Norwich. Instead, to continue on this route, turn right onto Route 2 and ride through Plainfield and East Montpelier. You can continue on Route 2 following the Winooski River into Montpelier.

If you're inclined to take a scenic detour, turn right onto Cherry Hill Road 1.1 miles past the blinking traffic light at the merging of Route 14 and US Route 2 in East Montpelier. Just follow the road, make a left turn at the T-intersection and ride down the hill on Upper Main Street to the center of Montpelier.

Montpelier is the end of Ride 7 and mid-point of Ride 4. You now deserve a reward, whether it's a beer in Charlie-O's (70 Main St.; 802-223-6820) or fine wine and dinner at the Main Street Grill & Bar (118 Main St.; 802-223-3188). Most riders choose to stay at the rather economical Econolodge at the top of the hill (101 Northfield St./Rte 12; 802-223-5258; www.econolodgevt.com), but the pricey Inn at Montpelier is undoubtedly the best bed in town (147 Main St.; 802-223-2727; www.innatmontpelier.com).

Ride 8　Lake Champlain and the Islands

Distance: *121 miles; four hours or more*
Highlights: *Islands of Lake Champlain, rolling hills through rural countryside, small villages, numerous places along the lakeshore beckon stops, including Saint Anne's Shrine.*

Lake Champlain is the sixth-largest body of water in the United States and it holds a number of surprises, though I doubt if "Champ," our local Loch Ness monster, is one of them. The world's oldest coral reefs are found in Lake Champlain and the U.S. Navy was born here, not on the Atlantic coast. The Lake Champlain Transportation Corporation is the oldest steamship company in the world and the steamship *Vermont* (c. 1809) was the first, after Fulton's *North River of Clermont,* to offer regular passenger service. The *Vermont* was built and operated by the Winan brothers in Burlington—one was a shipwright and the other the original pilot of the *Clermont.*

The northern bridge spans Lake Champlain between Alburgh, Vermont, and Rouses Point, New York.

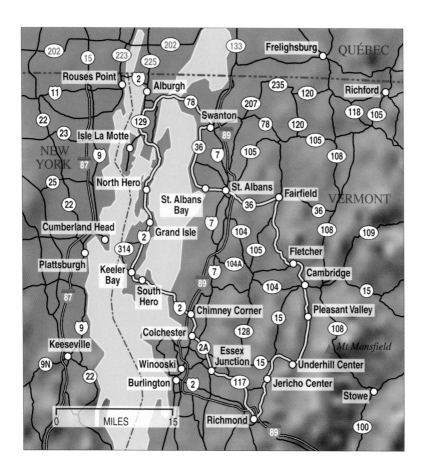

Samuel de Champlain explored the lake in 1609 and it became a strategic military position for the next two centuries. The Champlain Canal was built in 1823 and then, as now, a boat was able to travel from the St. Lawrence River to Manhattan. The luxurious steamships that traveled the length of the lake on their scheduled routes were one of the few things Charles Dickens praised during his tour of America in 1836, and these ships carried U.S. Presidents on a regular basis until the 20th century. Don't be surprised to find a bit of history wherever you stop along the lake.

Undulating roads wind through the hills that lie between Lake Champlain and the Green Mountains. The range of landscapes you will encounter on this particular ride will give you a new perspective on why I consider Vermont to have some of the best motorcycle touring in New England.

A logical place to begin this ride would be in Burlington, but since the mid-point of Ride 5 is the village of Richmond (pop. 4,090), we'll start

FROM RICHMOND, VERMONT

0	From the light at Richmond, head west on Rte 2
1.8	Past the entrance to I-89, take a right onto Rte 117
7.5	[Pass the junction of Rte 289 bypass on the right]
9.8	In Essex Jct. at the five corners, bear right onto Rte 2A
11.9	[Pass the junction of Rte 289 bypass on the right]
15.0	Bear right onto US Rte 2/US Rte 7
18.0	Left onto US Rte 2
23.1	[Pass through Sandbar State Park]
36.4	[Pass by Knight Point State Park]
45.5	Left onto Rte 129
48.2	Right onto West Shore Rd.
48.2	[If you want to explore Isle La Motte, follow Rte 129 left from this intersection]
51.6	Right onto Old Truck Rte (Town Hwy 1)
53.4	Cross US Rte 2 and proceed east on Rte 78 near Alburgh
63.2	Right onto Rte 36 (S. River St.) in Swanton
63.3	Left to continue on Rte 36 (Lake Rd.)
74.0	At the traffic rotary at St. Albans Bay, continue on Rte 36 (Lake Rd.)
76.9	At the junction of US 7, go right, then a quick left to follow Rte 36 (Fairfield St.) in downtown St. Albans
	Continue on Rte 36 through St. Albans to Fairfield
84.4	Right onto South Rd. in Fairfield (it becomes Fairfield Rd. after a couple of miles)
92.0	Continue on Fairfield Rd. in West Fletcher (Fairfield Rd. becomes Cambridge Rd., then Pumpkin Harbor Rd.)
98.7	Right onto Rte 15; cross the bridge
99.0	Left onto Lower Pleasant Valley Rd. at the green in Cambridge
103.0	At Pleasant Valley, bear right onto Pleasant Valley Rd.
109.6	At Underhill Center Pleasant Valley Rd becomes River Rd.
112.3	In Jericho, left onto Rte 15
112.8	Left onto Browns Trace Rd.
115.4	[Pass through Jericho Center]
116.3	Bear left to continue on Browns Trace Rd.
121.1	Arrive at US Rte 2 (Main St.) in Richmond ∎

there, which will guide you around the worst of the urban congestion. After all, the Greater Burlington area is home to more than 20 percent of the state's population, and is the undisputed business, cultural, and educational center of Vermont.

Riding westward from Richmond on Route 2, you'll turn right immediately after passing beneath I-89. Route 117 follows the Winooski River into

You'll find the oldest log cabin in the U.S. next to the high school in Grand Isle.

Essex Junction (pop. 8,591). Traffic congestion at the five corners in the center of Essex Junction can be avoided by using Route 289, a divided four-lane highway built as a bypass for employees of the IBM plant. It starts at Route 117 about two miles before you get to Essex Junction, crosses Route 15, and ends at Route 2A. If you need to stop at Frank's BMW Triumph Yamaha (802-878-3930;franksmotorcyclesales.com), exit from Route 289 and go right (east) on Route 15 (Center Road) to the blinking traffic light. If you go through Essex Junction rather than use the bypass, simply continue straight through the traffic lights at the five corners onto Route 2A. This in turn connects to the merged US Route 2/US Route 7, which then divides at Chimney Corner near Exit 17 of I-89. So, whether you rode north on I-89 from Burlington, or US Routes 2 and 7 from Winooski, or 2A from Essex Junction, you will be poised to follow US Route 2 through the Champlain Islands.

The wetlands on either side of the highway and the day-use-only Sandbar State Park are the delta of the Lamoille River. The causeway crosses to the town of South Hero (pop. 1,696) on Grand Isle. Route 2 runs along the edge of Keeler Bay, just one of many photographic vistas you'll encounter on the first segment of this ride. Stay on US Route 2 if you plan to camp at Grand Isle State Park (802-372-4300; vtstateparks.com/htm/grandisle.htm), which has 117 tent/trailer sites (but no electric hookups), 36 lean-tos, four cabins, and hot showers.

Route 314 loops out to Gordon Landing and the 12-minute ferry crossing to Cumberland Head, New York, which offers some great views of the Adirondack Mountains. Not only was Lake Champlain where the U.S. Navy was founded, it was the site of two of its most important early conflicts. In 1776, America's first hastily made and launched "fleet" of gun platforms engaged the advancing British Navy off Valcour Island. The ships under Benedict Arnold's command were driven back, but not before inflicting heavy damage, buying the Continental Army a crucial year to prepare for the war. The last battle in 1814, with the U.S. fleet under the command of Thomas McDonough, was victorious, as were our land forces, and the Battle of Plattsburgh proved to be the decisive point in the War of 1812.

One of the highlights of this trip is easy to miss. In front of the high school in the town of Grand Isle (pop. 1,955) is the Hyde Log Cabin, the oldest log cabin in the United States. Built by Jedediah Hyde in 1783, it remained in the family until the State of Vermont acquired it in 1945.

A drawbridge with a steel-grate floor spans the narrow crossing between Grand Isle and North Hero known as The Gut. As a teenager, Franklin D. Roosevelt was known to boast that he was the only civilian who could pilot steamships through this channel (his father was president of the Champlain Transportation Company). Although you can see folks fishing in many places, the very swift water concentrates the big fish—salmon, sturgeon, trout, pike, and pickerel—in the shallows. I've scuba dived here and can testify that brown eels can grow to eight feet in length and some northern pike are so large they look like green barracuda.

Across these lush fields can be seen the blue profile of Vermont's Green Mountains to the east and the purplish views of New York's Adirondacks to the southwest.

North Hero (pop. 810) is one of the places I once called home, and so I always get a special feeling upon entering this charming, tiny village. Trees shield the western view as the highway forms the shore on your right. Historically, smugglers would haul their shallow boats across the very narrow

A quirky sort of engine-uity is characteristic of the Green Mountain State.

West Shore Road curves along the edge of Lake Champlain.

neck of land that separates the eastern side of the lake from Carry Bay on the west; by the time pursuers had made it around the island, the illegal goods would be long gone.

After another short bridge you'll sweep around the corner and make a right onto Route 129. Watch for oncoming traffic on US Route 2. You will be at the Alburgh Tongue, one of only two places in the country where land is not attached to the contiguous Lower 48 states. The road follows the shore, then curves to the right onto West Shore Road or, for an interesting detour, turn left to cross the causeway onto Isle La Motte.

At the causeway, head north on West Shore Road to cruise along the Alburgh shore. Take the second right—this is the Old Truck Route—to US Route 2 at Route 78. Going left on US Route 2 will take you through Alburgh village and across the bridge to Rouses Point, New York. The second part of this ride begins by following Route 78 east.

Route 78 will go over the bridge to Hog Island. The delta of the Missisquoi River hosts an important wetland ecology, holding the largest

US Route 2—also known as the Roosevelt Highway—spans the lake not far from Sandbar State Park.

blue heron rookery in New England. The road will remind you of swamps in the deep South, minus the draping Spanish moss.

The quickest way to reach St. Albans (pop. 7,650) from Swanton (pop. 2,548) would be to follow Route 7, but the preferred scenic route is Route 36 along the shore of the lake. It goes south to St. Albans Bay, the original site of the town prior to the arrival of the Central Vermont Railroad.

Nearly a half a million years ago, the beautiful black building stone from the Fisk farm, one of the earliest quarries in America, was part of an ancient coral reef.

The northernmost action of the Civil War took place here on October 19, 1864. A group of 21 Confederate soldiers staged simultaneous robberies on the three banks in town, killed one man, and escaped into Canada. The British detained them, but determined their crimes to have been acts of war, and they were released, although the $88,000 they still had in their possession was returned to Vermont. Two years later, 3,500 Irish nationals, many of them Civil War veterans, coalesced under the banner of the radical Fenian Brotherhood and converged upon St. Albans to launch an invasion into Canada to set up an Irish Free State. The news of reinforced Canadian troops coming to meet them sent the Fenians into a disorganized retreat back to Ver-

Side Trip: Isle La Motte

From the causeway, take the second right by the public library, which leads to Saint Anne's Shrine (802-928-3362; www.saintannesshrine.org).

This interesting site is where Samuel de Champlain is alleged to have landed in 1609 while exploring the lake that is named after him. In 1666, a small French community under Captain Pierre La Motte built a fort and struggled in this wilderness until 1671, when the fort was abandoned. The land where the fort once stood was purchased by the Catholic Diocese of Burlington around 1890 and a small shrine was opened in 1893. There's a little museum containing a number of excavated artifacts; picnic tables are placed for all visitors to enjoy this lakeside retreat.

The oldest coral reefs on the planet can be found here—or at least their fossilized remains. When polished, the dull grey limestone takes on a beautiful black color flecked with the lighter-colored remains of trilobites and ammonites that lived hundreds of millions of years before dinosaurs roamed the planet. Limestone quarried from the Fisk Farm was used to build the Brooklyn Bridge, the facade of Radio City Music Hall, and the face of the U.S. Capitol Building.

Vice President Theodore Roosevelt was staying on Isle La Motte (which he frequently did) when he heard that President McKinley had been assassinated. He slipped across the lake and into the Adirondacks for a few days before showing up in Washington, D.C. to be sworn in as President of the United States. There must be an interesting story behind this episode, but I've yet to discover it.

This is a beautiful place; explore as far as you wish. Route 129 goes down the center of the island and the only way you can leave is to ride back across the causeway.   ■

Looking south from Route 129 on a foggy morning. Isle La Motte is to the right; Alburgh on the left.

mont, where U.S. troops had seized their camp and munitions. Locals were treated to an Army band concert as the Irishmen were escorted to the train depot and returned to Boston—all without a single shot having been fired.

Fairfield is a quaint little crossroads. It's also the birthplace of Chester A. Arthur, the 21st President of the United States. The two Vermont-born Presidents, Calvin Coolidge and Chester Arthur, were elected as vice presidents and succeeded to their presidencies upon the assassinations of the presidents-elect. Both served single terms. The location of the log cabin where Arthur was born has been lost to history, but the parsonage where he lived as an infant has been recreated and is now a State Historic Site (note the gravel road).

It will be a pleasant ride through Fletcher—don't look for a village—to Cambridge (pop. 235). Crossing the Lamoille River, make a left turn by the Cambridge Village Store onto the Lower Pleasant Valley Road. Once again, this won't be the shortest or the most direct way to reach Underhill Flats, but traveling along the east side of Mount Mansfield will be far more

Motorcycle touring doesn't get any better than the Pleasant Valley Road on the western side of Mount Mansfield.

aesthetically satisfying. Just be careful when you enter the small village of Underhill Center, because the stop sign by the Underhill Country Store will come as a surprise.

You will briefly—very briefly—rejoin Route 15 before making a left turn onto Browns Trace Road. Yes, as mentioned at the beginning of this ride, Route 15 would have been the fast way to return to Burlington and the Route 289 bypass, but this has been a day of exploring roads unfamiliar to most riders, and there's no reason to stop now.

The granite statue of Samuel de Champlain accompanied by his native guide was sculpted by F. L.. Weber in the Vermont pavilion during Montréal's Expo 67, which featured the theme of Man and His World.

At the green, opposite the general store in Jericho Center, you'll see a Vermont Historic Marker commemorating Wilson "Snowflake" Bentley (1865–1931), a farmer who used a large format camera and homemade microscope to photograph more than 5,800 snowflakes. He won worldwide recognition for proving that each snowflake is unique, and his glass negatives now reside in New York's Buffalo Museum of Science, with the Jericho Historical Society owning the broadest collection of his photographs (802-899-3225; www.snowflakebentley.com).

Bearing left at Jericho Center and continuing onto Browns Trace Road will lead you to the center of Richmond; bearing right and down the hill on Governor Peck Road will take you to the junction of Route 117 and US Route 2 in Richmond, where this trip began.

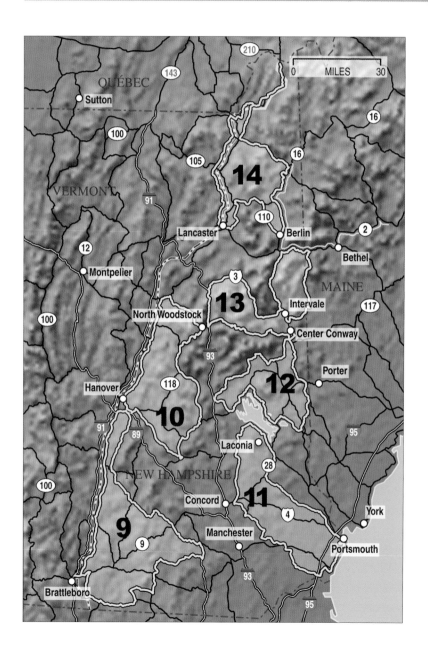

New Hampshire

New Hampshire has the smallest seacoast of any New England state—only 18 miles—and the highest mountain, Mount Washington at 6,288 feet. It measures 190 miles north to south, but just 68 miles at its widest point. Only four states are smaller in land area, but few offer as many miles of great touring roads as the Granite State.

It is a good-natured point of contention among me and my northern New England riding friends as to which state gets top honors. Although they can't be faulted for not living in Vermont, I can't deny New Hampshire has a strong case. In the end, of course, everybody wins.

The granite with which the state has chosen to identify was formed well below the surface during our earth's pre-history, when trapped magma cooled slowly enough for minerals to organize themselves into crystals; the coarser the grain, the more slowly the magma cooled. Light-colored Concord granite has a characteristic salt-and-pepper appearance, while Conway granite is typically more orange or pink in color—or even yellowish green—a result of its mineral composition. While both types of stone were named

Laconia Bike Week brings thousands of motorcyclists to New Hampshire every June.

for the places where they were first quarried, they aren't limited to those particular areas. Wherever granite is exposed today as surface bedrock, erosion has stripped away the miles of land forms that originally covered it. Without much effort, you can still see these forces at work today.

But what is it exactly about those flinty types from the Granite State and their Live Free or Die independence? The politics of their libertarian ideals go well below the mere surface of personal freedoms tempered with individual responsibilities. One feature unique to New Hampshire's history of recreational conservation is its property tax incentives for land enrolled under its Current Use statutes to remain in an undeveloped state. Assessment receives another hefty discount if a landowner allows low-impact recreation on his property, such as hiking and skiing, and is additionally freed of any liability for such activities. And unlike practices common out West, New Hampshire common law gives the public the right of access to land that's not posted—all of which has been attracting outdoor enthusiasts long before there were enough of them to label themselves as such. A lot of the original routes they followed, twisting and squeezing over and around the geography, will be what gives us the means to appreciate the wild solitude and beauty of New Hampshire's mountains and river valleys.

Seasonal folks have been flocking to the Lakes Region ever since Colonial Governor John Wentworth built a summer home near Wolfeboro in 1771. Henry David Thoreau documented his ramblings over the rugged peaks of the White Mountains just as railroad travel was beginning to popu-

For two days during Bike Week, the Mount Washington Auto Road is open only to motorcycles.

The dam at Lake St. Francis assures its place as the largest of the north region's many lakes.

larize the region's natural attractions as destinations for beating the summer heat and doldrums of points south.

The western boundary of the state, the Connecticut River, served not only as one of the first transportation routes into the New England interior, its flowing water powered the mills and industries that built a growing country—and which would ultimately threaten the landscape, through deforestation and its resulting erosion. It was the Weeks Act, passed in 1911, that provided for the establishment of the White Mountain National Forest and its consequent rebound into the multi-use resource we currently celebrate.

Today, few states are as rider-friendly as the Granite State, whose economy gets a shot in the arm each June when hundreds of thousands of motorcyclists saddle up to make the yearly pilgrimage to Laconia's Bike Week, and many, many more take the time to stay and savor the great roads. Restaurants and lodging welcome all, and the latter are often quick to offer small courtesies like shaded parking, kickstand plates, and old towels for wiping down your bike. If you haven't yet had the chance to experience and explore New Hampshire, you definitely have something to look forward to.

Ride 9   Bronson Hills and the Quiet Corner

Distance: *219 miles that will take all day*
Highlights: *The Connecticut River Valley with plenty of curves and lots of scenic views. The Saint-Gaudens National Historic Site, the longest covered bridge in the U.S., scenic colonial villages, several historic places, and perhaps even a pit stop for your motorcycle.*

I enjoy old roads, out-of-the-way strips of pavement that are practically void of traffic. The one that follows the eastern bank of the Connecticut River through the township of Westmoreland is simply called River Road.

Route 12 is the main highway in this part of New Hampshire. Until you begin to approach North Walpole and Bellows Falls, you'll catch only occasional glimpses of the river. Any of the bridges that cross the Connecticut River would link you to Ride 2, and you could weave back and forth between these two routes to create a tour of your own.

Great Falls was the original name for the village of Bellows Falls, Vermont, but the gorge is more readily visible from Route 12 on the New

Solitary Mount Monadnock was named for the Abenaki word that meant "mountain that stands alone," and geologists later adopted the term more broadly to designate any single mountain that is not part of a range.

Hampshire side. The gorge was much narrower when I was a boy, but since then the ledges have been dynamited to widen the channel. Even so, during the spring the raging water vibrates the ground, and nobody has ever survived the running of these rapids.

This was the northernmost point on the river for shad, and native Abenakis returned for the yearly salmon run until the early 19th century. Indian petroglyphs can be seen from the south side of the concrete bridge on the Vermont side. Their true meaning is a mystery, but I've always

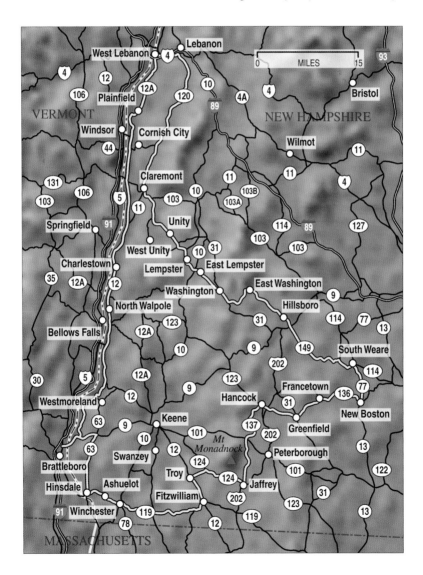

FROM BRATTLEBORO, VERMONT

0	From the US Rte 5/Rte 9 roundabout in Brattleboro, Vermont, go east on Rte 9
2.7	Left onto Brook St. to Main St. to River Rd.
11.4	Left onto Rte 63
13.7	Bear left onto Rte 12
23.8	In North Walpole, right to continue on Rte 12
35.6	Left onto Rte 12A (River Rd.)
43.2	Straight and continue on Rte 12A
48.5	At the Cornish-Windsor Bridge, straight to continue on Rte 12A
61.8	At the Powerhouse Mall in West Lebanon, right onto Glen Rd.
63.0	Right onto US Rte 4/Rte 10
65.4	At the green in Lebanon, right onto Rte 120 (School St.)
86.7	In Claremont, right onto Rte 11/Rte 103 (Broad St.)
86.9	Right, then left onto Broad St.
87.3	Left onto Chestnut St. (becomes 2nd New Hampshire Tpke)
101.8	Straight across Rte 10 onto Mountain Rd.
107.3	Bear right onto Rte 31 (S. Main St.)
108.4	Left onto E. Washington Rd.
119.1	In Hillsborough, bear right onto Center Rd.
121.7	Straight across US Rte 202 onto School St. (becomes Rte 149/Bridge St.)
134.6	In South Weare, right onto Rte 77 (Dustin Tavern Rd.)
140.3	In New Boston, hard right onto Rte 136 (Francestown Rd.)
156.3	Straight across US Rte 202 to continue on Forest Rd.
157.9	In Hancock, left onto Rte 123/Rte 137 (Main St.)
158.1	By the Hancock Inn, bear left on Rte 137
171.6	At US Rte 202 in Jaffrey, right onto Rte 124 (Main St.)
178.0	At Perkins Pond, left onto Troy Rd. (becomes Monadnock St.)
180.7	In Troy, left onto Rte 12 (S. Main St.)
184.5	In Fitzwilliam, right onto Rte 119
199.0	In Winchester, left to continue on Rte 119/Rte 10
199.6	Right to continue on Rte 119 (Ashuelot St.)
205.1	In Hinsdale, right onto Rte 63 (Kilburn St.)
213.4	Left (west) onto Rte 9
219.0	Arrive in Brattleboro, Vermont, at US Rte 5 and Exit 3 of I-91 ■

thought they were simply graffiti chiseled into the rock while waiting for the salmon to run. Maybe they say nothing more than BIG BEAR AND TWO EAGLES WERE HERE.

The first bridge to cross any point along the Connecticut River was also

The petroglyphs on the edge of the gorge at Great Falls have been attributed to Native Americans, who traditionally used this site for salmon fishing.

here, and the limestone structure that so crucially enabled the railroads to run from Boston to Chicago still serves that purpose.

The river follows an ancient fault line and marks the extent of the proto North American continent. Millions of years ago, the continent of Africa collided with North America, pushing ahead of it an archipelago of volcanic islands that acted like a bulldozer, plowing debris from the ocean floor that would become the mountains of Vermont; the remnants of those islands would become the hills in western New Hampshire, while the southeastern part of the state was once part of Africa.

Known as the Bronson Hill belt, this rolling topography used to be known for its mica mines (used as "isinglass" in wood and coal stoves and as electrical insulation), and abandoned feldspar quarries (an abrasive used in household cleansers) dot the now-forested landscape. Gem aquamarine, rose quartz, green fluorite, and jasper, as well as mica, quartz crystals, and black tourmaline fill my display cabinets from visits to these old mine sites.

Charlestown is a pretty little village that was settled in 1740 as Plantation No. 4, the northernmost British settlement along the river. In 1743 the settlers pulled six houses together, connected them with lean-tos, and built a stockade around them to protect themselves from Indian raids. The settlement became known as the Fort at No. 4; a bronze plaque mounted in a boulder on Main Street marks its original location. It was from here that Major Jeffery Amherst staged the assault that captured Montréal in 1760, and where Colonel John Stark gathered the local militia and rushed to Walloomsac, New York, to engage British Troops at the Battle of Bennington in 1777. Sixty-three buildings along the street are on the National Register of Historic Places, but the reconstruction of the fort is now located closer to the river.

Route 12A is a slow road—most of it is posted for 40 mph—but the bucolic countryside is among the prettiest along the entire length of the Connecticut River. There are industries discreetly located between Routes 12 and 12A, but you probably won't even notice them as you ride by.

The Cornish-Windsor Bridge, built in 1866, was the fourth covered bridge erected at this site. Listed as a National Historic Civil Engineering Landmark, the structure still stands as an example of the great wooden bridges that used to span the major rivers of the east. At 449.4 feet long, it's one of the longest covered bridges in the world.

The Cornish Colony was founded by Augustus Saint-Gaudens around 1885 and grew to more than 100 notable American artists and philosophers. Some of their names are still familiar: Ethel Barrymore, Maxfield Parrish, Frederic Remington, James Earl Fraser (*End of the Trail* and the "buffalo" nickel), President Woodrow Wilson, Paul Manship (*Prometheus,* Rockefeller Center), Isadore Duncan, Charles Platt (American Renaissance movement), William Zorach *(Spirit of the Dance,* Radio City Music Hall), and Daniel Chester French (*Abraham Lincoln,* Lincoln Memorial). Summers were an intense time of creativity and socialization.

Irish-born Saint-Gaudens was raised in New York and studied art and architecture in Europe. Perhaps best known for the realism with which he interpreted Civil War memorial commissions, including *Standing Lincoln* (Lincoln Park, Chicago), the David Farragut Memorial (Madison Square Park, New York) and the Robert Gould Shaw Memorial in Boston Common, especially notable for its true-to-life depiction of the African-Americans of the 54th Massachusetts Volunteer Infantry. At the request of Theodore Roosevelt, Saint-Gaudens created designs for two U.S. gold coins

The Fort at No. 4 has been authentically reconstructed at a site closer to the Connecticut River.

The Cornish-Windsor Covered Bridge is the second longest in the United States and the longest two-span covered bridge in the world.

minted from 1907 to 1933, the $10 Indian Head eagle, and perhaps the most beautiful U.S. coin of all time, the $20 Double Eagle, with a robed Liberty striding forth from the Capitol bathed in radiance, bearing a torch and olive branch.

Saint-Gaudens built his Cornish home and studios (www.nps.gov/saga/index.htm) in 1900 after returning from Paris, but he was soon to die of cancer in 1907. With views to the Connecticut River Valley and Mount Ascutney, guests likened the grounds of his beloved Aspet to the Italian countryside. Today the property is the only site in New Hampshire administered by the National Parks Service, and you can wander the grounds and enjoy more than 100 recastings of Saint-Gaudens's sculpture. Sadly enough, this gem is commonly overlooked, though I've noticed motorcyclists must be passing the word amongst themselves, as it is gaining in popularity; it really is a perfect low-key destination run.

Plainfield has a population of 2,241 people and a land area of 52.9 square miles, for an average of 43 people per square mile. In reality, the population distribution of this township, like most others in northern New England, depends more on topography than physical size. Main roads are often nothing more than a narrow strip cutting through municipalities.

This small village has an interesting church that looks more like a barn than the Federalist-style white-steeple houses of worship typically associ-

Augustus Saint-Gaudens's Cornish home and studios are the only site in New Hampshire administered by the National Parks Service.

ated with the region, but characteristic 19th-century architecture still predominates. It was here that Maxfield Parrish purchased his beloved house, The Oaks, on the tails of his earliest success as an illustrator of magazines, calendars, and children's books. The luminous and saturated colors that would come to characterize his later landscapes were achieved through painstaking layers of thin transparent oil and varnish, a dazzling technique that often defies print reproduction. Parrish's home burned in 1979 and was replaced by a similar looking house, but the artist's studio and famous gardens are intact, and portions of the place are now being opened to the public. For those who like to dig out little-known treasures during their travels: the stage backdrop in the town hall was painted by Maxfield Parrish.

Lebanon (pop. 12,598) is the economic hub of west-central New Hampshire and there'll be no shortage of fast-food restaurants as you ease into West Leb, but your patience will be well rewarded if you can wait until you get to Lebanon proper. As you are about to make the right turn onto Route 120, you'll be at one corner of Colburn Park. On the opposite corner will be Three Tomatoes Trattoria (1 Court St.; 603-448-1711), serving delicious wood-fired pizza, pasta, and rustic Italian cuisine consisting of fresh local ingredients and bold flavors.

By the mid-19th century, the abundance of water power from the Connecticut and Mascoma Rivers had fueled a characteristic boom in the Lebanon's mill trades, attracting workers from French Canada, but within a century, fate and circumstances had enforced an economic decline that has since been reversed, in part, by the routing of Interstates 89 and 91, along with the growth of nearby Dartmouth College, established by one of Lebanon's founders, Eleazar Wheelock.

In addition to the geologic fault line marked by the Connecticut River, the state boundary represents a political rubicon: the lack of sales tax in New Hampshire quite understandably lures Vermont's consumers across the border, a savings which is especially apparent in the purchase of alcoholic beverages. To facilitate such trade, New Hampshire's largest liquor outlets are (ironically) often located not far from the exit ramp of an interstate highway. Really.

If your motorcycle needs any consideration, the Lebanon area would be a good place to scout for what you need. About a half-mile beyond the intersection where you joined Route 4/Route 10, you'll find Granite State Harley-Davidson (351 Miracle Mile; 603-448-4664). Mason Racing (18-1/2 Mascoma St.; 800-677-5006) is a KTM dealer, but services all makes and models, plus has an extensive inventory of parts, supplies, and apparel. You'll find them just a block west of Route 120 by the green.

This ride follows Route 120 south from the green in Lebanon. However, if you were to take Route 120 north, you'd reach the 225-acre Dartmouth-Hitchcock Medical Center, one of only four Level 1 trauma centers in New England, with their choppers and advance response teams serving most of

Christ Community Church in Plainfield resembles a well-appointed barn, complete with silo, cupolas, and board-and-batten siding.

As construction began on the beloved Old Meeting House in Jaffrey, workmen could hear the cannon fire of the Battle of Bunker Hill. Over the years, it has served as a church, community building, town office, and high school.

the medical communities in the north country. It's also the beginning of Ride 10.

Regardless of which stops you made and which route you took, head south from the Lebanon green on Route 120. You'll ride into Claremont through a different part of Cornish, an old mill town built on a fast-flowing river . . . and then through Unity, Lempster, East Lempster, and on to Washington. The only thing that might disorient you is that no villages exist for Unity, Lempster, or East Lempster!

The village of Washington (pop. 1,123) could be described as a quaint New England town that seems to have been forgotten by history, and where the event of the day just might be your arrival. Every state must have a town named after our first president, but this was the first, although when the town was incorporated in December of 1776, George Washington was only the commander of the Continental Army. The town hall was built in 1787 and has been in continuous use for 225 years, albeit with a few upgrades, like indoor plumbing and electricity. The first Protestant congregation to observe a Saturday Sabbath was formed here in 1844, beginning what would become the first congregation of Seventh Day Adventists.

The second left turn south of the village leads to East Washington, and a wonderful country touring road to Hillsborough. Those who are interested

Mount Monadnock is one of the most frequently climbed summits in the world, and the only place from which you can view all six New England states.

in history might wish to continue from Washington on Route 31 instead, to view the Franklin Pierce Homestead (located just before the merger of Route 9 in Hillsborough; 603-478-0809). Built by Pierce's father Benjamin, it was the home of our 14th president from his early infancy until he married in 1834, and it remained in the Pierce family until acquired by the State of New Hampshire in 1925.

From Hillsborough (pop. 4,928) Route 149 twists through hills that typify the region. Old stone walls harken back to the days when most of this land was open farmland. The region is now predominately forest with a network of gravel roads that was established during an earlier century. Several highways lead to the town of Jaffrey and Route 149 is not the quickest, as it rambles through scenic villages like Francetown, Greenfield, and Hancock. Francetown looks like a postcard from the early19th century: Greenfield's Congregational Church (c. 1795) is the oldest meetinghouse in New Hampshire, and the John Hancock Inn is one of the oldest continuously operated inns in the state.

In Jaffrey (pop. 2,802), the Civil War memorial stands in front of the Romanesque Revival-styled public library, a scene replicated in small towns throughout New England. However, there are at least two things that set this town apart from all others: it is the only town in the world named Jaffrey—and it has Mount Monadnock.

It doesn't sound like much. Rising only 3,165 feet above sea level and a mere 2,100 feet higher than the surrounding terrain, solitary Mount Monadnock was named for the Abenaki word that meant "mountain that stands alone," and geologists later adopted the term more broadly to desig-nate any single mountain that is not part of a range. This hill is far from lonely, however; it's one of *the* most frequently climbed summits in the world, and the only place from which you can view all six New England states. More than 125,000 people hike its many trails every year, joining the ranks of Emerson, Thoreau, and Hawthorne, and countless other artists and composers whose works have paid tribute to this peak.

In many a small Yankee town, the most prominent public building will be the meetinghouse, church, or town hall, but many of these structures typically started as one and were later converted to another. So it was in Fitzwilliam, where the Congregational Church (c. 1816) was rebuilt as the town hall (c. 1817) after celestial lightning brought it down. There are many other historic buildings surrounding the green, but most are private residences. Fitzwilliam is also home to Rhododendron State Park (nhstateparks.com/rhodo.html), a 16-acre native grove at the bottom of Little Monadnock which blooms in mid-July.

Winchester is a few miles south of Keene on Route 10. Located on Route 10 in West Swanzey, MC Wheel (603-355-3901; www.mcwheel.com) is

The Fitzwilliam Inn, which opened its doors in 1793, is located at the crossroads on the green in the old village.

The two-span Ashuelot Covered Bridge in the Upper Village, an elaborate lattice construction with two sidewalks, was originally built to transport lumber across the river for use by the Ashuelot Railroad.

one of the few places in New England capable of truing bent motorcycle wheel rims, which is a handy thing to know.

Hinsdale (pop. 4,309) has claim to the oldest continuously operated post office in the United States, established in 1816, during the presidency of James Madison. With e-mail tolling the demise of traditional communication, you still have time to play a role on the stage of history by mailing a few postcards from the big tan building with the brown trim—before it's too late. A public park with shaded parking and picnic tables by the river is just beyond the turn onto Route 63.

From Hinsdale, Route 119 continues to Brattleboro. If you are staying in downtown "Bratt" this would be the route to take, otherwise a right turn onto Route 63 would be your best option for reaching the north side of town. A sweepy two-laner with minimal shoulders, Route 63 follows the boundary of the Pisgah State Park, which contains the entire watershed north of the Ashuelot River, along with seven ponds, four highland ridges, an old growth forest, and extensive wetlands. Eventually Route 63 intersects with Route 9; Brattleboro will be to the west and Keene to the east.

Ride 10   Western New Hampshire

Distance: *151 miles; plan on four hours*
Highlights: *The Connecticut River, mountains, a covered bridge, a mountain pass, a Redstone rocket, and a Shaker Village. But really the highlights are the roads and the scenery.*

The mileage for this ride begins at the green in Hanover (pop. 10,878), although all motorcycle services are located in West Lebanon, as are the greatest number of restaurants and modest-priced lodging. As the home town of Dartmouth College, Hanover has a wide variety of offerings, but they tend to be slightly more expensive.

The town of Hanover is not only a happening place, it regularly gains attention as one of the top ten Best Places to Live, its culture, diversity, and opportunities due in no small part to the Ivy League presence of Dartmouth College and its prestigious medical school. The much-acclaimed Hopkins Center for the Performing Arts faces the five-acre campus green at the end of Main Street. Next to it is the Hood Museum of Art (6034 E. Wheelock St.; 603-646-2808; hoodmuseum.dartmouth.edu), one of the oldest and

The Connecticut River Valley along Route 10 offers one bucolic scene after another.

largest college museums in the nation, with more than 65,000 catalogued objects, thousands of which are used each year by professors to enhance classes across the curriculum. The museum is known for its exceptionally good collections of West African masks and sculptures, as well as American portraits and landscapes, especially those of the White Mountain School, which depicted the now-familiar scenery you've been enjoying from behind the lens of history, when the presence of man had yet to reshape the potential of the wilderness.

Seventy-five miles of the Appalachian Trail between the Woodstocks is maintained by the Dartmouth Outing Club, as this 2,200-mile footpath passes right through the center of Hanover on its way to Mount Katahdin in

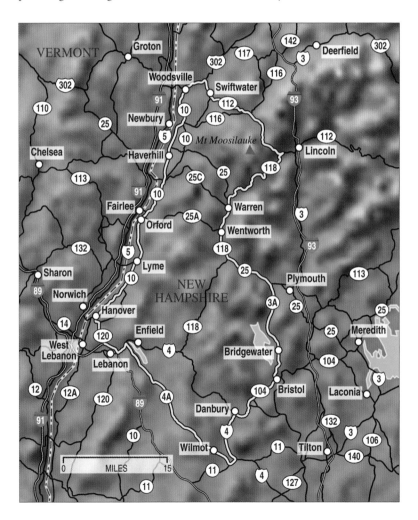

FROM HANOVER, NEW HAMPSHIRE

0	From Main St. in Hanover by the Dartmouth green, head east on Rte 10 (E. Wheelock St.)
0.4	Left to continue on Rte 10 (Lyme Rd.)
0.7	Right to continue on Rte 10 (Lyme Rd.)
17.9	Bridge to US Rte 5 in Orford
23.8	Rte 25 (Bradford Rd.) to US Rte 5
37.2	Bear right onto Rte 10/ US Rte 302 in Woodsville
39.8	Right onto Rte 112
57.7	Right onto Rte 118
70.6	Bear left onto Rte 118/Rte 25 in Warren
79.6	Straight on Rte 25
87.1	Right at roundabout onto Rte 3A
100.8	In Bristol, right onto Rte 104 (Pleasant St.)
110.0	In Danbury, left onto US Rte 4
117.0	Right onto Rte 11
118.1	Right onto Rte 4A
138.8	Enfield Shaker Village Museum
142.1	Left onto US Rte 4
143.6	Right, ramp onto I-89/Rte 10
145.6	Right Exit 18 ramp, right onto Rte 120
150.5	Left onto Rte 10 (E. Wheelock St.) in Hanover
150.9	Arrive at Dartmouth Green and Main St. in Hanover ■

Maine. Hikers with expedition packs and staffs are welcomed to town with helpful signage, community suppers, and brochures that detail mail and laundry services, public showers and Internet access, gear outfitters, and other little kindnesses that can be appreciated by any dirty and weary traveler.

Lyme (pop. 1,679) is a beautiful little village north of Hanover. The garages behind the church are horse sheds that date to 1810 and the Alden Country Inn opened for business in 1809 on what was then the Montréal-Boston stage route. The residents in this and other New Hampshire villages in the upper Connecticut River Valley have always been more closely associated with Vermont, and many of them joined the independent republic before George Washington's intervention brought them back into the United States fold. Even today, secondary school students from Lyme attend either Thetford or St. Johnsbury Academy in Vermont, while the Rivendell School System (K-12) encompasses both the town of Fairlee, Vermont, and Orford, New Hampshire.

Behind the white fences and green lawns of Orford (pop. 1091), a series of white clapboard homes sit on a small ridge. Known as the Seven Swans, they are considered the finest grouping of Federal-style residences in the nation. One of them was the home of Samuel Morey (see also Ride 3), one of the foremost American inventors of the early 19th century. In 1793 he invented the rotary steam engine and powered a boat with it; by 1797 he had a commercial steamboat operating in Greenwich, Connecticut. He super-

The five-acre Dartmouth Green in downtown Hanover, crisscrossed by gravel walking paths, is the emotional center of this Ivy League campus.

vised the building of the canal locks at Bellows Falls (1792–1802), and invented the modern water heater and fired it by devising a method of producing "water" gas (hydrogen) in 1817. He was heating and lighting his home with gas a half-century before it became popular in American cities.

You will cross the Ammonoosuc River only a quarter of a mile from Route 302 on Route 135 in downtown Woodsville, the largest village in the town of Haverhill (US Route 302 west links up with Ride 3). In the days when the river was the primary transportation route, Woodsville was the northernmost port.

The Bath-Haverhill Covered Bridge (c. 1829) is the oldest covered bridge in New Hampshire that still carries traffic. Ithiel Town patented this popular plank lattice truss in 1820, so this is a relatively early example of what would become the predominant style for covered bridge construction in North America. Town eventually became a wealthy man by using agents

Every colonial church would have had horse sheds nearby, to shelter the animals during the long worship services. This structure in Lyme is one of the rare ones to have survived.

Although beautiful homes surround the small common, the town of Haverhill isn't really a tourist stop.

to promote his design and exact royalties of one dollar per bridge foot; the fee was doubled for unlicensed bridges found built in this style.

The eastern portion of Route 112, designated as the Kancamagus High-way, seems to get the most attention from moto-pundits as being the best motorcycling road in the Granite State. I tend to favor the narrow, serpentine unnamed half of Route 112, especially where it follows the Wild Ammonoosuc River to Kinsman Notch, the westernmost of the major White Mountain passes. Most of these corners, especially in Swiftwater, are extremely tight and many are blind, so ongoing caution is advised.

As the road curves and climbs through a crease between Mount Moosilauke and Kinsman Ridge, note that many of the people who have parked in the turn-offs along the river might be panning or sluicing for gold in the cold, shallow water. Unlike some of the other, more famous notches, Kinsman leaves you with a real sense of having divined a route through a desolate and forbidding obstacle—a point that was probably all the more obvious to Asa Kinsman and his wife, who'd taken a wrong turn on the way to their new home, and found themselves needing to hack a path for their two-wheeled ox cart through the tortuous terrain.

At the top, there is a paved parking area that's a popular spot for riders to regroup. The ramparts of Mounts Blue, Jim, and Waternomee produce a soaring photogenic backdrop for the rockbound tarn of Beaver Pond; this tranquil spot is one of my favorites along the entire length of Route 112. The brook on the eastern side of Kinsman Notch disappears below the ground as it drains into the blocky tortured caverns and steep glacially carved walls of Lost River Gorge, a popular attraction since 1852, when the Jackman brothers literally stumbled into their discovery while fishing. Today, the area is owned and managed by a private non-profit that has up-

graded the boardwalks and stairways without losing the sense of subterranean, lantern-lit adventure and discovery that has attracted visitors
since its earliest days.

At the eastern end of the notch, make a tight right turn onto Route 118,
also known as the Sawyer Highway. Winding over the southern shoulder of
Mount Moosilauke through the White Mountain National Forest, how one
best makes use of this route can be as varied as the waxing and waning conditions of the pavement. Like many a historic roadbed, it suffers cracks and
heaves at the harsh hands of the weather. When coated in a velvety new surface, sportbike riders will find it irresistible, but the forest canopy also
courts a refreshing slow cruise on a hot summer day.

Just beyond the merging of Route 25 and Route 118 you'll see an unusual sight on your right. There are many New England village greens
graced by a cannon or an armored tank, but Warren's is the only one with a
Redstone rocket, a 70-foot ballistic missile used by the U.S. Army during
the Cold War, the same type that was used for the first nuclear missile test in
1958. (Despite the common myth, it's not the type of rocket that sent New
Hampshire native Alan Shepard into space.)

Before you head out of town, take special note of Calamity Jane's Restaurant (603-764-5288) on the south side of the village, and about a half-mile
farther, Fat Bob's Ice Cream (603-764-9047). While there ain't much to
compete with them around here, I'm not sure it would be worth anyone's
time to try, since both have earned destination status among all scattered

The porch at the Swiftwater Way Station is a pleasant place to stop and enjoy a snack.

Descending into the heart of the White Mountains, from Route 112 on the east side of Kinsman Notch.

souls within a reasonable radius. Located right on the snowmobile route that sustains them during the winter, Calamity Jane's dishes up hearty diner fare that keeps body and soul together, with rest rooms labeled for BUCKS and DOES, a small bar, and karaoke in the evening (one can only imagine). And be sure to leave room to top off your afternoon with one of Fat Bob's famously generous scoops of homemade ice cream or sherbet.

Blink and you might miss the village of Wentworth, named for the New Hampshire governor who in 1766 granted the fertile intervales to sixty settlers from Massachusetts. When a flood breached dams on upper and lower Baker Ponds in 1856, a three-mile torrent widened the channel by nearly 90 feet, undermining and completely washing away nine riverside mills, along with roads, homes, and barns.

From this point on, if you're tempted to twist the throttle, you should keep your eyes open for radar-equipped police vehicles, as Route 25 turns into a wide smooth highway. To link up with Ride 12, continue on Route 25 to US Route 3 south, otherwise bear right at the rotary west of Plymouth and ride south to Bristol on Route 3A along Newfound Lake, a spring-fed home to more than 20 species of fish. It's a pretty, sweeping forested ride,

Unlike most village greens, which might feature a cannon or perhaps even a tank, in Warren you'll find a Redstone rocket.

but be alert for moose and snapping turtles on the road; either could take you down.

Bristol (pop. 1,600) is a sweet little village situated just high enough in the hills to reap the benefits of both climate and scenery that have historically attracted seasonal visitors to the Granite State. As you turn left onto Route 104, note that Route 104 east goes directly to Meredith and this is one of the best approaches to Weirs Beach for Laconia Bike Week (see Ride 11). At Potter Place, turn right onto Route 11 and take the next right onto Route 4A.

The Enfield Shaker Village (603-632-4346; www.shakermuseum.org) on the shores of Mascoma Lake was established in 1793, the 9th of 18 original Shaker communities. The museum here is smaller than those in Hancock or Canterbury, but it is unique in that small groups can actually make reservations to stay in the original residential rooms of the Great Stone Dwelling (c. 1841), an impressive structure built to house church members and serve their daily communal needs.

Route 1A along the New Hampshire seacoast is popular with motorcyclists . . . and apparently musicians.

Ride 11　The Smallest Seacoast

Distance: *162 miles; plan on a full day of travel. Stopping in Portsmouth or the beach resorts will make this a two-day trip.*

Highlights: *A mix of rural and urban roads, forested hills to seaside resorts. Overlooks of Lake Winnipesaukee and New Hampshire's Atlantic beach resorts, historic sites and fine dining in Portsmouth, the Canterbury Shaker Village, and the New Hampshire Motor Speedway.*

"Laconia" is one of the big names in motorcycle rallies and every year several hundred thousand bikers head for the southern shore of Lake Winnipesaukee for a few days of Bike Week in mid-June. The hillclimbs from which the rally sprang are now miles from Weirs Beach in the Gunstock Recreational Area of Gilford, while the road races that used to be held at Gunstock are now even farther south at the New Hampshire Motor Speedway on Route 106 between Loudon and Belmont. The oval flat-track races take place much farther east in Rochester and many special touring events like Rally in the Valley and Ride to the Sky on the Mount Washington Auto Road are held far to the north. Regardless, the hub of activity around which all these far-flung events coalesce is known simply as Laconia.

There are numerous motorcycle dealerships in the area, but the influx of clientele during Bike Week gives Laconia Harley-Davidson (603-279-4526; www.laconiaharley.com) in Meredith and Conway the numbers to claim status as the largest H-D dealership in the state. Laconia has many popular spots to eat, but in my opinion (and those of countless others) the best place for breakfast (and a relative bargain, too!) is Café Déjà-Vu (211 Court St./US Rte 3; 603-524-7773; cafedejavunh.com). The Black Cat Café (603-528-3233) at the old depot also gets my patronage at least once a year.

From downtown Laconia, head south on Route 106 like I have countless times. The first stop will be the New Hampshire Motor Speedway, which features motorcycle and NASCAR racing, but also has a schedule for track days (www.nhms.com). At other times the Richard Petty Driving Experience allows people to get behind the wheel of a 600 hp race car while the Sports Car Driving Association offers programs to sharpen their high-performance and four-wheel driving skills. I'm not cut out to be a road racer,

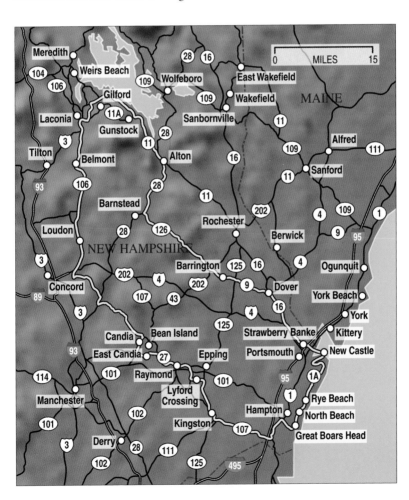

but the two-day Penguin Racing School course I attended there dramatically improved my highway riding skills. Although my old Beemer was constantly being passed by faster riders, I really learned how to approach a curve, brake properly, and follow a line, and discovered my bike could lean much farther than I ever imagined. Training for street riders is also offered by Tony's Track Days (www.tonystrackdays.com) throughout the riding season.

Opposite the entrance to NHMS will be Asby Road. This road is gravel, but it saves backtracking if you plan to visit the Canterbury Shaker Village. Otherwise, 2.5 miles farther, turn onto Shaker Road by the gas station and restaurant. This is one of the best-preserved Shaker villages (603-783-9511; www.shakers.org), all that remains of a community that once contained about 100 buildings. The Meeting House (c. 1792), the Dwelling (c.

FROM LACONIA, NEW HAMPSHIRE

0	From downtown Laconia at Rte 107, head south on Rte 106 (Main St.)
1.1	At the intersection with Rte 11/Rte3, straight to continue on Rte 106 (Belmont Rd.)
12.7	[New Hampshire Speedway on the left; Asby Rd. is on the right]
15.2	[Shaker Rd. is on the right by the gas station]
22.0	Stay on Rte 106, cross over I-393, then cross Rte 9
23.5	Near Concord, left onto N. Pembroke Rd.
29.4	Right onto Rte 28 (Suncook Valley Hwy)
30.6	Left onto Deerfield Rd. into Bear Brook State Park
40.0	Near Candia, right onto Rte 43 (Old Candia Rd.) to Deerfield Rd.
42.6	Left onto Rte 27 (High St.) to Raymond Rd.
46.2	Stay on Rte 27 (becomes Rte 27/Rte 107/Bus. 101)
52.3	At West Epping, bear right onto Depot Rd. (*not* right onto School St.) to Beede Hill Rd.
54.2	Left (east) onto North Rd.
56.5	Right (south) onto Rte 125 (Calef Hwy)
61.0	Rte 125 merges with Rte 107/Rte 111 in Kingston
62.6	Left (east) onto Rte 107
72.2	Left (north) onto US Rte 1
75.3	Right, ramp onto Rte 101 to Hampton Beach
77.5	Left onto Rte 1A (Ocean Blvd.) (one-way north)
83.0	[Pass through Rye Beach]
91.4	Right onto Rte 1B (Wentworth Rd.) (continuing on Rte 1A is a shortcut into Portsmouth)

(continued)

1793–1837), and Carriage House (c. 1825) won't likely hold any surprises, nor will the workshops and barns, really. What you probably won't be able to anticipate will be the evident scale of the organizational aspects of a communal society. The kitchen building is separate from the bakery; the large laundry has an extension for steam drying textiles. Buildings include woodsheds, offices, a theater, even the oldest hospital in New Hampshire (c. 1811–1840). Another structure was used as a syrup distillery, where one of the concoctions produced was the award-winning medicinal Thomas Corbett's Sarsaparilla Syrup. Although famous for their furniture, the Shakers produced many types of products for commercial sale to the general public, even the work of artists like Sister Cora Helena Sarle (1867–1956). A great spiritual experiment during the 19th century, the Shakers have been nearly forgotten except at heritage sites such as this, and those in Enfield, New Hampshire, and Pittsfield, Massachusetts.

Route 106 goes beneath I-393 on the outskirts of Concord, the capitol city of New Hampshire. You'll be looking for the second intersection and the left turn onto North Pembroke Road unless, of course, you have bike issues that require you to continue a short distance to visit Freedom Cycle for Yamaha, Honda, KTM, Kawasaki, and Can-Am (110 Manchester St.; 603-225-2779; www.freedomcyclenh.com); or Heritage Harley-Davidson (142 Manchester St.; 603-224-3268; www.heritageh-d.

CONTINUING INTO PORTSMOUTH

95.6	Bear right to stay on Rte 1B (Marcy St.)
95.8	Bear right (again) to stay on Rte 1B (Marcy St.); ride through Strawbery Banke
96.1	Right and loop beneath the Memorial Bridge
96.3	Right (first right) onto Bow St. to leave Portsmouth, or straight on Daniel St. for downtown
96.5	Right onto Market St.
99.9	Right, ramp onto US Rte 4/Rte 16 (north); stay on Rte 16
107.1	In Dover, right onto exit 8W onto Rte 9
107.5	Right to continue on Rte 9
116.2	In Barrington, bear right onto Rte 126
117.4	Bear left, continue on Rte 126/US Rte 202
117.6	Right to continue on Rte 126
131.4	In Center Barnstead, right onto Rte 28 (Suncook Valley Rd.)
140.5	Right, going counterclockwise around the gas station
140.7	Left onto Rte 11/Rte 28A into Alton; stay on Rte 11
153.6	[Lake Winnipesaukee overlook]
157.5	Left on ramp to Rte 11/US Rte 3
159.9	Right, exit ramp; turn right onto Rte 11A (Gilford Ave.)
161.2	Left on Rte 11A/Rte 107 in Laconia
161.8	Arrive at the intersection of Rte 11A/Rte 106/Rte 107 in downtown Laconia

There are numerous roads in southern New Hampshire that avoid busy commuter traffic.

Racing in the rain at NHMS.

com). If you are looking for Ducatis, Aprilias, or Moto Guzzis, you'll want to take I-93 south to Exit 5 in Derry to Seacoast Sport Cycle (208 Rockingham Rd./Rte 28; 603-437-5656; www.seacoastsport.com).

North Pembroke Road is a shortcut to Route 28, where you'll turn right (south) and then take the well-marked left turn to Bear Brook State Park and Campground. Unless you're planning to camp, you can ignore the park visitors booth and keep riding through the deliciously cool pine forest. There is a lack of directional signs, but the only place that might be confusing is at a certain Y-intersection, where you'll want to bear right rather than going up the hill. My directions provide names for the roads, but you won't see any posted, so don't bother looking for them. When you finally reach pavement with a painted line down the middle, it will be Route 43, onto which you should take a right and head south.

Even during mid-June when the big name routes are all but clogged with packs of two-wheelers cruising around the state, you'll likely find yourself almost alone on the fine network of local byways that wind through these stunted hills. Candia Four Corners, at the intersection of Routes 27 and 43, must have been busy once upon a time. Get a bit farther off the main highway and you'll find more forgotten places like Candia and East Candia Station. There are larger villages like Raymond and Epping, but also mere place names on the map where settlements once existed, places like Bean Island on Route 27 and Lyford Crossing on North Road.

Despite the lack of concentrated civilization, however, these roads are heavily settled and the speed limit is generally posted for 35 mph. Soon enough, Route 107 will take you to US Route 1 and all the strip development services you could ask for: restaurants, lodging, fast food, service stations, box stores, and Seacoast Harley-Davidson (17 Lafayette Rd./US Rte 1; 603-964-9959; www.seacoastharley.com) in North Hampton.

Note that Route 101 is the main highway leading to the New Hampshire seacoast, and if you've arrived on a Sunday morning in July during a heat wave, you could expect traffic to be backed up for two miles. Welcome to Hampton Beach!

Route 1A separates the beach from amusement arcades and fast-food joints where bathing-suit-attired customers stand in line at service windows. The back streets are jammed with hotels, rental cottages, and parking lots. As a teenager, this was one of my favorite summer destinations and I later enjoyed it with my own children. Wild roses will frame the sea as you cruise beyond the rocky point of land called Great Boars Head. Expect cars parked in every legal space along the road for miles, while others slowly trawl along like sea turtles looking for a nesting spot. During the worst of it, expect to be running the gauntlet in first gear, as Hampton Beach, North Beach, Rye Beach, and every state beach or bit of sand or rock between them fills with humanity. Early 20th-century mansions sit on tidy lawns between

North Beach is another popular strip of sand on the New Hampshire coast.

The Playland Arcade has been a feature of Hampton Beach for as long as I can remember.

tidal marshes and the sea, while more modern construction is often constrained to perch precariously on rocky points jutting into the Atlantic. A seawall has been erected as an eight-foot barrier between pavement and an ocean view. Why? Is it protection from erosion or perhaps tsunamis? Or merely to give runners a serpentine elevated path on which to ply their morning ritual?

Route 1A is the quickest way into Portsmouth, but Route 1B goes through New Castle as it crosses a succession of islands at the mouth of the harbor and provides a historical perspective not visible from other land approaches. Randomly scattered cedar-shingled homes on stilts give way to early 19th-century clapboard buildings lining narrow streets paved from doorstep to doorstep. The earliest settlement here was established in 1630 as Strawbery Banke, and the 10-acre Puddle Dock neighborhood is now maintained as a living history museum with costumed reenactors portraying the daily experiences of seaport life over the past few centuries.

Riding past Prescott Park, Marcy Street ends at State Street and the only option will be to turn right and loop beneath the Memorial Bridge and onto Congress Street.

This trip through downtown Portsmouth will be a big one-way, counterclockwise loop. At the eastern end you'll have the option of crossing Memorial Bridge into Kittery, Maine, or looping beneath it on Harbor Place. Church, Fleet, and Middle Streets connect Congress to State Street. The easiest way to leave downtown is to turn right onto Bow Street immediately after looping beneath the bridge (or if you miss it, take the third right onto Penhallow Street), then follow Bow Street as it curves left, then take a quick right (north) onto Market Street. It might sound confusing, but since

Portsmouth

In 1813, a disastrous fire destroyed the center of Portsmouth and—as would be repeated in countless New England towns—it was decreed that all future buildings were to be constructed of brick and have slate roofs, thus ensuring a harmony to the city's future architecture. From childhood I remember Portsmouth as a dark, dirty town, but it has since been restored beautifully and its wide sidewalks support busy outside cafés and boutiques.

Parking might be an issue, although it's not as scarce for motorcycles as for cars. There's parking between the entrance and exit ramps of the Memorial Bridge, at Prescott Park, and on Pleasant Street, where you can meet local riders gathering on Sunday mornings.

Portsmouth has numerous historic places to visit. For the last two centuries, St. John's Church (c. 1807) has preserved a chair on which George Washington once sat, perhaps to listen to the oldest working pipe organ in North America or the pealing of the bell cast by Paul Revere. Other structures with a story include the Moffatt-Ladd House (c. 1763), Gilman-Garrison House (c. 1690), Warner House (c. 1716), Jackson House (c. 1660), and the John Paul Jones House (c. 1758), which really belonged to Captain Gregory Purcell's widow, and was where Jones boarded in 1781 while his ship, *USS Ranger,* was being built.

Portsmouth Naval Yard was established on Seavey Island in 1800 and launched its first ship in 1815. It is now an active submarine base in the middle of a busy harbor, but security doesn't seem to be an issue. In fact, you can even tour the USS *Albacore.* There's so much to do that if you plan to spend the night or weekend in this historic city I suggest doing a little advance research (www.portsmouthnh.com). ■

The most scenic approach to Portsmouth is on Route 1B, which traverses a series of islands.

Enjoying the view of Lake Winnipesaukee from the overlook on Route 11.

almost all streets are one-way, it becomes rather obvious and you merely have to position yourself in the correct lanes.

From Portsmouth, your route opts for US Route 4 to Dover, then Route 9 to Barrington. In contrast to the bustle on the previous stretches, Route 126 between Barrington and Barnstead will offer enjoyable touring. There's never much traffic, even during Bike Week, and I've seen more wildlife along this road than any other place in the state.

The gas station that's located at the intersection of Route 11 and Route 28 in Alton is a convenient place to fill up the tank. Route 28 north goes to Wolfeboro and Ride 12. The last leg of this ride on Route 11 follows Alton Bay to Lake Winnipesaukee and back to Laconia. There are two overlooks along the road that provide great spots to deploy your sidestand and take in the view of the water.

Ride 12 Lake Winnipesaukee Ride

Distance: *134 miles and four hours (more during Laconia Bike Week)*
Highlights: *Twisty, pretty roads through forests and towns, occasional lakeshore views, Wright Museum, Castle in the Clouds, New Hampshire Boat Museum.*

This one is short and sweet and provides links to Rides 9 and 10. It will be particularly useful for anyone attending Laconia Bike Week or rallies in the White Mountains. As anyone with local knowledge will tell you, the traffic that might make you shy of this area typically can be avoided with a little creativity, timing, and knowledge. As a corollary benefit, when the un-clued are predictably clogged along the main fares, they won't be taking up valuable riding space on your road.

After telling you how to bypass Route 16 on Route 153, I may have to shoot you . . . or should that be that the locals will have to shoot me? Before you have finished waving goodbye to any chaos in your rearview mirrors,

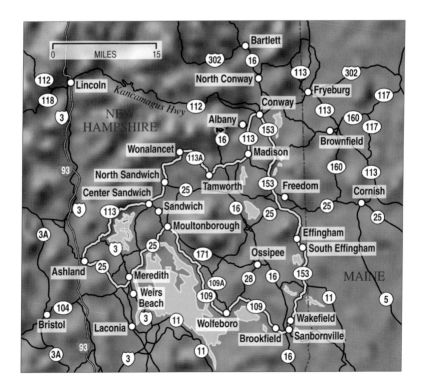

As the day draws to a close, a fiery blaze of color stands in dramatic contrast to the serenity of Squam Lake.

you will begin to feel the solace of boggy scrub and rising slopes reflected in mirror ponds and lakes. The first body of water of any note will be Dollof Pond (on your right), followed by the surreal shores of the Eaton town beach on Crystal Lake as the road sweeps around past the Little White Church, a beloved town landmark that reflects its non-denominational values of simplicity and community. From this point you'll pass Hatch Pond (on your left) and Long Pond on your way to Purity Lake and the family-friendly resort that capitalizes on its charm. The presence of other lakes, unseen from the vantage of the road, will suggest themselves in the coolness of the shaded forest as you ride past.

Bobby Sue's Homemade Ice Cream (603-539-5050), located on the highway in Freedom, makes an extremely wide range of flavors, the more familiar highlighted by exotics, such as white chocolate raspberry truffle or ginger. The South Effingham Country Store is a bit different: it has an old-fashioned dairy bar featuring frappes, floats, sundaes, and banana splits made with Bobby Sue's ice cream. They also serve a tasty breakfast and lunch at their Road Kill Grill.

An exhibit at the New Hampshire Boat Museum depicts the history of speedboat racing, which was once quite popular on Lake Winnipesauke.

From South Effingham, Route 153 briefly defines the New Hampshire-Maine border, meanders into Maine, and then back into New Hampshire as it follows the eastern shore of Province Lake. Depending on the time of year and whether or not the trees are in leaf you might catch glimpses of Belleau Lake, which is actually the Ossipee River Reservoir. Immediately after that you'll see Stump Pond on your left and again, depending on the foliage, Pine River Pond on the right side of the highway. In Sanbornville, turn onto Route 109 at the northern end of Lovell Lake. You might not even notice Kingswood Lake, but won't be able to ignore Lake Wentworth when the highway reaches it.

Wolfeboro touts itself as being the first summer resort town in America. In 1771 Colonial Governor John Wentworth—who took over the position from his uncle Benning Wentworth, who'd made a fortune selling grants in what would become Vermont—built an estate on the lake that bears his name. It was reputed to be the largest home in New England and naturally had all the support buildings—stables, gristmill, blacksmith shop, sawmill, carpentry shops, smoke house, and so on—associated with a grand estate. He also held the title of Surveyor of the Kings Woods in North America, which made it easy for him to have a road built from his home in Portsmouth to his summer place on the lake. Being a loyalist Wentworth had to flee New Hampshire to England during the American Revolution, but returned to the continent as the appointed governor of Nova Scotia. His grand house burned in 1820 and all that remains are stone foundations, a couple of historical plaques, and a story. Don't feel sorry for Governor Wentworth: he built an even grander mansion in Halifax, which still stands and is open to the public.

Route 109 merges with Route 28 on the northwest end of Lake Wentworth. On your left across from the big recreation field will be the New

Hampshire Boat Museum (397 Center St., Wolfeboro; 603-569-4554; www.nhbm.org), which is dedicated to the recreational and commercial boating heritage and lifestyle of New Hampshire's Lakes Region. They typically have an excellent rotating display of vintage mahogany and antique crafts, as well as an outstanding collection of inboard launches. Speed racing, which was once a popular sport on Lake Winnipesaukee is also represented, as are canoes, skiffs, rowboats, outboard motors, and other artifacts—making this a place that shouldn't be as overlooked as it sometimes is.

You really can't miss the Wright Museum in Wolfeboro: there's a Stuart tank breaking through its front brick wall (77 Center St.; 603-569-1212; wrightmuseum.org). A veteran of the Korean War, David Wright originally collected and restored more than 50 vintage WWII vehicles as a mobile exhibition he'd make available for parades and military functions. Having grown up during the end of the conflict, however, Wright always wanted to tell the full story of the war, which he knew included the contributions on the home front, and he has made that a much remarked part of the exhibits in his collection's permanent home. Among the military vehicles you'll find an Indian and a Harley-Davidson motorcycle, as well as a heavy Pershing tank, a White M16 Half Track with multiple Browning machine guns, a command car, cargo truck, ambulance, scout cars, and jeeps.

FROM CONWAY, NEW HAMPSHIRE

0	From Conway, head south on Rte 153 (Pleasant St.) at the intersection of Rtes 16, 113, and 153
15.1	Left as Rte 153 merges with Rte 25
16.1	Right to continue on Rte 153 (Effingham Trail)
36.3	In Sanbornville, right onto Rte 109
46.1	Left to continue on Rte 109/ Rte 28 into Wolfeboro Center
47.5	[New Hampshire Boat Museum]
49.0	[Wright Museum]
49.3	In downtown Wolfeboro, right to continue on Rte 109
64.6	Straight to continue on Rte 109 at the junction of Rte 171
66.9	Left onto Rte 109/Rte 25
67.4	Straight to follow Rte 25
77.0	Left onto US Rte 3 in Meredith
77.9	Bear right onto Rte 104
79.6	Right onto Winona Rd. at the traffic light and intersection
87.1	In Ashland, bear right, then turn right onto US Rte 3/Rte 25
91.0	Left onto Rte 113
102.8	Left to stay on Rte 113 in Center Sandwich
106.5	Straight onto Rte 113A (do not follow Rte 113) in N. Sandwich
119.7	Left onto Rte 113 in Tamworth
122.6	Straight across Rte 16 and continue on Rte 113
131.6	Right as Rte 113 merges with Rte 16
133.5	Arrive in Conway and the intersection of Routes 16, 113, and 153 ∎

A glimpse of Wolfeboro Bay on Lake Winnipesaukee is all you get from North Main Street in Wolfeboro, but this charming downtown has appeal and I always make a point to stop and walk around a little bit. There's a great ice cream shop, Bailey's Bubble, on the short street to the old railroad depot, which has public restrooms.

After passing through Wolfeboro, Mirror Lake will be seen on your right. Nineteenmile Bay is the next water the road touches, then, logically, Twentymile Bay follows. You'll never be far from water, even if it is hidden by the trees.

The easiest way to reach Castle in the Clouds is to turn right onto Route 171 near Moultonborough and ride two miles to the entrance on your left. The road by the gatehouse climbs a narrow switchback to the parking area. You have to take a shuttle or walk to the house.

Castle in the Clouds (603-476-5900; castleintheclouds.org) is the Lucknow estate built by Tom Plant around 1913. The millions he'd made manufacturing womens' shoes were used to build this 16-room mansion high on the side of the Ossipee Mountains. Every aspect of the place employed the finest craftsmanship and state-of-the-art technology when it was built, including such innovations as a central vacuum, brine refrigerator, and circular shower with a perforated nozzle. I especially like the kitchen

The festivities associated with Laconia Bike Week are spread across the Granite State, but the focus of activities is in and around Weirs Beach.

floor—it's actually a jigsaw puzzle—and while some people might be impressed with the Tiffany glass I think the hand-painted windows in the dining room are more interesting. And like any good mansion worth the name, this one has a "secret" room off the library. Plant ultimately lost his fortune due to bad investments. The estate and furnishings were auctioned off after his death, and subsequent owners have honored Plant's commitment to the integrity of the property, leaving things largely unaltered to this day.

This beautiful setting is also the watershed for Castle Springs bottled water which, unlike so many other brands, is actually spring water so pure it doesn't require filtration or any treatment. The 28 miles of hiking trails that traverse the 5,500 acres of the Castle in the Clouds property include routes to the summits of Bald Knob and Mount Shaw, at 2,975

The facade of the Wright Museum rates as one of the most creative I've seen in New England.

feet, the highest peak visible to the northeast, at the edge of a round, nine-mile range known the world over as the Ossipee Ring Dike. A fine example of this type of unique geologic formation, the dike was formed when the ceiling collapsed on an underground magma chamber, leaving a circular crack through which molten rock could erupt.

Route 25 weaves between Lee's Pond, Lake Kanasaka, and the extended bays of Lake Winnipesaukee on its way to Center Harbor and Meredith. Traffic on this road can be heavy during Laconia Bike Week, so those who are familiar with the region tend to use Route 25B from downtown Center Harbor to reach US Route 3/Route 25 through Meredith to get to I-93.

Meredith is a busy tourist town even when it's not Bike Week, but the events taking place on US Route 3 at Laconia H-D (603-279-4526; www.laconiaharley.com) and Hart's Turkey Farm and Restaurant (603-279-6212; hartsturkeyfarm.com) would guarantee delays if you happened to arrive with 250,000 other motorcycles. Immediately beyond these two popular establishments, the road divides and you should bear right (west) onto Route 104. (To link to the beginning of Ride 11 in downtown Laconia, bear left onto US Route 3 and bear right at the roundabout onto Route 106. To reach Weirs Beach, simply remain on US Route 3.)

At the first intersection on Route 104, turn right at the traffic light onto Winona Road, a stretch of twisty pavement so very beguiling that I must advise caution. Even well-steeled against its familiar temptations, I will still occasionally find myself drifting into an oncoming lane on a blind curve.

When you crest the hill into downtown Ashland stay straight—don't bear to the left—and turn right at the top of the hill onto US Route 3/Route 25. This follows the river and along the shore of Little Squam Lake. Turning onto Route 113 in Holderness, you will have arrived on the shores of Squam Lake, where the Academy Award-winning film *On Golden Pond* was filmed. The haunting tremolo of loons, which gave Katherine Hepburn's character so much pleasure, is still a common sound. These amazing birds, with their glossy black heads and speckled mantles, are well adapted to dive for fish, with dense bones, rearward set legs, and a relatively short wing-span—all of which also make them slow to take wing and ungainly on land.

Route 113 is an absolutely gorgeous narrow, serpentine road favored by motorcyclists, but residential homes and patrolling police make it advisable to keep forward velocity within the bounds of the posted limit.

The distinctive bare summit of Mount Chocorua rising behind the lake, as seen not far from Route 16, was chosen to represent the White Mountain National Forest on New Hampshire's America the Beautiful state quarter.

More than a quarter of a million bikers descend on New Hampshire during the second week in June, but great roads attract riders all season long.

Continue straight to get onto Route 113A in North Sandwich, which touches the southern border of the White Mountain National Forest in Wonalancet. This stretch of two-lane byway is known as the Chinook Trail, the only highway in the country named for a dog. When Yukon musher Arthur Walden returned to Tamworth after the Gold Rush, he set about breeding an ideal sled dog. A mastiff-husky cross who resembled neither of his parents, Chinook would have the exemplary characteristics Walden was looking for and would pass these traits to his offspring, siring half of the 100 dogs chosen for Admiral Byrd's Antarctic Expedition. Chinook himself was lost on that same trip, disappearing from the group on his twelfth birthday. Today, a few hundred examples of this unique breed are maintained by a small group of dedicated enthusiasts.

Upon reaching the hamlet of Tamworth, turn left to continue east on Route 113. The return to Conway is usually quicker via Route 16. On a clear day, the tranquil waters of Chocorua Lake, almost immediately visible to the left, will reflect the bare, uniquely recognizable summit of the same name. Timing, however, can make Route 16 a less desirable choice, since most of the tourism heading to that side of the Mount Washington Valley will avail themselves of this route; a Friday afternoon, especially before a holiday weekend, could be especially brutal. In that case (or in any case, should you prefer it), continue straight to stay on Route 113 instead before rejoining Route 16 for the last two miles home.

Ride 13 The White Mountains

Distance: *166 miles. Both loops can be ridden in a day, but it makes more sense to plan on two, especially if you want to take a side trip on the Mount Washington Auto Road.*

Highlights: *This ride is about mountains, but even the valleys are dominated by the landscape that rises above them. Most of the sights along this ride are natural wonders, but you could add a couple of railroad attractions or a visit to Whitehorse Gear's Warehouse Store.*

This ride is comprised of two loops that can be ridden in sequence or in combination with other nearby routes (Rides 12, 13, and 22) depending on your time and inclination. One highlight of this trip is the Kancamagus Highway (kank-a-MAW-gus), arguably the most popular motorcycle touring road in New England. In addition, this route bags three other notches

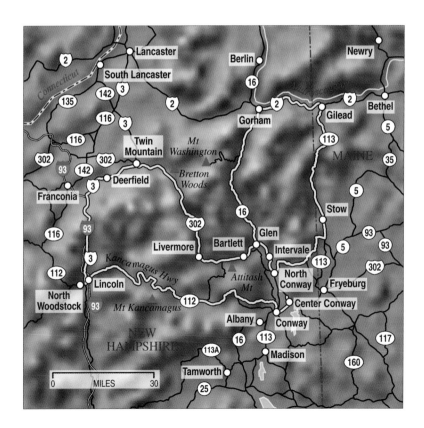

Lower Falls is perhaps the most popular public swimming spot on the Kanc.

through the White Mountain massifs, offering scenery that has been attracting visitors since the middle of the 19th century.

Whitehorse Gear (603-356-6556; www.whitehorsegear.com) in Center Conway is one of my homes away from home and it's also a destination for many touring riders visiting the region who are looking for a book, video, or must-have piece of riding gear. Coffee and local wisdom are always available and free. Yours will not be the first trip to have begun in their parking lot. Be sure to fill your gas tank before leaving Conway, because the 40 or so miles between there and Lincoln will have no services.

Named after the third and final chief of the Panacook Confederacy, the Kancamagus Highway traces the rough and rocky course of the Swift River through the White Mountain National Forest. The road was completed in 1959 and paved five years later.

As spectacular as the Kanc is (and it really is that), it suffers from the glare of its own popularity, and on a very busy summer day it's hard not to feel as if you are queuing up for a vehicular parade. With that in mind, I typically forego the easternmost end of the Kanc in favor of Passaconaway Road (which becomes Dugway Road). Instead of riding west at the traffic light in Conway and following Route 16/Route 113 to the junction of Route 112, take a right (north) onto Washington Street and bear left onto West Side

Whitehorse Gear's Warehouse Store has become a destination for riders enjoying the White Mountains. Coffee, technical advice, and local road tips are always free.

Road (the right fork would return you to Route 16 via a covered bridge over the Saco River). Passaconaway Road will be on your left about a mile beyond the traffic light in Conway. Newer and upgraded homes begin to peter out as pavement sweeps and rolls past Red Eagle Pond and some seasonal camps. Beyond the winter gate, the road is tight, narrow, and often shoulder- and guardrail-free, with dappled light obscuring the margins as they tumble in tangled abandon down to the bony river. You'll meet up with the Kanc just past the Albany Covered Bridge.

There are numerous campgrounds all along this stretch, but bring cash if you plan to stay because you'll be putting it in an envelope, not an attendant's hand. All of the state sites have potable water, bathrooms, picnic tables, and small fireplaces. There are also a few popular recreation spots along the Swift River from which humanity can potentially spill toward the roadway. Lower Falls, a complex of natural granite slides, pools, and small drops is a popular swimming hole, but swimming has been banned at the nearby Rocky Gorge Scenic Area since the early 40s, when a UNH student named Dorothy Sparks fell into the boiling pool and was trapped in the hy-

FROM CONWAY, NEW HAMPSHIRE – FRANCONIA LOOP

0	From Whitehorse Gear, ride east on US Rte 302 from E. Conway Rd.
0.9	Right onto Rte 113
3.0	At the traffic light in Conway Village, right onto Washington St.
3.2	Bear left onto West Side Rd.
3.9	Left onto Passaconaway Rd.
10.3	Left across the Albany Covered Bridge
10.4	Right onto Rte 112 (Kancamagus Hwy)
40.1	In Lincoln, right onto US Rte 3 after crossing the concrete bridge
44.7	The Flume in Franconia Notch State Park
45.5	Straight as US Rte 3 merges with I-93 through Franconia Notch
50.4	Exit 34B for the New England Ski Museum, Cannon Mtn. Tramway
53.5	Right onto Exit 35 to continue on US Rte 3
63.8	Right (east) onto US Rte 302 (Crawford Notch Rd.)
68.3	Fabyan Station; turn onto Base Station Rd. to the Cog Railway
69.0	Entrance to the Mt. Washington Resort/Bretton Woods
72.2	Saco Lake, Highland Lodge, Crawford depot
92.9	Straight as US Rte 302 merges with Rte 16 in Bartlett
96.4	[Information Center and scenic pull-off on right]

FROM NORTH CONWAY – HURRICANE MOUNTAIN ROAD LOOP

96.4	East on Hurricane Mtn. Rd. at US Rte 302/Rte 16 in Intervale. Caution.
100.0	[Top of the pass—lots of caution]
102.4	Left onto S. Main St.
106.3	Right onto S. Chatham Rd.
107.6	Left (north) onto Rte 113 (Stow Rd.)
118.2	Entering Evans Notch
128.9	Left (west) onto US Rte 2
140.1	In Gorham, left (south) onto Rte 16
148.0	Mt.Washington Auto Rd.
162.5	Left as Rte 16 merges with US Rte 302
166.1	Arrive in Intervale at the Information Center ■

draulic at the bottom. After three hours of fishing vainly with grappling hooks, most abandoned efforts to recover the body that night. A few labored on to divert the course of the water and lessen its grip until a pole noose could be slipped over Sparks's limp arm to haul her free—whereby she promptly regained consciousness, having been able to catch an occasional breath in her aerated watery tomb.

It's easy to be lulled by a relaxing cruise on this pleasant, wide highway, but you do need to stay alert for turning traffic, oblivious tourists, and moose, especially in the hours near dawn and dusk. Along the boggier stretches, a thick clot of haphazardly parked roadside vehicles can signal a sighting—and alert others to slow to an instantaneous rubbernecking crawl, or leap unheeding into the road from vehicles that could not yet be said to have come to a stop. You may temper any annoyance with the sort of smug that comes from easing by and realizing that the entire foolish train wreck unfolding before you was based on a rumor without any substance. There never was a moose, but at least the road curving before you will have been cleared of company.

When the nomenclature in New England does not reflect the stories of its more noteworthy European settlers or benefactors, it often adopted a version of the native appellation. Grandfather to Kancamagus, Papoose Conewa, the Child of the Bear, has become known to history as "Passaconaway," the powerful sachem who would unite 17 New England tribes to form the Panacook Confederacy in 1627. All that remains of the small village named after him is the Russell Colbath House on Route 112, where in 1891, Thomas Colbath told his wife he'd be back "in a little while." She placed a lantern in the window until her death 39 years later. Surprisingly, Colbath did return to the valley three years after that, but offered almost no explanation for why he left or why he came back.

Route 112 climbs the shoulder of Mount Kancamagus to the notch at 2,855 feet, cutting through a large part of the 770,000 acres that now make up the national forest, about 15 percent of which has been designated as wilderness, to be kept in as primitive a state as possible. From the numerous pull-outs, you can take in commanding views of Presidential Range-Dry River and Pemigewasset Wildernesses to the north, and the Sandwich Range Wilderness to the south as the road crimps tightly to scrub altitude before straightening to follow the Hancock and East Branches of the river into Lincoln, the crossroads of the White Mountains.

Whether you plan to follow this ride or motor over to Route 118 to continue on a portion of Ride 10, if it's close to midday, plan to get fuel for bike and body either in North Woodstock or at one of the many ski town services in Lincoln—even if it's only snacks you can enjoy at any of the innumerable spots that might tempt you to deploy a sidestand later on.

Railroad buffs might want to plan a later arrival, since one of my all-time favorite restaurants doesn't even board until 5 p.m. The Café Lafayette Dinner Train (603-745-3500; www.nhdinnertrain.com) is rolling stock complete with a converted military kitchen car that actually prepares excellent gourmet meals en route. Perhaps best of all, the elegant railway cars in

The Kancamagus Highway is New Hampshire's most celebrated motorcycle touring road.

Take care approaching the famous hairpin at the bottom of Mount Kancamagus.

Meals on the Café Lafayette Dinner Train are actually prepared en route in a custom modified galley car.

which you will be dining will have been restored and are maintained by the chefs, waiters, and conductors who will be serving you.

Route 3 goes north through Franconia Notch, a road replete with natural wonders that have attracted tourists for more than 150 years. The Flume is a narrow chasm of vertical walls 70 to 90 feet high and only 12 to 20 feet wide, the result of Flume Brook cutting into a softer dike of basalt that forced its way through faults in the granite.

As you probably know, the rocky profile of the Old Man of the Mountain succumbed to erosion stress in 2003, although it remains the ubiquitous symbol of the Granite State. The talus slopes of Cannon Cliffs provide a glimpse into the processes that shaped both this state and its emblem. As the subterranean granite dome that forms Cannon was eroded to the surface, it expanded and fractured, sloughing in layers from the southern and eastern exposures, a process aided by natural cycles of freezing and thawing. The top two of the five ledges that had made up the Old Man's profile had long been shored up against the worst effects of weather, but the inexorable forces that shaped these hills could not be stopped within the finite bounds of our known history.

If you live where you have to winterize your bike each year, you may appreciate the free New England Ski Museum at the base of Cannon Mountain, where you can peruse vintage photos, advertising, fashion, gear, and memorabilia, including the five Olympic gold medals of area native Bode

Miller. For those of us fortunate enough to be on two wheels, however, the best attraction will likely be the ride through the notch itself.

As you soak up a wealth of views seemingly unspoiled by the baser hands of men, it's worth remembering that these vast forests were all but clear-cut well into the 20th century, with huge tracts further destroyed by unchecked fires fueled by logging debris, making their ecological rebound even more spectacular.

US Route 3 arcs around the west side of Mount Washington and intersects US Route 302 in the village of Twin Mountain. The first few miles east on US Route 302 pass through a boggy area popular with moose. Watch for them.

You simply cannot miss the grand, red-roofed bulk of the historic Mount Washington Hotel as it sits bathed in alpenglow before the ramparts of the Presidential Range, the last of the luxurious old summer resorts that graced this region during the Gilded Age. It was state-of-the-art when it was built in 1902, with a hydraulically operated elevator, sprinkler system, and electrical wiring installed by Thomas Edison and the fledgling General Electric Company. Even today, the hotel still has its own telephone system and post office. The international financial consortium that recently purchased the property has chosen to restore, rather than update the place, to the extent of even replicating the patterns of the carpets with the original Belgian manu-

Even with a low ceiling of clouds obscuring its Presidential backdrop, the biker-friendly, five-star Mount Washington Hotel is a dramatic sight.

facturer! In spite of the opulent flair, you are more than welcome to wander in the public spaces and enjoy the view and a cool beverage from the wide veranda.

Behind the resort is the base station for the Mount Washington Cog Railway, where tiny locomotives push their railway cars to the summit of the northeast's highest peak. "Cog" is an old word for a gear, and these locomotives actually move by a combination of their standard drive wheels and a spoke gear that meshes with the crossties—like a powered ratchet that will only engage in one direction. With a maximum grade that exceeds 37 percent and averages 25 percent, a regular train would simply slide backward down the tracks. The tickets might seem pricey until you consider what must be the cost of maintaining one of the world's most unique feats of engineering in such an extreme environment.

The tiny pond on the east side of the road near Crawford Station is Saco Lake, the headwaters of the Saco River. When first discovered by a white settler around 1771, the narrow Saco River gorge at the north end of Crawford Notch was just wide enough for a mule to pass through. It was

The boilers on the Mount Washington Cog Railway were originally fired by wood, and then coal, before they added cleaner burning biodiesel locomotives in 2008.

One of the straighter sections on the Chatham side of Hurricane Mountain Road—but watch out for that dip!

blasted for the turnpike in 1806 and the railroad opened it even more in 1875. It's still a rather narrow passage, however, as you descend into this fabulous glacial canyon. Note the distinct gneiss bulge on the left of the road just beyond the body of water, which clearly resembles an elephant's head and trunk, complete with a large white quartz eye and brow.

Just beyond the height of land are two signed waterfalls that tumble and plunge more than 300 feet down the side of Mount Jackson to the road. The first, Flume Cascade, is not to be confused with the similarly named gorge in Franconia Notch; the second, Silver Cascade, typically garners more attention. Both are popular ice climbing spots in the winter. If your timing is fortunate, you may get to see the Conway Scenic Railroad's Notch Train oozing slowly along the sheer bluffs, a remnant of the Maine Central Railroad's Mountain Division Line. Gazing up at the sky above the verdant cliffs of this constricted pass can sometimes conjure in me a pang of vertigo as I pilot my motorcycle back toward Bartlett.

If you are hankering for a diversion, Bear Notch Road will take you from US Route 302 in Bartlett to the Kanc; this sweepy stretch of well-banked curves seems made for riding, with several scenic pullouts for regrouping and recapping. Another way to avoid the possible traffic between here and

Conway and North Conway

In addition to its long and historic devotion to the recreation and lifestyle that has long attracted so many to the White Mountains, the towns of Conway and North Conway function as a commercial hub for much of the area's hospitality services and retail businesses. New Hampshire's lack of sales tax has attracted factory outlet shopping to The Strip, and seasonal swells of visitors can make that stretch of Route 16/US Route 302 a busy place.

The town has the fortune of being located on a geologic shelf in a river valley. The Moat Range, which forms a lovely western backdrop to the historic old train depot, was named for the many beaver dams known to have proliferated near its foothills. The pinkish, backslashed shoulder of exposed Conway granite near the northern end is known descriptively as Red Ridge.

Rising from the modest slopes on the eastern side of town will be Mount Cranmore, a family oriented ski resort that did much to pioneer alpine skiing in North America, installing the first ski lift and inviting prominent Austrian skier Hannes Schneider to found a ski school in 1939 based on his Arlberg technique. Schneider arrived in North Conway as tens of thousands of other skiers did each year, on one of the many Snow Trains run by the Boston & Maine Railroad between 1931 and 1950. Today you

can get a taste of their steam-powered journey on the rolling stock of the Conway Scenic Railroad (603-356-5251; www.conwayscenic.com), which could include lunch in wicker armchairs in a restored Victorian Pullman.

Note that Rally in the Valley, an event that runs alongside Laconia, offers riders all the benefits of a less crowded base of operations from which to participate in Bike Week, and proceeds support scholarships for local students pursuing higher education in the trades. ∎

There's a paved access road to the top of Cathedral Ledge, one of two unattached bluffs that overlook the village of North Conway and the Saco River intervale.

Conway is to do what the locals do: take West Side Road, a right turn located after the Attitash Ski Area. This rural bypass runs along the western shores of the Saco River, more or less parallel to the main drag. At the lower end you will pass by the parking area for the short, very accessible trail to Diana's Baths, a multi-level cascade of drops and granite potholes on Lucy Brook that are great for cooling off on a summer day. After five miles on West Side Road, you will need to turn right at the large strawberry farm to continue to the covered bridge near where you began this route. This second half of West Side Road has signage for several good leg-stretchers, including an easy saunter around Echo Lake at the foot of Whitehorse Ledge, and the spectacular vista of the entire valley from the paved access road that winds to the top of Cathedral Ledge.

If instead you were to continue straight ahead onto River Road at Shartner's Strawberry Farm, you would pop out at one of the two traffic light intersections in the village. To bypass the busyness from this point, take any side street two blocks east to find the North-South Road, a blissful, limited-access road that returns to US Route 302 in Redstone, a village named for the old granite quarry whose flattish blocky face looms from the last peak in the little chain of hills you've been following.

If you have the daylight and are up to the challenge of a road whose features rival those in the European Alps, however, stay on Route 302 from Bartlett and after five miles or so, begin looking for the left onto Hurricane Mountain Road immediately before the scenic vista and information center in Intervale. After a few steep blips, you'll pass by some residences grouped around a rural crossroad that once denoted Kearsarge, a village of inns that

This is as high as you can go on land in the state of New Hampshire.

Ride to the Sky—The Mount Washington Auto Road

At the bottom of the mountain, it was 75 degrees and sunny, the blue sky flecked with puffy white clouds. By the time we reached 4,500 feet, it was sleeting, and there was no place to stop or turn around until reaching the summit. Most of the 200-plus riders were wearing tee shirts or denim jackets. I stopped in the parking lot just long enough to plug in my jacket liner and turn on my heated grips before descending. Most people don't know that this mountain has the worst weather in the world and more than a hundred have died on its slopes.

Weather changes rapidly on Mount Washington. The highest temperature ever recorded on the summit was 72 degrees and the average high in July is only 54 degrees, not considering windchill. In 1934, the manned weather observatory clocked winds of 231 mph, the second highest ever recorded on this planet. Hurricane-force winds blow more than 100 days a year and the average wind speed is somewhere around 50 mph. Snow falls year round.

Tourists have been trekking to the summit since the Crawford Path was created in 1816. The Tip Top House opened for overnight stays in 1852, the carriage road (now the auto road) in 1861, and the Cog Railway in 1869. All of these are still extant, although the remains of the squat stone bunk hut no longer hosts overnight guests. Today the summit also includes the weather observatory and visitors center with its museum and cafeteria. With more than a quarter of a million people each year making the trip to the summit via one means or another, solitude can be rare. Yet, the experience itself is unique enough to recommend it.

During the annual mid-June Ride to the Sky, the auto road is closed to all but motorcycles. This has become a Laconia Bike Week tradition, now expanded to two non-consecutive days (a weather consideration). On a nice day the experience is breathtaking. You'll also get the iconic bumper sticker trophy, "This Bike Climbed Mount Washington." ■

thrived on the summer rail trade. Once you're past the access gate, hang on tight—perhaps most tightly of all to your ego, as the trees grow right to the edge of a narrow ribbon of asphalt that pleats, folds, and humps its way up the slope by means of hairpin switchbacks and blind whoops that can launch you airborne or bottom your suspension. Note well that some of the white-knuckled drivers you could encounter will be unexpectedly in over their heads, cheating the center line, checking to see that the kids are buckled in tight, and leaving a slipstream of toasted asbestos in their wake. Other than all that, it's fantastic. *Have fun!*

At the end of Hurricane Mountain Road you'll connect with Route 113, which weaves back and forth across the New Hampshire-Maine border as it proceeds north. The Cold River and Basin Campgrounds in the national forest at the southern end of Evans Notch are typically much less crowded than others. From this point, Route 113 will narrow and become a long green tunnel of leafy canopy and dappled light that breaks out near the height of land on a sunny shelf overlooking Evans Brook. Another sweepy and secretive stint and you'll come out on US Route 2 just west of Gilead.

Gorham is the town of note that services visitors on this end of the Mount Washington Valley, and Route 16 south through Pinkham Notch, with its broad views of the majestic Presidentials, will stand in stark contrast to the quiet privacy of Evans Notch. Even without their white frosting, it's easy to discern the glacial cirques of (left to right) Tuckerman Ravine, Raymond Cataract, and Huntington Ravine. The tollgate for the Mount Washington Auto Road is just north of the pass. While this detour to the summit

Lightly trafficked, Route 113 through Evans Notch weaves back and forth between Maine and New Hampshire.

Looking down at Route 16 in Pinkham Notch from one of the summit parking lots on Mount Washington.

For motorcyclists in the eastern United States, the road to the top of Mount Washington is a rare opportunity to ride above tree line.

of the mountain is a mere 15.6-mile round trip, it requires at least half a day—weather permitting—but it's worth it.

Route 16 merges with US Route 302 in Glen, an intersection that would be of passing note if it were not so close to the popular amusement park of Story Land; when the gates close in late afternoon during the height of a summer weekend, you'll be glad to have options . . . but otherwise, no real worries. The rest of the way will be familiar by now as you go through Intervale to North Conway. Somewhere along this road is where you'll probably be sleeping tonight—you'll certainly have enough choices—but allow me to recommend camping at Glen Ellis (603-383-4567; www. glenelliscampground.com) on US Route 302 in Glen; Stonehurst Manor (800-525-9100; www.StonehurstManor.com), and the Colonial Motel (866-356-5178; www.thecolonialmotel.com) on Route 16 in North Conway. Delaney's (603-356-7776; www.delaneys.com) is a popular sports tavern; the only microbrewery in the area is the Moat Mountain Smoke-house and Brewing Company (603-356-6381; www.moatmountain.com); and the Black Cap Grille (603-356-2225; www.blackcapgrille.com), lo-cated farther south on the strip, also gets high marks.

Ride 14   The Bridges of Coos County

Distance: *180 miles; plan for an all-day ride*
Highlights: *Rivers, beautiful lakes, a mountain pass, and seemingly endless forests, the motorcyclist monument in Colebrook, the L.L. Cote Sports Shop in Errol, the Connecticut Lakes. You might spot a moose, a bald eagle, or even a bear.*

This ride could have easily been titled the Great North Woods Tour because that's another name for this region. Coos County (pronounced COE-oss) is an area larger than the state of Rhode Island, yet there are few roads, paved or otherwise. Part of this ride goes to the very source of the Connecticut River, and another part through the northern White Mountains. Tourism is pretty much limited to hunting, fishing, hiking, and getting away from people—although there is one annual motorcycle gathering that does draw a crowd. With fewer man-made distractions competing for attention, you'll have time to get to know a few of the interesting and historic examples of covered bridges in the area.

On a grey fall day, the brilliance of peak foliage can seem to be lit from within, as it is here in Dixville Notch, overlooking Lake Gloriette and The Balsams.

This loop starts in Lancaster at the intersection of US Routes 2 and 3. US Route 2 is the primary highway that runs east-west from the Vermont capitol of Montpelier to Augusta, the capitol of Maine. Lancaster is 28 miles east of St. Johnsbury—about a half-hour ride. With a population of about 3,500, the town offers a number of motels, restaurants, and gas stations, so it's a logical staging point.

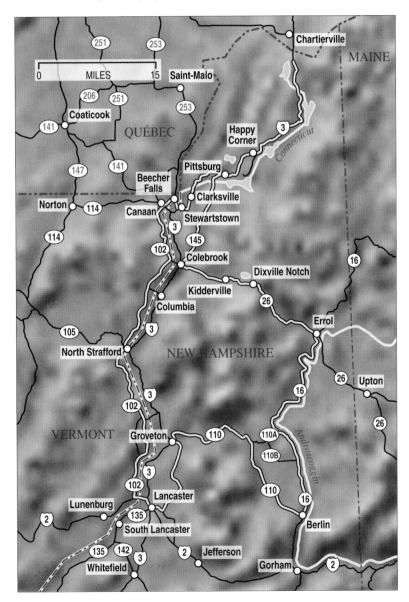

FROM LANCASTER, NEW HAMPSHIRE

0	From Lancaster, east onto Mechanic St. from the junction of Rte 135 on US Rtes 2 and 3
2.0	Left onto Grange Rd.
4.1	Left onto Lost Nation Rd.
13.1	Right onto Rte 110 in Groveton
26.6	In West Milan, continue south on Rte 110 toward Berlin
37.8	In Berlin, left (north) onto Rte 16 toward Errol
67.4	Left onto Rte 26 in Errol
78.4	[The Balsam Grand Resort, Lake Gloriette, and Dixville Notch]
79.1	[Entrance to the ski area on the left]
88.9	In Colebrook, left (south) onto US Rte 3
90.2	[*Motorcyclists at Prayer* monument; return north on US Rte 3]
91.7	Bear right onto Rte 145 (Park St.)
104.9	In Pittsburg, north onto US Rte 3
126.1	Turn around at the boat landing at Third Connecticut Lake and return south on US Rte 3
147.4	In Pittsburg, continue south on US Rte 3
148.3	[Pittsburg-Clarksville Bridge]
155.7	At Stewartstown, cross the river to Beecher Falls, Vermont, and turn left onto Rte 102 (south)
201.4	Near Lancaster, turn left onto Bridge St. to cross the river into Lancaster
203.1	Arrive at US Rtes 3 and 2 at Rte 135 and Mechanic St. in Lancaster ∎

Covered bridges are typically built of wooden trusses, triangular units whose connected elements distribute the forces of tension and compression along the structure. Other routes in this book found excellent examples of local bridges whose architectural pedigrees harkened back to designs well-known in the Middle Ages, such as kingpost and queenpost trusses. By the time roads were being built in the eastern United States, new versions were being claimed by their architectural inventors, including the popular Burr arch, Town's lattice, and the Howe truss. Different geographic regions seem to have favored particular styles, with the easily built and economical Town lattice being popular from the 1860 to 1890s, and the Howe truss, which can carry a bit more weight, gaining use during the late 19th and early 20th century.

One type of truss that's found only in the most northern areas of New England was developed by Peter Paddleford of Littleton, New Hampshire, in 1846. Paddleford modified a Long truss—consisting of vertical posts notched into parallel horizontal chords, and notched braces and counterbraces—so that the braces lapped over all the frame members and the counterbraces were set into tight-fitting channels, effectively "locking" the whole structure together under load and increasing its stiffness. Paddleford never patented his design for fear of court challenges threatened by the holders of Colonel Long's patent.

The light and airy Northumberland-Groveton Bridge is ideal for checking out the complicated joinery of its Paddleford truss design, to which have been added Burr arches for extra stability.

The Mechanic Street Bridge is the first covered bridge you'll encounter as you depart Lancaster. Built in 1862, this 94-foot, single-span Paddleford truss crosses the Israel River. Take note of its construction as you pass slowly though; although you won't notice anything on your bike, the stress of a heavy vehicle could disturb the dust on successive support timbers.

A very pretty bridge is the Northumberland-Groveton over the Ammonoosuc River near the junction of Route 110 at US Route 3 in Groveton. Built in 1852, this 126-foot white Paddleford truss has added Burr arches for increased stability. The reconstruction of Route 3 in 1939 bypassed this historic structure and today it is pedestrian-only. As one of the few bridges painted both inside and out, it's airy interior seems especially bright, making it ideal for checking out the complicated joinery of this style of bridge.

The next stop will be the Stark Bridge just off Route 110 by the church on North Stark Road. It crosses the Upper Ammonoosuc River and has

gone through so many re-
pairs, revisions, and restora-
tions that I'm not sure how to
classify its present construction, though it began as a two-
span Paddleford truss. Its proposed replacement in the
1950s with a more modern
concrete and steel bridge created such an outcry that the
plan was scrapped. Its location, adjacent to a pictur-
esque, steepled white church,
has secured its standing as one
of the most iconic and photographed places in the state;
the light is especially good at
this site in the morning.

In West Milan (MY-lin),
stay on Route 110 into Berlin
(BER-lin). High on the hill
overlooking the town is the

*If you've been hankerin' for a mooseburger,
check out Northern Exposure in Errol.*

Holy Resurrection Russian Orthodox Church complete with onion-domed
spires. In 1915 there were 300 Russian men working the lumber camps of
the Coos, but only 32 had families. To encourage women from the Minsk
region to emigrate to the north woods of America, a group of these men organized a church and school. To get there from Route 16, turn left at Mechanic Street and make another left at the traffic light. Turn right onto
Exchange Street/Mount Forist Street (before the post office), cross the railroad tracks, bear right, and climb the steep hill. Turn left onto Russian
Street and you'll see the church.

Berlin has a population of 10,000 people, although not all of them live in
the city. The entire county has only 33,000 people, and this includes larger
towns like Jefferson, Gorham, and Whitefield on the southern boundary. It
also comprises several unincorporated areas like Sargent's Purchase on the
summit of Mount Washington, which was covered in Ride 13.

The ride north on Route 16 follows the Androscoggin River, the highway often hugging its western bank to and through Thirteen Mile Woods,
known for its sweeping curves and abundant wildlife. The extensive
wetlands on the other side of the river are prime moose habitat. A normal

size cow weighs around 900 pounds and a large bull is twice that. These huge animals won't get out of your way and if their long legs don't clue you to the fact that moose can move quickly, just take my word for it. If you see one up ahead by the side of the road, brake and stop. Don't try to sneak around the animal and don't saunter up to take a picture.

You can't miss the L. L. Cote Sports Shop (603-482-7777; www.llcote. com) in Errol (pop. 291)—since there aren't many other things of that size to compete for your attention at the intersection that functions as the center of activity. A real "general store" for the north country lifestyle, at Cote's you can not only pick up a Subway sandwich, but also a wide array of firearms, warm clothing, power tools, camping gear, or even a canoe with an outboard motor. Their in-house collection of taxidermy features many rare albino versions of northland critters, the crowning glory of which is a stuffed white-and-grey bull moose.

Ride 22 also touches Errol and its humble selection of necessary amenities make it a hub stop for sportsmen, cyclists, canoers, and motorcyclists—and all of them chow down on the mooseburgers at Northern Exposure (603-482-3468). Don't forget to top off your tank before getting back on the road.

Over on Route 26, the citizens of Dixville Notch and Kidderville get together in the Ballot Room of Balsams Grand Resort every four years to elect the President of the United States. This tiny town has had first-vote status since 1948. With 10 votes cast in 2012, it didn't take long to tally the results for the national media (it was a tie, 5-5).

Of more interest is the wonderful road that goes through this mountain

Organized in 1915 by Russian lumbermen hoping to encourage marriageable young women from the Minsk region to emigrate to the Great North Woods, the Holy Resurrection Orthodox Church stands high on a hill overlooking Berlin.

At Our Lady of Grace Shrine in Colebrook, a granite sculpture stands in memory of a horrific motorcycle crash that took place during Laconia Bike Week.

passage at 1,887 feet above sea level. It's not a new one: The Coos Trail was established through the notch in 1803 and you're now riding on a 200-year-old highway. The temptation is to crack the throttle, but radar-equipped police cars are often parked by Lake Gloriette at the entrance to the Balsams and you won't see them until it's too late.

Colebrook is a busy little town, but in mid-June it seems positively packed as 10,000 motorcyclists arrive for the annual Blessing of the Bikes. It can now be said that "Laconia" stretches from the New Hampshire seacoast to the Great North Woods. What began as a rather small affair in 1976 grew in size and popularity once it was scheduled for the end of Bike Week and organized as the Great North Woods Ride In (blessingofthebikes.tripod.com). The event takes place at the Shrine of Our Lady of Grace on US Route 3 south of town. There are 50 monuments on this site, one of the most famous of which is the granite sculpture *Motorcyclists In Prayer.*

Route 145 is a road used mostly by residents—not that there's much traffic between Pittsburg and Colebrook. You'll go through Clarksville (pop. 265), a place name on the map, but you won't find a village. People in this neck of the woods like to spread out a bit. I think Route 145 is more interesting than US Route 3, even though the pavement isn't maintained quite as well.

Pittsburg (pop. 869) is the northernmost town in New Hampshire, the only New Hampshire town to border Canada, and the only town that borders both Vermont and Maine. It's also the largest township in New England with a total of 291.4 square miles; although a number of people live in the village, other homesteads are scattered along backroads. I recommend that you continue riding north on Route 3 to the Connecticut Lakes and then return to this point (a 43-mile round trip). My philosophy is that you might never come this way again, so see it now. The northern section of this

Despite a few modern improvements, the road through Dixville Notch, plotted more than 200 years ago, retains much of its original character.

The Columbia Covered Bridge is one of the prettiest on the Connecticut River.

road (near the Canadian border) is known locally as Moose Alley. Whether your goal is to spot a moose or avoid them, note that they are most often sighted near dawn or dusk.

The Connecticut River originates at the Third Connecticut Lake and runs through the Second, the First, and Lake Francis (the lakes were numbered in the order of their discovery—south to north—not in the direction of the water flow). This is an outdoorsman's paradise so you'll see signs for lodges and camping areas. Tall Timber Lodge is one of the fancy places and it's located on the shore of Back Lake (609 Beach Rd.; 800-835-6343; wwww.talltimber.com). Their Rainbow Grille restaurant serves up excellent fare. In spite of all they offer, however, I'll admit to having camped just off the road on more than one occasion, accommodations that you may find especially well suited to this beautiful, wild place.

The Pittsburg-Happy Corners Bridge was built in 1869 as a Paddleford truss with Burr arches added to the 60-foot span. This one is located 0.3 mile off the highway on Hill Road (5.5 miles north of Pittsburg on the right) and is open for regular traffic. Remember that whenever you leave the highway you'll be on a gravel road.

The Pittsburg-River Road Bridge (c. 1858) is a 50-foot, single-span queenpost that's no longer in use, but is still the northernmost covered bridge on the Connecticut River. The modern concrete and steel bridge runs parallel to it, so access and photos are easy to obtain, but it's located 1.2 miles off US Route 3 on River Road (6 miles north of Pittsburg on the right).

Pull into the boat launch area at the Third Connecticut Lake and dip your feet in the water. I don't know how long it will take, but the water around your ankles will end up in Long Island Sound. The Canadian bor-

der is only a mile up the road, but this is a good place to turn around and begin your trek back to Groveton or Lancaster.

Just south of Pittsburg on US Route 3 is another covered bridge. The
Pittsburg-Clarksville is a single-span Paddleford truss to which Burr arches
have been added for additional strength. Built in 1876, it is 88 feet long and
is now open only to pedestrians. Also just south of Pittsburg you might
notice a historic site marker on the side of the road. You've just crossed the 45th
Parallel and you are now halfway between the North Pole and the equator!

Stewartstown is directly across the river from Beecher Falls, the easternmost town in Vermont. Even though this chapter focuses on New Hampshire, I recommend that you cross over the river at Stewartstown and turn
left onto Vermont Route 102 for the ride to Lancaster. It is a more enjoyable
motorcycling road than busy Route 3.

And as this particular route winds to an end, the last covered bridge or two
offers up yet another variation on the styles you have seen up until now. The
145-foot Columbia Bridge, built in 1912, is a rather modern covered bridge,
and a classic example of a Howe truss. Similar in appearance to the Long and
Paddleford trusses described earlier (in that it uses wooden braces and counterbraces), the vertical elements in this design were made of pairs of iron tension
rods. And with that, your tour of the bridges of Coos county is concluded.

*At the northernmost place in New Hampshire reachable by road, this idyllic spot is just
a mile from the Canadian border on Third Connecticut Lake.*

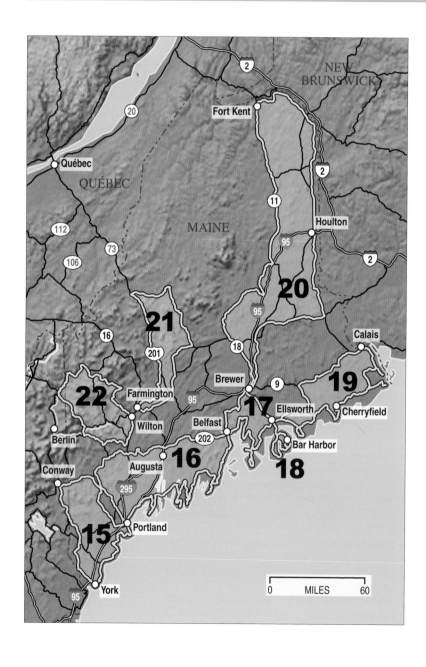

Maine

Maine is almost as large as all the other New England States combined. It encompasses 35,387 square miles, but 4,523 of these are covered with water. With a population of about 1,300,000 and most residents living in cities and towns located in the coastal lowlands, there's plenty of blissfully undeveloped landscape. About half the land area of the state is unorganized territory, meaning these 424 townships have no local government and are administered by the state. There are 6,000 lakes, 32,000 miles of rivers, and 17 million acres of forests. Even if you had the time to travel all 22,000-plus miles of Vacationland's maintained highways, you'd still only be sniffing around the peripheries of everything there is to see and do. This state is bigger than it appears when looking at a map. You might be surprised to learn that Portland, Maine, is closer to New York City than it is to Fort Kent.

From Kittery to Eastport is only 293 miles, yet Maine has more than 3,500 miles of coastline—some sources put this as high as 5,550—and depending upon which reference you consult, 400 to 2,000 Atlantic islands within its boundaries. Someone figured out that the deep inlets on the Maine coast could harbor all the navies in the world simultaneously. These same features are a haven for lobster, and 90 percent of all lobsters caught in

Welcome to Maine.

the United States are from Maine. With this much jagged coastline you'd expect lighthouses, and there are 63 of them—more than any other state—but only ten of these are accessible by motorcycle.

The image of the eastern white pine appears on both the state seal and flag, and the tassel from its cone is the official state flower. During colonial times, the tall, straight, light trunks of these trees were essential for the masts of large sailing ships. All white pines of a certain diameter were marked as expressly reserved for the King's navy—an extremely unpopular (and much flouted) regulation that would set the tone for British-American relations until well into the 1800s.

The first sea battle of the Revolutionary War took place around Machias, shortly after British troops had retreated from the Battle of Lexington and Concord, to be held under siege in Boston. A merchant emissary with armed reinforcements was dispatched specifically to trade for lumber, but the deal was derailed at a point, and several twists and turns later, local militia armed with muskets had boarded and captured the warship, adding it to a growing makeshift fleet that would continue to intercept British ships. In fact, England's aggressive propensity to secure Maine's timber, which con-

Wild lupine is common throughout the north country, spraying the hillsides with violet early each summer.

Maine lowbush blueberries are a great source of phytochemicals and antioxidants.

tinued through the War of 1812, prompted the building of Fort Knox at the mouth of the Penobscot River to protect the resources around Bangor. Until the border between Canada and the United States was established in 1842, tensions over logging rights in the disputed territory nearly erupted in bloodshed during the state-declared Aroostook War, which was ultimately resolved with diplomacy.

Even counting Alaska, the state of Maine has the highest percentage of forested land in the country, with most of the wood today harvested to make paper. It's big business, and just so you know, logging trucks have the legal right-of-way; allow them to pass as you would a fire truck or ambulance. But these days, the wars that have been raging over the future of logging in Maine's North Woods have been no less acrimonious and heartfelt. In 2011, philanthropist, Mainer, and former owner of the Burt's Bees line of natural care products, Roxanne Quimby offered to donate 70,000 historic acres she had acquired between Baxter State Park and the East Branch River to establish a North Woods National Park, as well as an equal and adjacent parcel to be set aside for traditional recreation, like hunting and snowmobiling. Whether Quimby's controversial vision for the land will come to pass will be anybody's guess, but that the woodlands of Maine are a treasure worthy of a fight has never seemed to be the issue.

Roadside icons like this one in Freeport still exist, a throwback to the 1950s.

Ride 15 Southwestern Maine

Distance: *213 miles; at least a full-day trip*
Highlights: *Rolling hills, lakes, and coastal beaches, lighthouses, the Wells Auto Museum. Portland, Maine; York, Maine; Conway, New Hampshire.*

The first leg of this ride is an enjoyable tour through scenic countryside from Conway to York Beach, avoiding large towns. In fact, you don't even have to deal with a town until reaching Berwick. The ride is not filled with dramatic scenery or compelling points of interest, but these low-key country roads will be a pleasure to ride. Route 153 from Conway to East

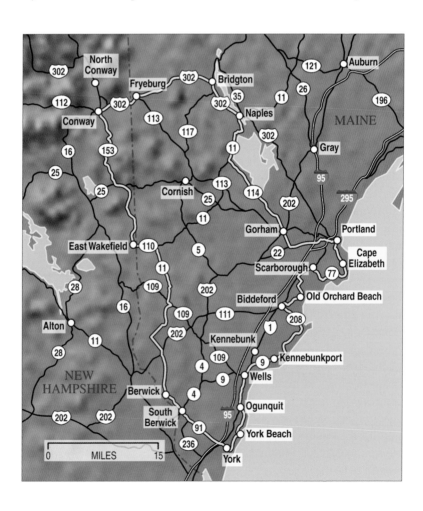

Wakefield, New Hampshire, is very popular with motorcyclists. Route 11 in Maine is less well known, but equally enjoyable.

Berwick and South Berwick are 19th-century mill towns that simply haven't become tourist destinations. If you like the ambience of small town communities, I think you'll like both of these. From South Berwick to York the properties will become more "gentrified."

The delightful Route 91 (York Woods Road) will end at US Route 1, a fast highway that offers seemingly endless choices for hotels, restaurants, and services. Route 1A, however, is a far more scenic way to experience the southern coast of Maine. From any route, though, expect peak summer weekends to up the local traffic considerably.

The first chartered city in America was Gorgeana in 1642, the capitol city of the province of Maine under lord proprietor Sir Fernando Gorges. After his death, Massachusetts reclaimed the territory, which was renamed for York, England, although New England and New France continued to squabble over control, with the latter often employing Native Americans against colonial settlements. The Old Gaol in York Village dates to 1719

Cape Neddick Light on the Nubble—known almost exclusively as Nubble Light—is the most photographed beacon in the state.

FROM CONWAY, NEW HAMPSHIRE

0	From Conway Village, head south on Rte 153 from Rte 16
15.2	Left onto Rte 153/Rte 25 east
16.2	Right on Rte 153 (Effingham Trail)
28.9	Left (east) onto Rte 110 (Wakefield Rd.)
32.6	Right onto Rte 11 (Bond Spring Rd.)
43.3	Left onto Rte 11/Rte 109
44.2	Right onto Deering Ridge Rd. to Lebanon Rd.
48.2	Straight at intersection onto Bakers Grant Rd.
49.4	Bear left onto Heath Rd.
49.5	Bear right to stay on Heath Rd.
51.7	Left at intersection onto Center Rd. (south)
54.8	Straight to cross US Rte 202/Rte 11 onto Long Swamp Rd. to Pine Hill Rd.
63.0	Bear right (one-way) onto Eleanor's St. in Berwick
63.0	Left onto Rochester St.
63.1	Right, left onto Saw Mill Hill
63.5	Right onto Rte 236
66.8	Continue through South Berwick on Rte 236
68.9	Left onto Rte 91 (York Woods Rd.)
76.6	Left onto US Rte 1 east
76.8	Right onto US Rte 1A (York St.)
78.3	Arrive at Rte 103 in York Harbor
78.3	South on Rte 1A (York St.) from the junction of Rte 103 in York Harbor
78.8	[Harbor Beach Rd. on the right goes to the public beach]
81.8	Right onto Nubble Rd.
82.7	[Sohier Park and Nubble Light]
83.7	Right onto US Rte 1A (Long Beach Ave.) to Ocean Ave.
84.7	Bear right onto Shore Rd.
90.2	Bear right onto US Rte 1
97.3	Bear right onto Rte 9 (Port Rd.)

(continued)

and served as the royal prison for the entire province. Debtors made up a large part of the incarcerated population, especially after the Revolutionary War, with other crimes running from slander and drunkenness to arson, grand theft, and murder. Regardless of offense, all were originally housed together in two very primitive rooms—although the turnkey and his family didn't rate much more than that.

There are far too many turn-offs and scenic vantage points along the Maine coast for me to try to catalog them in any meaningful way, but I'll mention this first one merely to introduce you to the possibilities that exist. From Route 1A, half a mile beyond the junction of Route 103, bear right onto Harbor Beach Road to York Harbor. You'll discover paved parking, public restrooms, and a nice beach—the southern one percent of the Maine coast can claim 90 percent of its sand beaches. The raggedy edge of the Maine coastline can be attributed to its consisting of bedrock that has eroded unevenly over the millennia. North and east of Portland, however, the foundation is more metamorphic than igneous, and the deeply worn embayments that have produced sandy beaches will be giving way to more dramatic confrontations between the turf and tide.

Turning onto Nubble Road and into Sohier Park to Nubble Light

CONTINUING . . .

101.8   Right on Rte 9 (Maine St.) in Kennebunkport

102.0   Left on Rte 9 (School St.)

109.4   [Fortune Rocks Rd.]

115.5   In Biddeford, right on Rte 9 (Clifford St.)

115.8   Left onto Water St.

116.0   Bear right on Rte 9 (Main St.)

116.7   In Saco, right on Rte 9 (Beach St.)

117.6   Left onto Old Orchard Rd.

118.8   Straight onto Rte 5 (Saco Ave.)

120.6   Right onto Old Orchard St.

120.8   Arrive downtown Old Orchard Beach; return via Old Orchard St.

121.0   Bear right onto Rte 98 (Portland Ave.)

121.3   Bear right to stay on Portland Ave. (leave Rte 98)

124.2   Left onto Old Blue Point Rd.

125.3   Right onto US Rte 1

128.7   In Scarborough, right onto Rte 207 (Black Point Rd.)

131.7   Left onto Rte 77 (Spurwink Rd.)

137.1   [Two Lights Rd. leads to Two Lights State Park]

138.9   [Pass Shore Rd. on right]

141.8   In South Portland, left onto Rte 77 to the Casco Bay Bridge

143.2   In Portland, bear right onto York St.

143.3   Right (next right) onto Park St.

143.3   Left onto US Rte 1A (Commercial St.)

143.9   Arrive downtown Portland at Market St. and Long Wharf

143.9   From Market St. at Long Wharf, head away from the wharf on Market St.

144.2   Left onto Congress St.

145.2   Right onto Rte 25 (Deering Ave.)

145.4   Left (west) onto US Rte 1 (Blue Star Memorial Hwy)

146.0   Straight under I-295 and onto Rte 22 (Congress St.)

152.3   In North Scarborough, Rte 22 merges with Rte 114

153.1   Right onto Rte 114 (South St.)

154.0   First right (straight) at roundabout; stay on Rte 114 (South St.)

181.7   In Naples, left onto US Rte 302

204.8   In Fryeburg, left onto US Rte 302/Rte 5

213.3   Arrive at Rte 113/Rte 16/Rte 153 in Conway, New Hampshire   ■

(c. 1879), it will appear as if this was the destination for most of the riders who chose to endure Route 1A. This happens to be my favorite lighthouse in Maine. It's also the most photographed lighthouse in the state; just be-

Rowboats in Perkins Cove wait to take lobstermen to their craft in the marina.

cause I have my own photos that date back over several decades won't deter me from taking several more. Actually, the official name of this lighthouse is the Cape Neddick Light and it is on a small rocky island called the Nubble. Just up the street is Brown's Ice Cream (232 Nubble Rd.; 207-363-1277), another famous stop on the southern Maine coast. All the ice cream is made on the premises and sometimes you'll find unusual flavors. Try the "tornado," which contains every type of candy used in other specialty ice creams.

Looping around Cape Neddick will bring you to the village of York Beach. The Goldenrod (207-363-2621; www.thegoldenrod.com), a restaurant that has been owned by the Talpey family since 1896, is located on US Route 1A in downtown York Beach next to the public parking lot. Their famous saltwater taffy is made in the front window, but the soda fountain, with its frappes, floats, sundaes, and even banana splits, will take you right back to the early 60s.

From York Beach, Shore Road goes past the Cliff House Resort, the Ogunquit Museum of American Art, and Perkins Cove, one of the most frequently painted landscapes in Maine. The wooden pedestrian drawbridge in Ogunquit (located directly behind the motel) that crosses the harbor is a

Low tide in Wells.

photo op and leads to the Marginal Way, an exceptionally beautiful mile-long pedestrian path along the shore from Oarweed Cove to Ogunquit Beach. Ogunquit (pop. 1,000) is a summer resort town famous for its artists and fantastic three-mile-long beach. It has lodging for 2,500 visitors, but on holiday weekends during the summer 50,000 people show up, which means you'd best have reservations if you plan to stay there.

I highly recommend the Wells Auto Museum (US Route 1 by the shopping plaza in Wells; 207-646-9064; www.wellsautomuseum.com). As with any automobile collection, my favorites are probably not going to be yours. The 1918 Stutz Bearcat is one of the crown jewels of this collection, but the 1954 Bentley is my favorite. Historically important oddities include a 1908 International High Wheeler (International Harvester once made cars and trucks), a Smith Motowheel (it's incorrectly attributed to 1909, a year before the Wall Auto Wheel was invented and five years before the A.O. Smith Company purchased its manufacturing rights), and a 1923 Ford Model T Snowmobile (a conversion kit introduced in 1922).

I should mention Fisherman's Catch (207-646-8780; www. fishermanscatchwells.com) located on Harbor Road just off US Route 1 in Wells, overlooking the salt marsh. Countless restaurants will call themselves a lobster pound, but this is the real deal: generous portions of fresh seafood, perfectly prepared, their fried platters complemented with a light and crispy batter. Lacquered picnic tables, fishing nets and buoys, and tableside paper towel holders complete the requisite decor. If there is a long line out the door, some might be locals waiting for take-out. Unless you just *have* to have a lobster, try their crabcakes or seafood chowder. They are delicious.

Next, you'll be turning onto Route 9 toward Kennebunkport, which means you'll be foregoing the opportunity to go antique shopping in Kennebunk or partying at Bentley's Saloon (US Rte 1; 207-985-8966; www.bentleyssaloon.com), a biker-owned establishment—bar, restaurant, motel, and campground—with live bands, pig roasts, lobster feeds, and an all-you-can-eat breakfast.

The Kennebunks were established as a fishing outpost in 1602 and became famous for shipbuilding during the 19th century. The original town center at Cape Porpoise still harbors a working fleet of fishermen. Kennebunkport received more recent fame as President Bush's Summer White House, although that vacation home had been in his family since 1903. There are numerous large, very exclusive estates here, but you'd be lucky to even catch a glimpse of a few.

Side Trip: Trolley Museum

Devoted enthusiasts of electric railroading have helped the Seashore Trolley Museum (www.trolleymuseum.org) in Kennebunkport to grow from a single open trolley car retired from the Biddeford & Saco line to its present international collection of more than 200 transit vehicles housed in several buildings on 300 acres. When Route 9 makes a right turn in Kennebunkport, turn left onto Maine Street, which will become North Street. Continue straight onto Log Cabin Road until you arrive at the trolley museum. From US Route 1, turn right onto Log Cabin Road and ride south to reach the museum.   ■

North of Biddeford, Old Orchard Beach began as Thomas Rogers's apple orchard in 1657, but it was the arrival of the Grand Trunk Railway in the mid-19th century that transformed it into a summer resort for tourists from Montréal and Boston, which it remains to the present day. This is the archetypal seaside resort, with seven miles of sand, amusement rides, and the third incarnation of its famous pier. There are motorcycle-only parking spaces—as there have been for at least 40 years—pizza, cotton candy, cheap tee shirts, and sunglasses for sale. It's a great place for teenagers and families with young children.

The quickest way to reach Portland is to stay on US Route 1, but I recommend you turn onto Route 207, ride through Scarborough, and make a right to follow Route 77 around Cape Elizabeth. Samuel de Champlain first visited Richmond Island on the southern end of the promontory in 1605. When John Smith presented Charles I with his map of New England, many of the native designations were replaced with English names, but this one, honoring Charles's sister, is one of only four such tributes to have survived history.

Following signs, you should have no difficulty finding Two Lights State Park, perched on the rocky headlands above Casco Bay. "Where is the other lighthouse?" asked the Japanese tourist who'd parked behind me in a NO

Old Orchard Beach is the archetypal seaside resort.

The Casco Bay Bridge connects South Portland to the Back Bay near Commercial Street and the Old Port.

PARKING space. "There's only one," I reply. A few camera clicks later and he was headed back to the highway. His confusion was understandable; there were originally twin lights at the end of the road. The easternmost beacon, the now-automated Cape Elizabeth Light, is an active Coast Guard facility and not open to the public; the western light ceased operation in 1924 and is now a private home. Maine has 63 lighthouses, more than any other state, but only ten of these are easily accessible by motorcycle. However, I know where another one is located . . .

President George Washington commissioned construction of the Portland Head Light in 1787, the first such structure built by the fledgling U.S. Government (c. 1787–91) and, naturally, it's on the National List of Historic Places. It's located on the grounds of Fort Williams Park, the site of a defensive battery created during the late 19th century. These days, it may be as well known as the terminus of the Beach to Beacon 10K, the largest road race in the Pine Tree state, begun more than 15 years ago by Cape Elizabeth native and Olympic gold medal marathoner Joan Benoit Samuelson to bring runners to her favorite training grounds.

Fort Williams Park is off Route 77 on Shore Road; Shore Road will become Cottage Road and a left onto Broadway will put you back on Route 77 where you'll cross the Casco Bay Bridge into Portland. Before you do so, consider that most of the affordable lodging and restaurants, as well as most of the services, are located in South Portland along Broadway between Route 77 and US Route 1.

Portland has so many restaurants and cafés that you will have no trouble finding something that suits your fancy, but if you want the best in seafood, eat where the fishermen do, at Becky's Diner (309 Commercial St.; 207-773-7070; www.beckysdiner.com), one of those places with a long counter and chrome stools with red vinyl cushions. Located at Holyoke Wharf, Becky's breakfasts are fit for a lobsterman who has spent hours tending his traps.

Portland had the good sense to renovate its downtown while retaining a working port. On one side of Commercial Street are restaurants, boutiques, and galleries; on the other are fishing and transportation wharfs and piers. The primary downtown area extends for several blocks up the hill from the docks. FYI: the Portland Regency Hotel is on Milk Street and the Hilton Garden Inn is at 65 Commercial Street, while the Eastland Park Hotel and Holiday Inn will be found on High Street near Congress Street and the

The automated beacon on Cape Elizabeth is an active Coast Guard facility and not open to the public.

*Motorcycles tend to
cluster on the
causeway in Naples
to enjoy the view.*

Portland Museum of Art. Other hotels will be found near the airport or just off Exit 5 of I-295/US Route 1.

The Portland Museum of Art (7 Congress St.; 207-775-6148; www. portlandmuseum.org) features the work of such quintessential American artists as Edward Hopper, Rockwell Kent, Winslow Homer, Andrew Wyeth, John Singer Sargent, and European painters including Renoir, Matisse, Picasso, and Degas. It's a fine art museum that one would associate with a much larger metropolitan area. Winslow Homer's studio was at Cliff Path on Prouts Neck of Cape Elizabeth and the Wyeth family's summer home was in Cushing, so the Pine Tree State is well represented among this pantheon. Another important figure in Maine's history was Henry Wadsworth Longfellow. The family home where the poet lived for the first 35 years of his life was the first brick home constructed in Portland and is now the oldest surviving structure in the city (489 Congress St.; 207-774-1822; www.mainehistory.org/house_overview.shtml).

The Portland Observatory (138 Congress St.; 207-774-5561; www. portlandlandmarks.org/observatory) was built in 1807 and is the last 19th-century signal tower in the country. Located on top of Munjoy Hill, there are 102 steps to the top of the 65-foot-high tower and, as you would suspect, it offers a wonderful view of the harbor. This was the first tourist attraction in Portland, but it also allowed merchants to see when their ships were about to enter port.

There are numerous other points of interest in this big little city. Markers for the Freedom Trail (a.k.a. Underground Railroad) and the John Ford Memorial (at the intersection of Pleasant and Fore Streets) are noteworthy. The latter commemorates a local boy who not only rose to the rank of rear admiral in the U.S. Navy, but also became one of Hollywood's most influential and prolific directors, making 130 films between 1917 and 1965, including *Stagecoach, The Searchers,* and *The Man Who Shot Liberty Valance.* Although his epitaph reads, "I Make Westerns," his six Academy Awards had nothing to do with this genre.

The ride from Portland to Conway could also be ridden in reverse as the first leg of Ride 16. While I recommend taking Route 22 (Congress Street) to reach Route 114, you certainly could do the same using Route 25 (Brighton Avenue). The idea is to take the more scenic western shore of Sebago Lake rather than following US Route 302 on the eastern side. Both arrive at Naples, the crossroads of western Maine.

There are many fine touring roads in the southwestern corner of the state, but on weekends riders tend to fill the long lakeview porches at Rick's Café (207-693-3759; www.rickscafenaples.com) in the old casino building at the intersection of US Route 302 and Route 11. There's ample parking along the causeway directly across the road. As you leave Naples, on the left side of US Route 302, there's also a picnic area with roofed tables and decent views of Long Lake. Naples Custom Motorsports (20 Kansas Rd.; 207-693-4025; www.naplescustommotorsports.com) services all makes and models and they even have a free biker breakfast the last Saturday of every month during riding season.

The remaining thinly-settled miles to Conway should be a pleasant, easy ride.

Riders chill on the wide porches at Nick's Café in the old casino building.

Ride 16   The Mid-Coast

Distance: *375 miles; more if you start exploring the many peninsulas. This route can be ridden in two days, but with stops and exploration it can easily develop into a week-long vacation.*
Highlights: *Rolling hills, gentle valleys, and lakes, with both urban and rural settlements. Lighthouses, windjammers, fishing harbors, Bath Iron Works, Maine Maritime Museum, Owl's Head Transportation Museum, Farnsworth Art Museum, Fort Western, shopping, and much more.*

The state of Maine claims 3,500 miles of coastline and has so many deep harbors that all of the world's navies could simultaneously dock here. Long inlets force US Route 1 inland with state highways branching south to reach the rocky headlands of a succession of peninsulas. You could easily spend a couple of days exploring the fishing harbors and scenic ocean views that lie between Casco and Penobscot Bays.

It's very likely that you'll depart Portland by crossing Back Cove on I-295/US Route 1A. Whether you continue on I-295 or take Exit 9 onto US Route 1 is simply a matter of choice. Route 88 branches from US Route 1 to go through Falmouth Foreside, but all of these roads lead to Yarmouth. Just so you know: Street Cycles in Falmouth is 5 miles north of Portland on

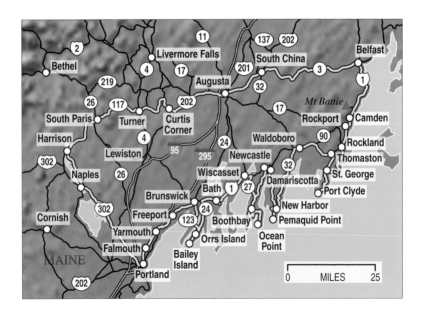

The largest rotating globe in the world, Eartha, is located at DeLorme's headquarters in Yarmouth.

US Route 1 (207-781-4763; www.streetcycles.com), servicing Suzuki, Triumph, and BMW.

Immediately after passing beneath I-295 or from Exit 17, turn right into the parking lot for DeLorme's world headquarters. The company's three-story glass atrium provides the setting for Eartha, the world's largest rotating and revolving globe, a humbling compilation of data and technology designed to depict Earth as it is seen from space, complete with 3-D landforms. Whether you are a fan of printed maps or GPS gear, this stop offers more cartography for sale than any other shop I know. The Maine State Visitor Information Center, with restrooms and free maps, is across the street.

There are no locks on the doors of L. L. Bean since they are open 24-7-365, and this major outdoor retailer in downtown Freeport receives more than 3.5 million visitors each year! Add to this the traffic generated by numerous other opportunistic factory outlets, and then imagine a cascade of pedestrians with tunnel vision spilling off the sidewalks to reach the welcoming entrance doors of retail heaven on the opposite side of the street. And I won't even mention the turning traffic or parking space seekers. If you wish to experience the mayhem firsthand, just remain on Route 1 through Freeport. However, I usually try to avoid most of the activity by bearing right onto South Freeport Road just one and a half miles east of DeLorme headquarters. Everyone really should make the pilgrimage to Bean's at some point, however, and if this is your chance, try turning left from South

FROM PORTLAND, MAINE

0	In Portland, from US Rte 1A (Franklin Arterial), take Exit 7 onto Rte I-295 north
11.3	Right at Exit 17
11.5	Right onto US Rte 1
12.7	Right onto South Freeport Rd.
16.1	Right onto Porters Landing Rd. (becomes Lower Mast Landing Rd.)
17.3	Right onto Bow St. to Flying Point Rd.
18.0	Bear left onto Pleasant Hill Rd.
24.1	Bear left onto Maine St. into downtown Brunswick
25.3	Right onto Rte 24 (Bath Rd.)
25.5	Right onto Rte 123 (Harpswell Rd.)
32.0	Left onto Mountain Rd.; watch for signs to Rte 24 (Orrs Island)
34.5	Right (south) onto Rte 24
39.3	Arrive Bailey Island; return on Rte 24 (north)
52.5	Right ramp onto US Rte 1 (north) in Brunswick
57.6	Right exit US Rte 1
57.7	In Bath, right onto Rte 209 (High St.)
58.6	Left onto Rose St. (although almost any cross street is okay)
58.8	Left onto Washington St. (Maine Maritime Museum and Bath Iron Works)
59.8	Right onto Commercial St.
59.9	Straight on ramp for US Rte 1 and Carlton Bridge
73.6	Right (south) onto Rte 27
83.1	In Boothbay, bear right onto Corey Ln. (by the monument)
83.4	Bear left onto Lakeside Dr.
85.5	Left onto Rte 27 (Western Ave.) into Boothbay Harbor
87.1	Arrive downtown Boothbay Harbor
87.7	Right at the traffic light onto Rte 96 (Ocean Point Rd.)
92.9	Straight on Rte 96 (becomes Crooker Rd. in Ocean Point Rd.)
95.7	Left onto Rte 96, return to Rte 27
100.8	Right (north) onto Rte 27
105.0	Right onto River Rd.

(continued)

Freeport Road onto South Street (instead of right on Porters Landing Road) then approach via Bow Street; it'll be easier than using US Route 1. To reach downtown Brunswick, you must make a right turn onto Porters Landing Road (which becomes Lower Mast Landing), a right onto Bow Street, then bear left onto Pleasant Hill Road, and make another left onto Maine Street.

The 13th child of an outspoken religious leader, Harriet Beecher Stowe

CONTINUING FROM NEWCASTLE, MAINE

115.0 Bear right onto Bus. Rte 1 in Newcastle; cross the Damariscotta River

115.6 In Damariscotta, bear right onto Rte 129/Rte 130

118.5 Straight to continue on Rte 130

127.0 In New Harbor, right onto Huddle Rd.

128.2 [Colonial Pemaquid State Historic Site]

128.3 [Pemaquid Beach]

129.2 Right (south) onto Rte 30

132.2 Arrive Pemaquid Point Light; return on Rte 30 (north)

135.3 Right onto Rte 32 in New Harbor

135.9 [Shaw's Fish & Lobster Wharf]

154.9 Right onto US Rte 1

166.3 [Maine State Prison Showroom in Thomaston]

167.4 Right onto Rte 131 (High St.) by General Knox Museum

181.7 Arrive Port Clyde; return via Rte 131

190.6 In the village of St. George, right onto Rte 73

198.6 [Museum St. and the Owl's Head Transportation Museum]

199.4 [N. Shore Dr. leading to Owl's Head Light (7-mi. round trip)]

201.3 Straight onto US Rte 1 into Rockland (turn right for Lighthouse Museum)

207.4 In Rockport, right onto West St. at the junction of Rte 90

207.7 Left onto Pascal Ave.

207.8 [Harbor View Dr. to the harbor is on the right]

208.0 Right onto Central St.

208.2 Bear right onto Russell Ave. to Chestnut St.

210.1 Right onto Frye St. and down the hill

210.2 Left onto Bay View St.

210.2 Right between the buildings leads to the harbor in Camden

210.3 In Camden, right onto US Rte 1 (Main St.)

212.0 [Mt. Battie Rd. is on the left]

227.1 Right onto Northport Ave. into Belfast

228.5 Arrive at Main St. in downtown Belfast

(continued)

had a vision for the novel *Uncle Tom's Cabin* while attending the First Parish Church in Brunswick. Published in weekly installments over the better part of a year, the book's emotional portrayal of the country's "peculiar institution" galvanized abolitionists and heightened animosity toward the South. Stowe's husband, a theology professor at Bowdoin College, would often invite favored students to their home to discuss chapters prior to publication,

The open checkerwork arrangement of the granite of the Cribstone Bridge, held in place by gravity alone, is strong enough to withstand violent tides and storms.

among them Joshua Chamberlain, the future general whose gallant defense of the Union flank at Little Round Top would bring the 20th Maine Volunteer Infantry Regiment home as the heroes of the decisive Battle of Gettysburg.

East of Brunswick, the coastline becomes a series of long, narrow, jagged peninsulas with hundreds of islands separated by deep inlets and a multitude of hidden bays. While this is a haven for fishermen and lobsters, the irregular topography forces US Route 1 inland. State highways and town roads run south from Route 1 to the rocky headlands of these peninsulas and back, and most are worth exploring if you have an extended amount of time.

From Bowdoin College, Route 123 runs down Harpswell Neck and there are so many named coves, bays, and sounds that it would be an exercise to list them. The town of Harpswell alone has 216 miles of coastline, more than any other town in the United States, yet you'll rarely get the sense that you're riding down a narrow finger of land. The signs are very clear for the turn to Orrs Island and Route 24. From this point, the road undulates and you'll have views of the sea, but the narrow channels between islands and peninsulas make the ocean look more like a river. You'll cross the famous Cribstone Bridge, a 1,150-foot span whose construction is unique in the world. Built in 1927 and refurbished in 2010, the open checkerboard arrangement of the granite is held in place by gravity alone and yet is strong enough to endure relentless tides and violent storms.

Beyond Orrs Island is Bailey Island, a charming settlement at Land's End. The Bailey Island Motel (207-833-2886; www.baileyislandmotel. com), while it could use a bit of updating, has a wonderful location at the end of the bridge. The Bailey Island General Store will have all that's needed, and its small kitchen delivers a great breakfast and a small lunch menu at extremely reasonable prices. On my last visit, I purchased one of BIGS's BLTs and a cold Lobster Ale from their ample selection and rode to the island's principle "tourist" attraction, the Giant Staircase, a natural series of wave-eroded shelves. I kicked back, poured a beer the color of cooked crustaceans, and watched the world turn to golden hues in the setting sun.

On the next leg of the trip, you'll leap over the next peninsula to reach Bath, whose shipyards on the Kennebec River have been plying their trade since 1762. During World War II, the Bath Iron Works built more destroyers than Japan. And the newest class of Navy destroyers, the DDG 1000 Zumwalt, is currently being fabricated here. I wanted a photo of the largest construction crane on the East Coast, but signs on the chain-link fence surrounding BIW state NO PHOTOGRAPHY—SECURITY TAKE NOTICE and NO ENTRY—DEFENSE CONTRACTOR. This seemed a little ridiculous, since everything was readily visible from the bridge or the other side of the river, and public tours of the facility are conducted on almost a daily basis.

Farther down Washington Street is the Maine Maritime Museum that includes the Percy & Small Shipyard and Apprenticeshop (243 Washington St.; 207-

CONTINUING FROM BELFAST, MAINE

228.5	From High St. in Belfast, left (west) onto Main St. to Rte 3
260.5	Straight; Rte 3 merges with US Rte 202 in South China
272.1	Left onto US Rte 202/US Rte 201
272.7	First right on roundabout onto Corey St. and cross the bridge into Augusta
273.1	Left onto Rte 11/Rte 27
273.6	At roundabout, first right onto US Rte 202/Rte 100
289.5	Right onto Bog Rd. (if you miss it, take Rte 106)
291.2	At Curtis Corner, left and cross the RR tracks onto Rte 106
294.6	In Leeds, left onto Church Hill Rd.
302.5	At Turner Center, bear left onto Rte 117 (Turner Center Rd.)
321.3	In South Paris, continue on Rte 117
335.3	In Harrison, left (south) onto Rte 35
346.4	In Naples, left onto Rte 35/US Rte 302
362.8	Continue on Rte 302 as US Rte 202 intersects
374.9	In Portland, arrive at the end of US Rte 302 at Exit 6 of I-295 ■

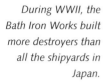

During WWII, the Bath Iron Works built more destroyers than all the shipyards in Japan.

443-1316; www.mainemaritimemuseum.org), the last surviving intact shipyard in the country to have built large wooden sailing vessels, including seven of the eleven six-mast schooners constructed in the United States. Two pieces of steel sculpture depict the prow and stern of the last of these, the *Wyoming*, at its actual size, an astonishing 450-feet long. Unlike clippers, which were narrower and used only for time sensitive or extremely valuable goods, schooners were built for cargo capacity. Alas, even when internally braced with steel, such large wooden vessels were prone to deform in rough seas, and that was the fate of the *Wyoming*, lost off the coast of Nantucket after fifteen years of service.

If you want to explore more of the terrestrial fingers near Bath, you can start with the Town of Phippsburg and move on to Popham Beach State Park. Next would be Georgetown Island, a short hop south of Arrowsic Island, reached by taking Route 127. By taking Route 144 you can explore Westport, another island. From Bath to Wiscasset is less than 12 miles, but to cover these three peninsulas would require at least 100 miles of riding and no fewer than four hours.

Montsweag Roadhouse (207-443-6563; www.montsweagroadhouse. com), located between Woolwich and Wiscasset on US Route 1, is a biker-owned, family-friendly restaurant during the day and a popular pub with live music in the evenings. To follow the mapped route, ride through Wiscasset, cross the Sheepscot River, pick up Route 27, and ride south to Boothbay Harbor. If you stop at the information center in Boothbay, you can inquire about the most scenic roads and pick up some maps and local wisdom from the resident experts. Bear right at the monument and you'll end up on Lakeside Drive, then head north on Route 27 along the beautiful harbor for which the village is named.

Entering Boothbay Harbor, I was impressed by the quality of the docking, the abundance of lodging and dining options, and its two camping areas, which have tent sites. Downtown has a number of interesting small boutiques, shops, and galleries; excursions on schooners, lobster boats, and sightseeing motor launches are also readily available. You will not want for things to do, but when the road finally beckons, turn onto Route 96 to East Boothbay and the next peninsula.

Route 96 goes to Ocean Point on Linekin Neck and it is *scenic.* Taking Shore Road, you'll slowly cruise along a narrow, winding strip of pavement that will be unmarred by even a single painted line. There may be pedestrians, bicyclists, and people who simply have stopped their cars and are sitting on folding chairs in the middle of the road, admiring the view. Between the twisty road, the fellow gawkers, and the arresting seascape, you may never get out of second gear.

Back on Route 27 and heading north, keep your eyes peeled for River Road. Although named for the Damariscotta River, the route actually runs along the ridge and not the shore, so you'll end up riding through forests and past small farms and rural homes without a glimpse of water. However, it is a thoroughly enjoyable road filled with elevation changes and corners. Since most of the road is shaded, this is an especially sweet ride on an otherwise sultry day.

The last intact example of what were numerous shipyards along the shoreline during the Age of Sail, the Maine Maritime Museum preserves the art of building wooden schooners.

Fort William Henry is the reconstruction of a series of forts that guarded the oldest English settlement in America.

Once you're back on US Route 1 in Damariscotta, make a right turn and head south on Route 129, following the eastern side of the Damariscotta River. About 3 miles south of Damariscotta, bear left onto Route 130.

People come to the coast of Maine for different reasons and they often return to the same place year after year. Pemaquid was where I would come to scuba dive, so many of my favorite places I simply can't show you. One that I can is Fort William Henry, the oldest permanent English settlement in America.

It was fishermen from Pemaquid who sent food to Plimoth Plantation in 1602, allowing that famous Massachusetts settlement to survive its second winter. In 1625, a year-round trading post was established and by 1665, the settlement had 30 houses. Pemaquid, like many other early settlements in Maine, was attacked and burned to the ground several times despite having successive forts built on the site. The last one was named Fort Frederick (c. 1729–30) but it was dismantled in 1775 to prevent the British from using it as a base. In 1908 the fort was reconstructed and is now referred to as Fort William Henry.

Pemaquid Light was built in 1835 and still uses the fourth-order Fresnel lens installed in 1856. The keeper's house was added in 1857 and now contains a small museum and a one-bedroom apartment that can be rented on a weekly basis. If you ever wanted to live the fantasy of being a lighthouse keeper, this would be your chance, but don't expect solitude: it's a busy place. Just beyond the keeper's house there is a bronze plaque mounted on a boulder that commemorates John Cogswell and his family's first setting foot in America on August 14, 1635—and the same for Ralph Blaisdell and his family, although they landed the following day after the *Angel Gabriel* was shipwrecked in the Great Colonial Hurricane. I love finding these bits of history.

The best fish chowder I've ever eaten was at Shaw's Fish & Lobster Wharf Restaurant (207-677-2200) in New Harbor. When I was there years ago, it was a beat-up fisherman's eatery. Today it's a bit more upscale, but it's still the place to come if you want crab cakes, chowder, a lobster roll, or a full-on crustacean gorge.

Behind the brick facade and picture windows of the Maine State Prison Showroom in Thomaston (392 Main St./Rte 1; 207-354-9237) lies a unique retail store. The items offered for sale are made by the inmates participating in the Prison Industries Program. Some items are merely souvenir trinkets, but others are works of art. The best wooden model ships I've seen outside of museums can be purchased at very reasonable prices, but the gem of my last visit was a life-sized sculpture of a biker on a chopper with a mermaid on the pillion.

The stark white mansion on the hill looks a bit out of place. It turns out to be the re-creation (c. 1929) of the house General Knox built on this site. Henry Knox was a Boston bookseller with a passion for military history who became Chief of Artillery during the Revolution and the first U.S. Secretary of War in President Washington's cabinet. He retired in 1795, moved to Thomaston, built his mansion, and died after choking on a chicken bone. General Knox's home marks your turn onto Route 131 for a run down the St. George Peninsula.

The Maine State Prison Showroom in Thomaston retails the work of inmates who are participating in the Prison Industries Program.

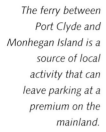

The ferry between Port Clyde and Monhegan Island is a source of local activity that can leave parking at a premium on the mainland.

Port Clyde, at the end of Route 131, is a working harbor, but the ferry to Monhegan Island makes this small village a tourist destination where parking is at a premium. The ferry carries mail, supplies, and passengers, but no vehicles—hence the source of the problem. I like the honest chaos the ferry brings to this small village, but I advise you to head to the Marshall Point Light before the small crowd disembarks (follow the signs). This tiny lighthouse (c. 1857) is only 31 feet high and has a long wooden walkway leading to it. The keeper's house (c. 1895) and lamp house (c. 1905) are part of this site and the grounds are open to the public. Amid the profusion of wild roses, a black marble memorial has been erected to the local fishermen who have been lost at sea.

Moving north on Route 73, Owl's Head Transportation Museum (207-594-4418; www.owlshead.org) is located at the end of Museum Street on the western edge of the airport. This is one of my favorite transportation museums, especially during Vintage Motorcycle Days over Labor Day weekend, when thousands of motorcyclists arrive on machines old and new. This museum has so many aircraft in its collection they have their own airstrip, but there are incredible transportation gems of all kinds in the hangers, including an original bi-wing Ornithopter—a heavier-than-air vehicle that attempted flight by means of flapping wings—made by James W. Clark during the first decade of the 20th century. Lawrence Ricker's famous 1901 electric-powered torpedo race car and an extensive collection of pre-WWI automobiles are exhibited in the hangar along with unusual pieces, like a 1935 Stout Scarab and a 1938 Eliot Cricket. The 1913 Scripps-Booth Bi-Autogo is one of my favorites in the motorcycle collection, powered by a V-8 and stabilized by wheeled outriggers. Some of the 19th-century bicycles are also amusing; for instance, the 1968 Velocipede Boneshaker was named

The Owl's Head Light still uses the fourth-order Fresnel lens installed in 1852, although it's now illuminated by electricity instead of whale oil.

more for the condition of the roads than its lack of suspension. Another favorite is the 90-ton, 600 hp Harris-Corliss steam engine of 1895, but other engines in the engineering room are just as fascinating.

The Owl's Head Light is another popular destination on this peninsula. Built in 1852, the fourth-order Fresnel lens that was installed in 1856 is still in use, although it's now illuminated by electricity instead of whale oil. The grounds are open to the public, but the lighthouse tower, which is still an active navigational beacon, is open only three days a week.

One of the best places to learn about the history and operation of lighthouses is the Maine Lighthouse Museum (1 Park Dr.; 207-594-3301; www. MaineLighthouseMuseum.org) in Rockland. Their collection of lighthouse lenses is impressive, especially considering how many of these 19th-century Fresnel lenses are still in use.

Sheltered by a mile-long breakwater, Rockland has one of the busiest pleasure craft moorings on the mid-coast.

The Farnsworth Art Museum (16 Museum St.; 207-596-6457; www. farnsworthmuseum.org) in downtown Rockland specializes in Maine-related American fine arts. Works by Winslow Homer, George Bellows, Andrew Wyeth, and more contemporary artists and photographers grace their collection. The Wyeth Center is part of the museum, but is located in an old church building on Union Street. This is where the works of three generations of Wyeths—N.C., Andrew, and James—are exhibited. It is interesting to see how each son was influenced by his father, yet developed his own style.

Moving up the coast, Rockport Harbor is one of the best places I know to view wooden schooners, and I rarely pass this way without going down to the public wharves to see what's afloat. On my last visit, I watched the 86-foot windjammer *Appledore II* leave the harbor under sail.

The area from Thomaston to Rockport became known as the Lime Capitol of the World. Originally laid down as deposits of seashells and the like, limestone, after being burned to remove carbon dioxide, becomes lime, which was used for plaster, mortar, and fertilizer. By 1828, demand was so high that Rockport was producing a million casks of lime a year, a process that needed a prodigious amount of cordwood to feed the kiln fires. You can spot some of the tailings and a few of the surviving kilns along the waterfront, as well as a Vulcan steam locomotive similar to those that hauled limestone from the quarries to the site.

Andre the harbor seal was a Rockport legend in his own time, wintering at the Boston Aquarium during the 1970s and early 80s. Released every spring in Boston, he would swim to Rockport Harbor for the summer where he would join his trainer and entertain visitors and locals alike. The granite statue of Andre the Seal was unveiled in Rockport in 1978, eight years before his death.

From downtown Rockport at the head of the harbor, head to Camden via Union Street or Russell Avenue. Camden harbor has paved motorcycle-only parking, public restrooms, a few nice restaurants, and an information center where schedules are posted for windjammer and motor-launch tours. To find it, turn right off US Route 1 (Main Street) and make an immediate left—going downhill between two brick buildings—to the harbor. Megunticook Falls can be seen from this vantage point, but the main attractions will be the wooden schooners you'll find moored here.

The summit of Mount Battie is only 790 feet above sea level, but it still provides an unparalleled view of Camden and the coast. To make it even easier, you'll find coin-operated binoculars by the parking area. This is part of the Camden Hills State Park and is the best place to camp in this area ($25 non-resident; 207-236-3109) and one of the few affordable spots to lay your head during peak tourist season.

The town of Belfast is a place that has been passed by—and that's unfortunate. Once the armpit of the mid-Maine coast with a chicken processing plant, it is now transforming itself into a town of nice B&B inns and special events. On my last visit there I met up with Jim LeClair—who with his wife, Patti, own and operate the Maine Coast Welcome Center—and we

Once part of a major industry, the remains of the kilns which helped to transform limestone into lime are preserved along Rockport's harbor.

The best place to view Megunticook Falls is from the Camden Harbor parking area.

headed down to the local sports bar—beer, chili, and baked potato skins type of fare—and had a very good time. I'm not sure whether being by-passed by US Route 1 has done this town a favor or not, but until it gets "discovered" it's likely to remain a pleasant and affordable stop along the busy coast.

The next leg of the journey will return to central Maine via Route 3 to US Route 202 through the capitol city of Augusta. Route 3 will merge with US Route 202/Route 9 in South China. You'll pass North Country Harley-Davidson/Honda (207-622-7994; www.northcountryhd.com) and Farrin

Fort Western in Augusta was built in 1754.

Power Sports (207-622-6006; www.eastcoastmotorcyclestore.com) on US Route 202/Route 9/Route 3 east of Augusta. When the routes divide, stay on US Route 202/Route 9.

I enjoy riding through Augusta just to check out what is new. At the first roundabout you can take the first right to go downtown or the second right to stay on US Route 202/US Route 201 to avoid it. Either way you're going to cross the Kennebec River.

Old Fort Western (207-626-2385; www.oldfortwestern.org) will be on Cony Street just before the bridge—you certainly can't miss the palisade and blockhouse as you come down the hill. Built in 1754, this is the oldest wooden fort in the state, but soldiers were stationed here only until 1767. James Howard purchased the fort, established the post store, and converted the barracks into his home. The house and the store are furnished and stocked according to probate records of 1799.

Water Street through downtown Augusta is one-way. You'll have to take the second left onto Commercial Street—which runs along the back of the downtown commercial buildings—and loop around the block to ride up Water Street in order to check out the store fronts. The capitol city of Maine is especially easy to get in and out of, so don't hesitate to explore.

Paul Blouin Performance (Suzuki, Triumph, Victory, Kymco; 207-626-3500; www.paulblouinsuzuki.com) is on Route 202 just beyond Augusta. Your next destination will be South Paris, and from here your route will depend upon whether you wish to enter New Hampshire via US Route 2 or US Route 302, or follow US Route 302 east back to Portland where this trip began. That last segment of this ride is frequently used to travel between Conway, New Hampshire, and Portland, Maine.

Ride 17   Deer Isle, Blue Hills, and Bangor

Distance: *178 miles; five hours without stops*
Highlights: *Rolling forested hills, coastal roads, city streets. The Penobscot Narrows Bridge and Observatory, Fort Knox, the village of Stonington, the Cole Land Transportation Museum, and Bay Brew Ice Cream.*

My last experience in this particular neck of the woods was memorable for all the reasons one travels on two wheels, one of those times when the serendipities of an inconvenience begin a new story. This one began at the Maine

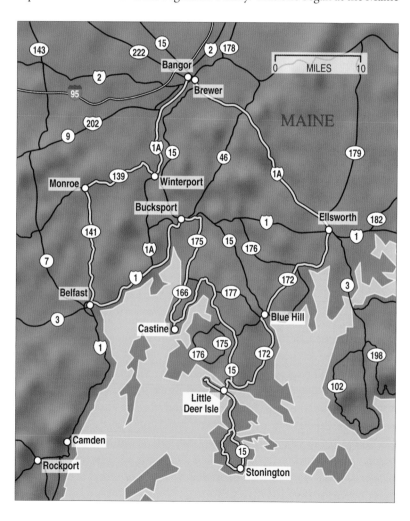

Coast Welcome Center (www.maine-coast-welcome-center.com), where owners Jim and Patti LeClair offered me some shelter from the rain so I could repair my front sprocket. And, as road luck would have it, there was an extensively stocked hardware store just across the highway. Jim's advice helped me fine-tune the mid-coast portion of the itinerary. And, of course, the rain stopped just as I was finished making my repairs.

The technological elegance of the Penobscot Narrows Bridge will be all the more striking for its sudden appearance among the natural beauties of the coastline. Its cradle-stay system was originally employed in 2007 as an expedient and economical way to replace the suspended Waldo-Hancock Bridge, which had deteriorated badly. The unique features of its engineering seem to offer advantages over more traditional methods of design. Instead of being bundled, the long steel cables within the stays are held in a cradle that allows them to be inspected and replaced individually, and they have begun to experiment with and monitor carbon composite cables. The two granite pylons that support the 2,120-foot span deliberately resemble the familiar grey obelisk of the Washington Monument, granite for which was quarried on nearby Mount Waldo.

The innovative cradle-stay system of the Penobscot Narrows Bridge was originally employed in 2007 as an expedient and economical way to replace the suspended Waldo-Hancock Bridge, which had deteriorated badly.

FROM BELFAST, MAINE

0	From the Maine Coast Welcome Center east of Belfast, east on US Rte 1
14.2	Follow US Rte 1 over the Penobscott Narrows Bridge
15.7	Continue through Bucksport on US Rte 1
17.4	Right onto Rte 175 (Castine Rd.)
25.5	At the intersection of Rte 175 and Rte 166, continue straight to stay on Rte 166
27.3	Bear right onto Rte 166A
31.1	Right onto Rte 166 into Castine
32.6	Arrive Castine; return north on Rte 199
40.1	Straight at the junction with Rte 175 on Rte 199/Rte 175
46.9	Straight onto Rte 176
49.3	Straight onto Rte 15
52.2	Straight as Rte 175 merges with Rte 15
55.1	Right to continue on Rte 15
57.2	Bear left on Rte 15 on Little Deer Isle Rd.
58.3	[Beach on Deer Isle]
67.9	In Stonington, right onto Main St.
68.2	Right onto School St.
68.5	Bear left onto Sunset Ave. to Burnt Cove Rd. to Sunset Rd.

(continued)

At the top of one of the towers sits a 13 x 25 foot observation room with a 360-degree view that rolls to a horizon that may be a hundred miles away on a clear, dry day. An extremely fast elevator will whisk you to the top, where stairs ascend two levels above the deck to an even loftier vantage point. To maximize the experiences of their visitors, observatory tickets are time-stamped, but you can explore Fort Knox while you wait for your turn.

Fort Knox (c. 1844–69) was strategically constructed at the narrows to prevent the British from invading the Penobscot River Valley for its valuable timber resources—something it had done during both the American Revolution and the War of 1812. Ironically, this was the first fort in Maine that wasn't constructed of wood, and never having seen a battle, these granite fortifications are extremely well preserved. Route 175 follows the east bank of the Penobscot River, then turns inland toward the hamlet of Penobscot on your way southward toward the Blue Hill Peninsula.

Cross the suspension bridge over the Eggemoggin Reach onto Little Deer Isle and ride across the winding causeway to Deer Isle, which was only connected to the mainland in 1939. Perhaps you've already seen a bit of Deer Isle without recognizing it. The granite quarries on this island supplied the stone for the Boston Museum of Fine Arts, the Smithsonian Institution, the U.S. Naval Academy, the Manhattan Bridge, and President John F. Kennedy's tomb. My first stop was at a sand beach alongside the road, to wonder if John Steinbeck had stopped in a similar fashion to take in the scene on his way to Dunham's Point to launch the odyssey that was to be

Travels with Charley. You will have to determine for yourself the meaning of his statement, "One doesn't have to be sensitive to feel the strangeness of Deer Isle." Or if you prefer your oddities delivered as a more amusing catalog of characters, pick up Linda Greenlaw's *Lobster Chronicles,* set a mailboat hop away on Isle au Haut, one of the many less-accessible terrestrial oases that spangle the waters off the northern coast of Maine.

If you have the time, deploy a sidestand at Nervous Nellie's Jams & Jellies (589 Sunshine Rd.; 207-367-2777; www.nervousenellies. net), where during the season they produce more than 300 homemade jars of fruity spreads each and every weekday from their tiny cottage kitchen, 90 percent of which is sold on Deer Isle. Peter Beerit's whimsical sculptures of wood and dump-found metal share the space and provide a fun backdrop for creative people who have chosen to do business without taking themselves too seriously.

CONTINUING FROM STONINGTON, MAINE

75.2	Left onto Rte 15 and return to Little Deer Isle
80.3	On Little Deer Isle, bear left onto Eggemoggin Rd.
83.0	Bear left onto Lighthouse Ln.
83.4	Arrive at viewpoint for the Pumpkin Island Light; return to Rte 15, turn left and cross the bridge
88.2	Straight onto Rte 175 (Reach Rd.)
91.7	Left onto Rte 172
100.2	Right onto Rte 172/Rte 175/Rte 15 into Blue Hill
100.9	Straight, stay on Rte 172 (ignore the others)
114.3	In Ellsworth, straight onto US Rte 1/Rte 3
114.5	Left onto US Rte 1A (State St.) to Bangor Rd.
140.4	Follow signs for US Rte 1A in Brewer
141.2	In Bangor, left onto Bus. Rte 1A/US Rte 202 (Main St.)
141.9	Straight, continue on US Rte 1A (south)
154.2	Right onto Rte 139/Rte 69
156.5	Left to stay on Rte 139
164.7	In Monroe, left onto Rte 141
177.9	Arrive at US Rte 1/Rte 3 by the bridge in Belfast ∎

Route 15 ends at the wharf in Stonington, a quintessential Maine fishing village and tourist destination, with lobster boats and fishing gear competing with pleasure craft for harbor space. Aside from the appealing atmosphere of the town itself, Stonington has an opera house, summer boutiques displaying work by artisans, and a couple of hotels along the narrow shore road that doubles as the transportation route for the daily catch and the local tourist promenade. But none of it is glitzy, and this I like.

Returning to the bridge, continue straight to explore a bit of Little Deer Isle. The end of the road will bring you to a public boat launch with a view of Pumpkin Island Light (c. 1854). Complete with the keeper's house, boat-

Sand Beach on Deer Isle.

house, and oil house, this privately owned property is not accessible to the public even if they arrive by boat.

Blue Hill Peninsula is touted as being something very special—and while it certainly is nice, travel experience will teach you that the places that are most earnestly aware of promoting their finest qualities rarely have a corner on any particular experience. What you can enjoy in abundance, however, is the leisurely peace and quiet of blueberry covered slopes, charming coves and

While you wait your turn for the the observation room at the top of the bridge tower, you can explore Fort Knox, whose stone fortifications are in great shape.

Side Trip: Castine

Although our main route for this trip doesn't go to Castine, a visit to this isolated village is well worth a detour. Before you leave the east bank of the Penobscot River, Route 175 intersects Route 166. To reach Castine, take Route 166 south to its northern junction with Route 166A, then Route 166A to its southern junction with Route 166. From there, ride south to Castine.

Established seven years before Massachusetts's Plimoth Colony, Castine is arguably one of the oldest permanent settlements in New England, where its strategic importance as an entry point to the fur- and timber-rich interior along the Penobscot River made it an ongoing target for invasion and occupation by the French, Dutch, and British. It had begun to decline after the Civil War, when steamships and railroads began to impinge on harbor transport, but was revived in the late 1800s by an influx of well-off summer "rusticators," urban guests seeking recreation in the mild seaside climes. No doubt that some of the romanticized accounts of the past from such literary figures as Harriet Beecher Stowe and Henry Wadsworth Longfellow were partly kindled by the local atmosphere. More recently, the village has been enhanced by the growth of the Maine Maritime Academy, a four-year college producing engineers and officers for the merchant marine. When you are ready to resume your main trip itinerary, head north on Route 199 to the junction of Route 175 and proceed east from there.   ■

inland marshes, and rollercoaster backroads that wind inexplicably back on themselves or end with astonishing suddenness at a vista of crashing waves.

In contrast, Ellsworth will be a piece of the modern world, a place where you can straighten out a bank card problem, find an essential piece of gear, purchase replacement batteries, and get a broadband Internet connection. It's also the beginning of Rides 18 and 19. Ellsworth to Bangor will be a straight shot along Route 1A and it's a busy road. If your intention is to follow this loop, it'd be best to stay on US Route 1A. If you plan to continue on to Ride 20 then Business Route 1A would be a better choice.

Bangor's location at the mouth of the Penobscot River ensured its place in the lumbering history of the Pine Tree State, where timber felled inland could be shipped to Boston, New York, the Caribbean, or even to California via Cape Horn, as demand outstripped production in the early days of the

A lobster house on the edge of Penobscot Bay in Stonington.

Gold Rush. Bangor logging barons flaunted their wealth with elaborate mansions in the Broadway section of town. Ironically, the city is also known for its fine canopy of shade trees. By the 20th century, the pulp and paper mills that would begin to dominate the Maine woods would rely more on railroad than river transport, but their ongoing presence would ensure that the north country would remain unsettled to this day.

Although Bangor is the crossroads of eastern Maine, the downtown area will be practically deserted after people leave their offices. The social center seems to be the malls on the west side of the city. Some have attributed this to a misguided Urban Renewal Project in the 60s which destroyed local landmarks like the old town hall and train station, shifting focus from the city center to big-box retail on the periphery. With the re-development of its waterfront, however, Bangor's cultural life has been slowly returning to its historic roots downtown.

One place of special interest is the Cole Museum (405 Perry Rd.; 207-990-3600; www.colemuseum.org), located on the south side of the intersection of I-395 and I-95. To reach it from US Route 1A/Route 9 turn left onto the ramp for I-395 west. I-395 ends after passing beneath I-95 and, at the traffic light, turn left onto Route 100 (Odin Road), then the next left onto Perry Road. After crossing beneath I-95 it will be on the left. The museum focuses on Maine-related transportation, and the warehouse-style exhibition space is jammed with vehicles that represent the full range of that spectrum, from bicycles and baby carriages to a rare GM diesel-electric locomotive, and even the entire Enfield railroad depot. There are old Harley and Indian motorcycles, and interesting cars of various vintages. But perhaps most unique to the Cole is its collection of snow-removal equipment (the largest in the country) which includes some rare specimens like the Linn with its wooden cabin and tractor treads. The 1964 GMC tank van, a special custom made for Cole Transport, sported a 3,300-gallon fuel tank behind the tractor cab, allowing the driver to deliver heating fuel to the northern reaches of the state and fill the empty trailer behind with potatoes, paper, or any other market goods for the return trip. Ingenious. You'll find a tank, helicopter, and other military vehicles, too. I've always been fascinated by half-tracks; the museum has one made by White, still fitted with a 50-caliber machine gun.

US Route 1A continues south from Bangor to US Route 1, but your route will follow the more interesting Route 139, which happens to begin across from the gas station and by the Penobscot Bay Brewery in Winterport (279 S. Main St. at the junction of Rte 139; 207-223-4500; www.winterportwinery.com), where they brew up Old Factory Whistle Scottish Ale, Whig Street Blonde, and Half Moon Stout—good beers one and all. However, their microbrewery twist is their Bay Brew handmade ice creams, like Half Moon Stout with a swirl of chocolate. Can you be arrested for operating under the influence of too much ice cream?

Route 139 goes west, passing by the Winterport Dragway (www.winterportdragway.com) to the small village of Monroe. From there Route 141 goes directly south to Belfast. Both offer such a pleasant ride you'll probably never use US Route 1A again.

The scenic Park Loop Road on Mount Desert Island is best ridden early in the morning, for both the quality of the light and the lack of traffic.

Ride 18   Mount Desert Island

Distance: *107 miles that can be ridden in 3.5 to 4 hours; realistically, plan for all day*

Highlights: *Stunning coastal roads, forests and villages. Bar Harbor, Acadia National Park, Park Loop Road, Cadillac Mountain, Seal Cove Auto Museum, Bass Harbor Light, and fantastic scenery throughout.*

Mount Desert Island isn't exactly unexplored territory. Indian tribes lived there 6,000 years ago and English fishermen were based on nearby Pemaquid Point by 1602, but it was a slight mishap with a rocky shoal and subsequent repairs in a sheltered cove that put this island on the map. In his journal entry of September 5, 1604, Samuel de Champlain referred to this place as "Isle des Monts Desert" and the name stuck.

Mount Desert Island is the sixth-largest island in the contiguous United States and the third largest on the East Coast, but the short bridge and causeway from the mainland—just beyond the airport—goes by almost unnoticed, as if you were merely crossing a small river. The town of Bar Harbor and Acadia National Park have become synonymous with Mount Desert Island.

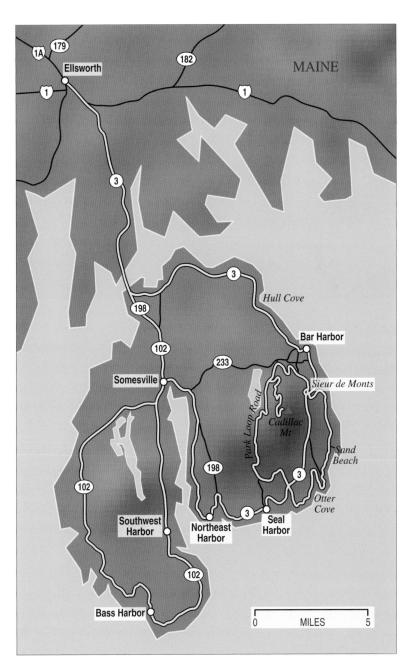

There's seemingly no shortage of places to stay between Ellsworth and Bar Harbor, but the shopping centers and service stores are located along the first couple miles of this ride. There are more than 70 restaurants in Bar

The town of Bar Harbor has become nearly synonymous with Mount Desert Island and Acadia National Park.

Harbor, but you can easily put together an elaborate picnic lunch by shopping at the supermarket on Cottage Street, then walking down to Agamont Park to check out the ships. The four-mast schooner *Margaret Todd* is usually moored there and you can purchase tickets for a short tour. You might even discover a mega-yacht or a cruise ship docked among the lobster boats. There are so many lodging places that choosing one is often determined more by which ones have vacancies. Try the Eagle's Lodge Motel (278 High St.; 207-667-3311; www.eagleslodge.com) in Ellsworth or the Belle Isle Motel (910 Rte 3; 800-782-9235; www.belleislemotel.net). I recommend the Castlemaine Inn (39 Holland Ave.; 207-288-4563; www. castlemaineinn.com), a biker-friendly B&B that's within easy walking distance of everything in downtown Bar Harbor. There are a few campgrounds, with Bar Harbor KOA (136 County Rd.; 207-288-3520; www. barharborkoa.net) having its own beach, a shuttle into town, and a heated pool.

When—or if—ferry service is re-established to Nova Scotia, it will probably originate here. Over the years, many of my numerous trips to Mount Desert Island have been for the purpose of catching the ferry to Yarmouth, but there is much more to this fascinating place than the ferry terminal. For starters, you'll want to mount up early in the morning to ride the Park Loop.

FROM ELLSWORTH, MAINE

0	From Ellsworth, south on US Rte 1/Rte 3 at US Rte 1A
1.0	Straight to continue on Rte 3
9.5	Bear left to stay on Rte 3
17.1	[Hulls Cove entrance and visitor center for Acadia National Park]
19.5	Left onto Rte 3 (Mt. Desert St.) into downtown Bar Harbor (right is Rte 233/Eagle Lake Rd.; straight is Kebo St. and the entrance onto the Park Loop Rd.)
20.0	Arrive Main St. in Bar Harbor
20.0	In Bar Harbor, south on Main St. (Rte 3) at Mt. Desert St.
22.1	[Sieur de Mont entrance to Park Loop Rd.]
37.9	Right onto Cadillac Summit Rd.
41.3	Arrive at the summit of Cadillac Mt.; return down the mountain
44.6	Right onto Park Loop Rd.
48.1	Exit right at Sieur de Monts
54.2	Stanley Brook entrance for the Loop Rd. at Seal Harbor
57.1	Left onto Rte 198
57.9	In Northeast Harbor, bear left onto Main St.
58.1	Bear right onto Neighborhood Rd.
58.5	Right onto Manchester Rd.
59.5	Manchester Rd. becomes Sargent Dr.
62.7	Left (north) onto Rte 3/Rte 198
65.3	In Somesville, left onto Rte 102 (Main St.)
66.2	Bear right onto Rte 102 (Pretty Marsh Rd.)
71.9	[Seal Cove Auto Museum]
78.4	Straight onto Rte 102A (Rte 102 is a shortcut)
79.4	[Bass Harbor]
80.0	[Straight to visit Bass Harbor Light]
80.6	Arrive at Bass Harbor Light; return to Rte 102A
81.2	Right onto Rte 102A
83.8	[Seawall Motel]
87.1	[Southwest Harbor]
93.4	At Somesville, straight onto Rte 102/Rte 198
95.4	Bear left (north) to remain on Rte 102/Rte 198
97.6	Straight, onto Rt 3 north
107.3	Arrive in Ellsworth at US Rte 1/US Rte 1A ■

The first national park established east of the Mississippi River was Lafayette National Park in 1919, whose name was changed to Acadia in 1929. Thirty-two thousand acres of the park are on Mount Desert Island. Over two million visitors arrive every year, most of whom come during the peak

Thunder Hole's booming is the result of air being trapped and compressed by incoming waves.

months of July and August. Much of its most intimate corners are best explored on foot or by bicycle, which you can easily rent.

There are three road systems on Mount Desert Isle: public, national park, and carriage. The 57 miles of carriage roads that grace the eastern side of the island are off limits to motor vehicles. These were built through the efforts of John D. Rockefeller Jr. (son of the founder of Standard Oil and father of Nelson A.), who personally purchased the land and supervised the design and construction of the roads from 1913 to 1940 before donating them to the National Park Service. The Park Loop Road, however, was built specifically for motorized vehicles by the National Park Service between 1925 and 1941 with Rockefeller's financial support.

The road and its landscaping were designed by America's premier landscape architect, Frederick Law Olmstead, who also designed the grounds of Central Park in New York City, Shelburne Farms in Vermont, and Biltmore in North Carolina. Two-thirds of the 20-mile Park Loop Road consists of a one-way counter-clockwise loop around Cadillac Mountain. Public highways—which include state Routes 3, 233, 102, and 198—also run through the park, along the coast, and to scenic harbor villages.

I suggest following Main Street (Route 3) south out of Bar Harbor to reach the Sieur de Monts Entrance to the Park Loop Road. There are other primary entrances—from the visitor center on Route 3 north of Bar Harbor, and the Cadillac Mountain Entrance on Eagle Lake. The Individual Entrance Pass costs $5 and it's good for a week, but if you arrive early in the morning before the gatehouses open, you can pay later.

Most of the famous grand "cottages" and hotels on the island were lost in the Great Fire of 1947—only Highseas (c. 1912) survived. In contrast with the spruce and fir which typically dominate the landscape, the woods have recovered with an especially notable growth of deciduous trees, which produces some of the most brilliant fall foliage on the coast of Maine.

There are numerous overlooks and trailheads along the Park Loop Road, but parking is permitted only on the right side of the pavement almost everywhere there is one-way traffic. Sand Beach is a popular swimming spot. At Thunder Hole, the echoing booms made by waves rushing into the cave are loudest during mid-tide. The road briefly divides at Otter Cliffs—you take the high road and I'll take the low road—both offer excellent views. This is where Samuel de Champlain had his little mishap on September 5, 1604, when his ship struck the shoal. From this point, you will be riding into an area untouched by the historic conflagration, and spruce trees regain prominence. Otter Cove, its causeway built in 1939, was where Champlain stopped for repairs and made his memorable journal entry.

The causeway over Otter Cove marks the spot where Samuel de Champlain stopped to make repairs to one of his ships, which he recorded in a diary entry that quite literally put Mount Desert Island on the map.

The first bridge you'll pass under carries Route 3 traffic; the second is the Triad-Day Mountain Bridge for carriages. After the second bridge, you'll see the well-marked left turn that leads to Route 3 and Seal Harbor. *Caution:* from this point onward, the Park Loop Road will have two-way traffic. You'll pass one of the gatehouses for the carriage road, the Jordan Pond Gate Lodge on your right, a European-hunting-lodge-inspired design built in 1932 by the influential American architect Grosvenor Atterbury.

A right turn will put you on the 3.5-mile road that winds across the north and west faces of Cadillac Mountain to reach the summit at 1,527 feet. This is the highest point on the Atlantic coast, one of the most-frequently visited mountaintops in America, and one of the first places in the United States to see the rising sun (from October 7 to March 6 it is *the* first place). You'll have the best views early in the morning or at other times when humidity is low.

Continuing on the Park Loop Road, you'll want to turn left to return to Bar Harbor via Route 233. Staying on the park road will carry you back to Route 3 south of the village, or you can simply do another circuit and take the Stanley Brook exit for Seal Harbor.

Route 3 cuts through the park from Bar Harbor to Seal Harbor and then follows the coast to the head of Northeast Harbor. Southwest Harbor is only a crow-flying mile-and-a-half from Northeast Harbor, but to reach it by land is at least a 14-mile ride. Your route heads out of Northeast Harbor on Sargeant Drive, a delightful, narrow road that runs along the eastern shore of Somes Sound, where trucks are banned and traffic is sparse. Somes Sound is the only true fjord in the eastern United States, with buoys only a few feet from shore marking lobster traps resting more than a 100 feet be-

Both schooners and lobster boats ply the waters of Somes Sound, the only fjord in the eastern United States.

The Indian motorcycle collection at the Seal Cove Auto Museum is small, but important.

neath the surface. On my last visit there, I actually stopped in the oncoming lane, turned off the engine, and waited for a lobster boat to slowly ease into position to pull its traps. Photos taken, I continued on my way, without having seen another vehicle. Sargeant Drive is certainly as scenic as the coastal portions of the Park Loop Road.

Somes Sound cuts Mount Desert Island almost in half, and you'll be heading to what is called the West Side. The first New England settler arrived with his family in 1762 and the community around Somesville grew to become the economic center of the island. Then, in 1855, Charles Tracy, a New York lawyer and the father-in-law of J.P. Morgan, arrived with 26 friends for a month's outing, one of whom was the landscape painter Frederic Church. His artwork and published diary of the stay introduced Mount Desert Island to wealthy city dwellers and thus began the tourism that continues to this day. Somesville is no longer an economic center, but simply a bucolic little village just north of the division of Route 102. Note that Route 102 makes a complete loop, with the western portion of Acadia National Park filling most of its circumscribed area.

The only thing that will suggest that the unimposing, blue metal pre-fab building might be a museum are the stationary gas—not gasoline—engines set by a walkway. The old saying "you can't judge a book by its cover" certainly holds true for the Seal Cove Auto Museum (207-244-9242; www. sealcoveautomuseum.org). From what I've been told, this deceptively modest facade is very much like that of Richard Paine, the man who assembled the magnificent collection within. Immediately after opening a very ordinary commercial door and stepping into the expansive interior, I was hooked. I'd hazard a guess that the only place where you'd find more Stanley steam cars would be in Jay Leno's garage.

To get this iconic shot of the Bass Harbor Head Light, you'll need to follow a path from the parking lot through the woods and down some stairs to a viewing platform.

The museum has a 1903 and a 1904 Knox made in Springfield and a 1909 Steven-Duryea from Chicopee Falls. There are very early models made by Olds, Pope, Cadillac, Ford, and even a 1909 Corbin. Classics like the American Underslung, the Maxwell, Locomobile, and REO are represented. The rarest car in the collection is one made by the Finley-Robertson-Porter Company of Port Jefferson, New York—it's unlikely you've heard of them. In four years they managed to produce nine cars and this one (serial number 5) is the only survivor. My favorite, however, is based solely on aesthetic appeal: the 1910 Stoddard Dayton is a jewel, with polished brass fittings, a circular windshield, an auxiliary spotlight, and up to 28 coats of paint, each of which was hand-sanded and rubbed. This was a very fast car and, like all of the company's top-end models, prior to being sold, the engine was completely disassembled, checked, and reassembled after an initial 400-mile factory road test!

Seal Cove bills itself as an auto (not a motorcycle) museum, but the bikes it does own are of special interest: a restored 1904 Indian, the first to have a twist grip; and an original 1913 single fitted with an acetylene headlamp. The following year would see the introduction of electric lights and the ill-fated electric starter/generator on the Hendee Special. Although it would be sold as the least expensive model for the next couple of years, this was the last single-cylinder Hedstrom engine produced by the company. Needless to say, I had a great time.

There are other unique motorcycles in the collection; for example, a 1911 Pope—actually sold as a "Columbia"—and a "1911" Flying Merkle. The shape of the gas tank on the Flying Merkle and the existence of the hand shifter are clues that this is probably a 1910 model, the last year in which belt-drive was standard. In comparison, the 1912 Pierce Four seems almost futuristic, with a shaft drive, T-head four-cylinder engine, gear-driven magneto, and a clutch that simultaneously engaged the shift lever on the handgrip. Furthermore, the oversized 3.5-inch frame tubes were sectioned to hold both oil and gasoline. The $400 retail price tag made it the most expensive motorcycle of its time.

After your return to Route 102, feel free to explore the various side roads, seeking out photo ops and stopping often just to ogle the natural beauty and striking contrasts of light and texture. In spite of the sensory overload, you will be riveted by the sight of the Bass Harbor Head Light clinging to the edge of the forested cliff more than 50 feet above the mean high water. This lighthouse was built in 1858 and is currently the private residence of a U.S. Coast Guard family and not open to the public. A well-traveled path leads down to the lighthouse where a succession of people queue up for their obligatory photo in front of the tower. For the classic postcard view however, you'll need to hike a bit to the stairs down to a vantage point on a viewing platform. On my last visit, I fell into conversation with other riders, one from New Hampshire, four from Illinois, and two from Michigan. With their five machines making up a third of the vehicles in the lot that day, one might surmise that motorcycle tourism is alive and well.

The Seawall Motel is located on the edge of the park, across the road from a beach made of round stones. Known as "cobbles," the stones from these beaches were once loaded into ships as ballast and then sold in ports like Boston to pave the streets. Here, the tides have created a natural seawall barrier that rises above the road. After violent storms, however, the highway crews have to plow the cobbles from the pavement.

The next morning, as you shuffle from your room to sit on the rocky seawall, a mug of hot coffee in hand to welcome the possibilities of the day, consider heading Down East after your return to Ellsworth. After all, you've come this far . . .

Ride 19 Goin' Up Down East

Distance: *307 miles, including side trips; plan for five hours to (most likely) all day.*
Highlights: *Views of the Atlantic and blueberry fields, Acadia National Park on Schoodic Peninsula, Quoddy Head in Lubec, and Eastport.*

The phrase "down east" is used so casually 'round heah that it's easy to forget how odd it might sound to someone hearing it for the first time. Before steam power, ships would sail from southerly ports to Maine and the Grand Banks fishing grounds by going east with the prevailing wind (downwind), and the term Down East came to designate the coast between Mount Desert Island and Eastport. To return to Boston, one had to tack against the wind (upwind) so heading south became "going up" to Boston or Gloucester, an artifact of speech you'll still hear today. This ride through the region does both, going down to Eastport and up to Ellsworth.

If you've ever ridden to Canada's maritime provinces, the chances are good that you've traveled the primary routes of this ride. Once past Ellsworth, you'll feel that you've escaped the heavy tourism of the southern

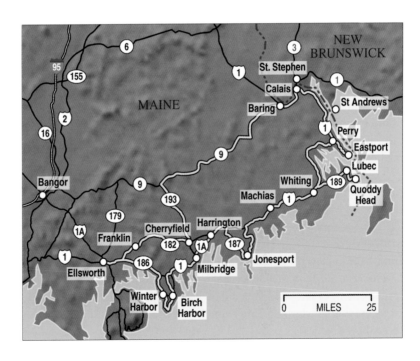

I doubt there is another place in Maine that prepares lobster as many ways as Ruth & Wimpy's Kitchen in Hancock.

and mid-coast regions and have left the state's big cities in your wake. There are many peninsulas begging to be explored, but the first departure from US Route 1 will be to see the mainland portion of Acadia National Park, a section visited by only 10 percent of the tourists who get to Mount Desert Island. Route 186 will head south on the Schoodic Peninsula to Winter Harbor, so named because its deep water rarely freezes and is protected from the fierce nor'easter storms. The more than seven miles of park road are one-way beginning at Frazer Point, where you'll find barbeque pits, picnic tables, and restrooms.

The highest point on the peninsula, Schoodic Head, is located up a narrow gravel road. Beyond it on the park road is Schoodic Point, reputed for the drama of giant pounding waves that toss softball-sized rocks onto the road. On a nice day, it can be stupendous, but I strongly recommend against your taking the ride in high weather or strong winds.

After exploring Schoodic Peninsula, return to US Route 1 by way of Millbridge. US Route 1 follows the Narraguagus River north to Cherryfield, but you'll want to take Route 1A to Harrington, bypassing several more peninsulas. It's unavoidable: the coast of Maine pretty much consists of a fringe of terrestrial fingers interspersed with long, narrow inlets.

Maine is the largest producer of lowbush blueberries in the world, with a

FROM ELLSWORTH, MAINE

0	From US Rte 1A in Ellsworth, head east on US Rte 1
1.0	Left to continue on US Rte 1
18.2	Right onto Rte 186
24.7	[Winter Harbor]
26.9	[Beginning of Park Rd. (one-way)]
29.1	Left onto Blueberry Hill Rd to the Schoodic Head lookout
30.2	From the lookout, return to the Schoodic Scenic Byway
31.3	Left onto Schoodic Scenic Byway
32.1	Right toward Schoodic Point and Education Center
32.7	From the Point, return to Schoodic Scenic Byway
33.2	Right onto Schoodic Scenic Byway
37.7	Right to return to Rte 186
44.9	Right (east) onto US Rte 1
55.1	In Milbridge, right onto US Rte 1A
62.9	Straight onto US Rte 1
68.5	Right onto Rte 187
79.1	[Pass the bridge to Beals Island in Jonesport]
91.3	Right (east) onto US Rte 1
117.1	Right onto Rte 189
128.2	Arrive at the International Bridge in Lubec; return (or take the bridge onto Campobello Island, New Brunswick)
129.4	Left onto Boot Cove Rd.
132.1	Left onto Quoddy Head Rd.
134.2	Arrive Quoddy Head Light and State Park; return to Rte 189
138.9	Left onto Rte 189
148.8	In Whiting, right onto US Rte 1
169.2	Right onto Rte 190 to Eastport
176.4	Arrive in downtown Eastport; return to US Rte 1 (or via the ferry to Deer Isle, New Brunswick)
183.8	Right onto US Rte 1
204.1	Arrive in Calais, one block from the bridge to St. Stephen, New Brunswick

THE FAST TRACK WEST

204.1	From downtown Calais, ride south on Rte 9
211.0	Left to continue on Rte 9
258.7	At Beddington, left onto Rte 193
277.8	At Cherryfield, right (west) onto Rte 182
301.3	Right (west) onto US Rte 1
307.0	Arrive at US Rte 1A in Ellsworth ■

Maine 227 **3**

quarter of the total U.S. crop. Unlike their larger cultivated counterparts, these wild native bloobs have evolved to thrive in stressful environments through a natural concentration of protective phytochemicals—the same ones touted for their health benefits in humans. And not only do they pack more piquant potency per purple pill, they don't leave large soggy holes in your muffins and pancakes. It's no contest.

Wild blueberries are propagated via underground runners which sprout new clone roots and stems. Crops are managed on a two-year cycle, pruning or burning fields after the late-July-through-August harvest, and encouraging vegetative growth the following year. A billion commercial bees are called upon each

The sign says it all.

spring to supplement the native population of pollinators. Even where the picking is still done traditionally with hand-held rakes, winnowing machines make faster work of removing leaves and twigs, allowing the berries to be washed and individually quick-frozen before they have time to lose any of their goodness. Think back on these harsh barrens the next time you are enjoying blueberry pancakes or jam.

Most of Maine's 2,000 or so islands aren't accessible by road or ferry, and there are only a couple dozen or so where you can arrive by motorcycle. One of these is Beals Island, which is reached by taking Route 187 to Jonesport, a working fishing village. Eighty percent of the township is under water; Beals Island, accessible by a bridge, is part of the landed 20 percent. It's a pretty place that appeals to those who wish to get away from it all, but amenities are very limited. Three and a half miles from the bridge, the pavement ends on Great Wass Island, a major nesting site for seabirds.

Back on US Route 1, Machias looks like just a stop along the road, but every place has a history; this town of 1,300 residents is no exception. On June 12, 1775, the first naval battle of the American Revolution took place

Looking across to Campobello Island from Lubec.

here, though it was no Hollywood image of broadside duels; more like an armed British frigate being pursued by two coastal sailing vessels of irate townsmen with hunting muskets, pitchforks, and scythes. Yet a battle did occur, men died, and history books were written. What interests me is the tavern (c. 1770) where these local men planned the attack on the British who threatened to confiscate their lumber—lumber essential to naval shipbuilding. The Burnham Tavern Museum (207-733-4577; www.burnhamtavern.com), furnished circa 1780, is in almost original condition, and provides an accurate glimpse into our colonial past.

Lubec is the easternmost *town* in the United States and the most southern entry point into New Brunswick. It also marks the beginning of the Bay of Fundy, the most extreme tidal environment on the planet.

Route 189 runs east from US Route 1 near Whiting. Lubec is a small village (pop. 1,500) at the tip of a finger of land. The FDR Memorial Bridge crosses to Campobello Island and the Roosevelt Campobello International Park. Riders traveling to St. John, New Brunswick—including those heading to Nova Scotia—should note that the ferry from Campobello Island to Deer Isle costs $8 for motorcycles, and the one from Deer Isle to Eastport is the same (877-747-2159; www.deerisland.nb.ca/ferries.htm). Fuel surcharges might apply. Although wholly in Canada, the park is managed by an international commission that's affiliated with both the National Park Service and Parks Canada. Regardless, you'll still need your passport to return to the U.S. and all Canadian customs rules will apply.

Franklin Roosevelt inherited the Shingle-style house from his mother, and his family summered there from 1909 to 1921. It was here, at the age of 39, that he contracted the polio that would leave him paralyzed. After he became president, Roosevelt only returned for three short visits, but his wife continued to enjoy the 34-room cottage with children and friends. During the height of interest in FDR, the park hosted more than 150,000 visitors a year, a number that has dropped steadily over time, and was further impacted by tightened post-9/11 border security. Most recently, park officials have been actively courting visitors with creative programs such as Tea with Eleanor, a twice-daily seasonal event that relates her life on the island.

You wouldn't have made this trip if you weren't interested in visiting the easternmost piece of land in the United States (N 44.48.55 W 066.57.04), which is the scenic setting for the West Quoddy Head Light (207-733-2180; www.lighthouse.cc/westquoddy). Quoddy Head State Park is essentially an island connected to the mainland by a short neck of terra firma. The archetypal red-and-white beacon tower, complete with a white keeper's cottage, makes photos of this lighthouse instantly recognizable. Although the station was established in 1808, this lighthouse was constructed in 1857 and the third-order Fresnel lens—still in use—was installed the following year.

Your next destination on this trip will be the easternmost *city* in the United States: Eastport. Turn off US Route 1 in Perry and follow Route 190

The distinctive red-and-white candy stripes of the West Quoddy Head Light make it a recognizable landmark in generic posters and calendar shots of the New England coast.

St. Croix Island may not have been an ideal place to try and establish a town, but history was written in the attempt.

until it ends. This city will feel much larger than the town of Lubec, but in reality its population exceeds it by less than two-dozen individuals. Perhaps the feeling comes from the brick downtown port area that was built after a disastrous fire in 1886 destroyed Eastport's wooden structures. Then again, perhaps it is because you arrived there on the Fourth of July.

Eastport holds the largest Fourth of July celebration in the state and thousands of people come to the party. Since 1905 it has become a tradition for the U.S. Navy to dock at this port each year to celebrate the nation's birthday. Downtown will be swarming with vintage cars. Among the many shops and restaurants cashing in on the trade will be Raye's Mustard (83 Washington St.; 800-853-1903; www.rayesmustard.com). This is the last stone-ground mustard mill in existence and has been owned and operated by four generations of the same family. Originally built to supply mustard to the now-defunct sardine industry, the business has been adapted to serve gourmet markets and produces 21 different varieties, including some international award-winners.

Eastport is on Moose Island, although as you ride over the causeway you won't get a sense that you're island hopping. Piers, docks, and fishing sheds are built on high pilings or wharves with floating decks, since the tides can run 20 to 25 feet at the mouth of the Bay of Fundy, compared to 8 to 12 feet in southern Maine; tides at the northeastern end of the bay can exceed 40 feet! One of the effects of such massive amounts of water moving around is the Old Sow, the second-largest whirlpool in the world, located between Moose and Deer Islands. Although the whirlpool has reputedly diminished since the causeway was built, it's still not a safe place for a small boat during ebb tide. Regardless, a small ferry makes the crossing between the islands and, if timed correctly, this is the best vantage point for viewing the phenomenon.

Back on US Route 1 and about a mile and a half north of the village of Perry there is a pull-off area with picnic tables and a weathered pink granite marker denoting the 45th Parallel, the oldest North American marker for this latitude.

Settlement of North America began in 1604 on St. Croix Island, where an unprepared party of French came to these shores to set up a trading base. Half of the settlers died that first winter and in the spring, a member of the group, erstwhile explorer Samuel de Champlain, began scouting for a new settlement for the survivors (they went to Port Royal, New Brunswick). There is no public access to this tiny island at the mouth of the St. Croix River, and the international site is managed by the National Park Service in consultation with Parks Canada. The signs on US Route 1 will lead only to a parking area from which a person can gaze at an otherwise insignificant rocky island.

With the largest Fourth of July celebration in Maine, downtown Eastport gets transformed into a vintage auto show.

Calais (pronounced CAL-ess) is a border town with St. Stephen, New Brunswick, just across the now-narrow St. Croix River. The Calais Visitor Center (39 Union St.; 207-454-2211) has maps, local information, and clean restrooms; parking is on pavement in front of the building. There also will be plenty of local stores to serve your needs. Although there are several international crossings into Canada, the one in downtown Calais is more convenient and usually quicker than the one on Route 9 north of town.

Fans of GPS, GIS mapping, and historical navigation might find the Calais Transit Stone to be of interest. The Calais Observatory was established in 1857 for the purpose of taking longitude measurements required for laying the transatlantic telegraph cable. Astronomical transits were very precise telescopes used for measuring star passages. Coupled with an astronomical clock, these devices allowed for the precise positioning of a spot on the Earth's surface. Electrically connected to other observatories by telegraph, and using triangulation, a third location could be determined. This mid-19th-century technology essentially does what your GPS unit does. Both the transit and the clock were typically mounted on granite stones and the transit stone in Calais is one of the few that has survived. You can find the observatory site across from Dunkin' Donuts on North Street.

For practical reasons, the second half of this loop begins in downtown Calais. The primary international border crossing is located two miles farther west to better link Route 9 to NB Route 1. Seven miles from downtown Calais, US Route 1 divides from Route 9 in Baring. Don't look for a village, Baring is just a place name on the map, but there is a gas station where riders can rendezvous to continue on Ride 20 to the Four Corners Park in Madawaska or meet up en route to the Gaspè Peninsula.

The information center is located in the Downeast Heritage Museum in Calais.

The bridge in downtown Calais spans the approach to St. Stephen, New Brunswick.

Route 9 begins as Airline Road, which is appropriate since most traffic will be flying to reach Bangor. You're not going to find services on this stretch, so be sure to fill the gas tank at the station in Baring. The highway will continue on to Bangor—and so will most of the traffic. Maps show the names of towns along Route 193; there will be none. Maps show an airport landing strip; there isn't even a terminal building. However, you will find a plethora of resident moose, deer, and other wild creatures, so manage your speed accordingly. I actually rather like the isolation of these old forgotten highways.

Crossing the Narraguagus River in Cherryfield onto Route 182 will be another ride through forest. The road winds between lakes—although the only one that becomes visible is Fox Pond—making this a much cooler option on a hot summer day than taking US Route 1 back to Ellsworth. The uniformity of the trees will indicate that this is another forest plantation, however, with the land poised someday to become blueberry fields or such. After passing through Franklin, the highway often touches the shore of Hog Bay, which is more estuary than bay, before it will join US Route 1 at the northern end of Kilkenny Cove. From here it'll be only three miles to Ellsworth.

Ride 20   The Northeast Corner

Distance: *484 miles; plan for a couple of days*
Highlights: *Forests and potato fields, lakes and rivers. A tour of the "solar system," the official northeast corner of the United States, Fort Kent, and roads with little traffic.*

This ride begins in Brewer on the eastern shore of the Penobscot River directly across from Bangor, and will follow the river north to Lincoln. I-95 runs along the western side of the valley so there will be little but local traffic on US Route 2.

Except for the village of Lee, Route 6 runs through forests and fields, but on the southern shore of East Musquash Lake there will be a nice paved pull-off where you can admire the view. The orderly rows of trees are proof that this area was clear-cut in the past, while other sections will have been harvested more recently. Forestry remains one of the primary industries in this state. Although 90 percent of America's toothpicks originate from this area, most trees are felled for paper pulp.

Just outside of Danforth you'll enter Aroostook County. About the size of Connecticut and Rhode Island combined, this is the largest county east

About a million flattish acres in Aroostook County are devoted to growing spuds.

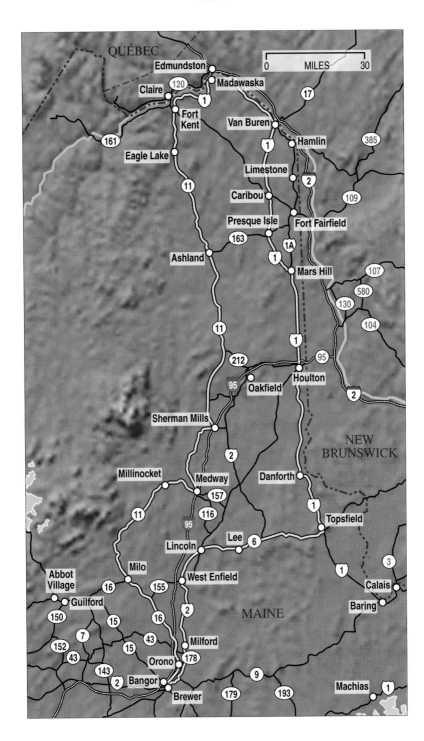

New Brunswick lies on the opposite bank, across the upper portion of the Saint John River, which forms the international border with Canada.

of the Mississippi River. Eighty percent of its five million acres is forested, with the remaining million or so devoted primarily to potato farms. Traditionally, harvesting these acres of spuds has been a local, generational affair, with adults often scheduling their vacation time accordingly, and students being freed from school for several weeks while the crop was secured. As modern agriculture erodes the necessity of this practice, the harvest recess has been fighting to remain a relevant and unique part of County life.

Houlton is the crossroads of eastern Maine, with I-95 passing just north of town and US Route 2 going through the center of it. Canada begins just a couple miles east of town and the Houlton International Airport terminal is only 500 yards west of the border of New Brunswick. The highway is straight, the land is flat, and if you happen to ride through in July when the potatoes are in blossom it will be a beautiful sight; otherwise you'll be left to admire large barns under a big sky.

The largest wind farm in New England is located on Mars Hill Mountain, a 1,700-foot prominence on the border of Canada. Each of the twenty-eight 1.5-megawatt G.E. turbines stands more than 400 feet tall and has a wing span comparable to a Boeing 747. Despite its opening the door to the renewable energy industry in Maine, the project has not been without controversies, with excessive noise being one of the biggest complaints.

In Mars Hill you have to decide whether to continue straight on US Route 1A or follow US Route 1 through the cities of Presque Isle and Caribou. If you wish to avoid traffic, US Route 1A would be the better choice and, despite a few additional miles, it's quicker. However, this tour takes US Route 1 to continue on to the center of the world's largest scale model of the solar system.

You actually entered the orbit of Pluto back in Houlton and passed three

FROM BREWER, MAINE

0	From the intersection of Bus Rte 1 and Rte 9 in Brewer, ride north on Rte 9/Rte 178
4.1	Left to continue on Rte 178
13.3	In Milford, bear right onto US Rte 2
35.9	In W. Enfield, straight as Rte 6 merges with US Rte 2
47.9	In Lincoln, bear right to continue on Rte 6
88.3	In Topsfield, left onto US Rte 1
170.2	In Mars Hill, straight onto US Rte 1A
219.4	In Van Buren, left to stay on US Rte 1
244.1	[Pass by the bridge in Madawaska that connects to Edmunston, New Brunswick]
244.3	[Four Corners Park in Madawaska]
263.2	[Junction of Rte 161, entering Mile One of US Rte 1]
263.7	In Fort Kent, arrive at the junction of US Rte 1 and Rte 11
263.7	In Fort Kent, south on Rte 11
279.4	[Pass through Eagle Lake]
312.2	In Ashland, continue on Rte 11 [Rte 163 goes to Presque Isle]
368.5	Near Sherman Mills, right to continue on Rte 11 [bear left for Exit 264 of I-95]
393.5	In Medway, right to continue on Rte 11 [left onto Rte 157 for Exit 244 of I-95]
404.1	In Millinocket, continue on Rte 11
443.1	In Milo, left onto Rte 11/Rte 16/Rte 6
445.3	Bear left to continue on Rte 16/Rte 6
467.1	[Pass Exit 199 of I-95]
475.6	In Orono, bear right onto US Rte 2
483.1	In Bangor, left onto Broadway to Oak St.
483.6	Arrive in Brewer at Bus. Rte 1A and Rte 9 ■

recently discovered "dwarf" planets since leaving Topsfield. Using a scale of one mile to represent one Angstrom Unit (A.U.), the Sun has a 50-foot diameter and Pluto is a sphere a mere one inch in size. Pluto can be found at the Maine Visitor Center next to I-95 in Houlton and the sun is incorporated into the Northern Maine Museum of Science building at the University of Maine in Presque Isle, 40 miles away. You'll have to keep on the lookout for the distinctive poles that hold most of the planets, as they are placed on private and commercial properties along US Route 1. Jupiter and Saturn are not difficult to spot, but the distance between the inner planets means they will be located in the more densely populated area of Presque Isle. The Earth (east side of the highway at Percy's Auto Sales) is only one mile from the Sun, and Venus (west side of the highway at the Budget Traveler Motor Inn) is 0.7 miles away. Mercury, at the beginning of the UMaine campus (Burrell's Garden), is located a mere 0.4 miles from the museum.

If you think that nothing much happens up here you'd be wrong. In 2011 Bill Warner became the first man to break the 300 mph barrier on a conventional motorcycle. The Loring Timing Association (www.lta-lsr.com) holds sanctioned land-speed races at the former Loring Air Base in Caribou where they have a nice straight strip of asphalt 2.5 miles long. On July 17th, Warner and his supercharged Suzuki set the land-speed record for a conventional motorcycle at 311.945 mph! And you thought you had to go to Bonneville!

If you have taken scenic Route 1A along the Maine-New Brunswick border through Fort Fairfield and Limestone, it's easy enough to cut west on Route 161 or Route 233 to Caribou should circumstance necessitate it. Whether you took US Route 1 or Route 1A, you'll rejoin US Route 1 in Van Buren. If you are headed to the Gaspè, you'd cross the border onto Route 17 and follow it to Campbellton, New Brunswick.

During the Great Expulsion that took place in Nova Scotia from 1755 to 1763, the British forcibly deported the Acadian population in what we would now term "ethnic cleansing." Families were broken apart and sent to different parts of the world, with a third of the population dying in the process. Some Acadians fled and formed communities in Louisiana (Cajuns) and along the upper reaches of the Saint John River. You'll hear Acadian being spoken on the streets of Van Buren and Madawaska so this isn't all ancient history. To learn a bit more, stop at the Acadian Village (www.connectmaine.com/acadianvillage/tour.html) on US Route 1. Some of the buildings in the museum are reconstructions and others are originals that have been moved to the site. Note that on the streets of Madawaska you're as likely to hear French spoken as

The Fort Kent blockhouse is a visible reminder of the war that almost was.

If you are continuing on to the Gaspè, you'll probably want to cross the border in Van Buren.

English. And that language you can't quite identify? Well, that would be Acadian or perhaps a unique dialect called Brayon or "Valley French."

The Aroostook War is an almost forgotten conflict that nearly caused a third war between the United States and Great Britain. It's an interesting story about company greed, commodity speculation, conflicting territorial claims, refugees, and extremist groups escalating disagreements to the point of armed conflict. The U.S. border remained in dispute until the Webster-Ashburton Treaty in 1842 established it along the south bank of the Saint John River. The Republic of Madawaska was coined during these troubled times as an exasperated response to an overly inquisitive French official, and members of parliament further popularized the concept in references to their constituents, and added such details as a flag and coat of arms. Today, the republic good-naturedly encompasses both sides of the border, with the title of president traditionally bestowed upon the mayor of Edmundston, New Brunswick.

Madawaska is at the most northeasterly corner of the United States, and in recent years, the famous SCMA Four Corners Motorcycle Tour has put this small city on the map. The Madawaska Four Corners Park (213 W. Main St., four blocks west of the international bridge and opposite the wind turbine; N47.21.362 W068.19.958; www.madawaskafourcorners.org), with its granite benches and illuminated fountain, is the first park dedicated to long-distance motorcycle touring, honoring official tour finishers with a 12-foot-high Norwegian blue-pearl granite monument and paving-stone markers engraved with their names. To participate on this self-guided endeavor, you must be a member of the Southern California Motorcycling Association and pay the $100 fee (www.usa4corners.org). You are given 21 days to visit the four official checkpoints—San Ysidro, California; Blaine,

Washington; Key West, Florida, and Madawaska, Maine—but you can tag them in any order you choose.

There are a couple of hotels in Madawaska, but a much wider choice of lodging and restaurants are just across the border in Edmundston, New Brunswick (you'll need a valid passport or augmented drivers license to return). Martin's Motel (98 Main St.; 207-728-3395; www.martinsmotel. org) is basic, but inexpensive. Camping could be an option, except for that miserable six-week period starting in mid- to late-May known in the northern woods as "black fly season," If tenting it otherwise suits you, try the Lakeview Restaurant & Camping Resort in St. Agatha (9 Lakeview Dr. off Flat Mountain Rd.; 207-543-6331; www.lakeviewrestaurant.biz).

Mile One of US Route 1 begins at the international Claire-Fort Kent Bridge. From there it's only 2,377 miles to the end of the highway in Key West, Florida (one of the other Four Corners checkpoints). The other place of note is the blockhouse for which the town is named. It was erected in 1840 during the Aroostook War and named for Edward Kent, the Governor of Maine who so precipitously declared war on Great Britain. The two-story structure is one of the few original blockhouses in the country. This National Historic Site is open to the public and is maintained by local Eagle Scouts.

The University of Maine (U of ME) has a campus here so it should come as no surprise to find a number of fast-food chains on Main Street, where you can get pizza, Chinese, Mexican, subs, and even a hamburger.

Although eighty percent of Aroostook County is forested, the remainder supports a verdant patchwork of agriculture.

Unfortunately, the privately owned Golden Road to Mount Katahdin, the highest peak in Maine, is closed to motorcycles.

Route 161 heads west from Fort Kent, and over the years I've followed it for many miles. The Maine Northwoods Region is the largest wilderness east of the Mississippi, with 3.5 million acres, including the famous Allagash Wilderness Waterway. It's my recommendation not to venture into the Allagash without an off-road bike, camping gear, and extra gasoline, since it is a maze of wilderness roads (and no directional signs).

Route 11 begins in Fort Kent, but before heading south make sure you top off your gas tank; it's 105 miles to Sherman, although you might get lucky and find a working pump at Eagle Lake. After Sherman you won't find another gas station until reaching Medway. If you like long stretches of highway with almost no traffic you'll be in for a treat. Just don't expect scenic vistas, because you literally can't see the forest for the trees.

Route 163 goes east to Presque Isle and Route 212 leads to US Route 2 and I-95 in Oakfield, should you wish to ride east to Houlton. You have the option of getting onto I-95 south at Exit 264 near Sherman Mills, where there's a gas station with premium fuel, or at Exit 244 in Medway. You're now 130 miles south of Fort Kent and about to make a big loop to the west only to return to I-95 at Exit 199. This will give you the choice of a 45-mile ride on the big slab or 74 miles on Routes 11 and 16 through more forest and small towns.

From Medway, Route 11 goes west to Millinocket, and the eastern terminus of the Golden Road, a private gravel byway through the Maine woods which touches the southwestern corner of Baxter State Park near Mount Katahdin, the highest peak in the state, before arcing southwest to Route 15 in Greenville. Unfortunately, however, motorcycles are banned, and they mean it.

Route 11 merges with Route 16 in Milo and connects with Ride 21 in Abbot Village. From Milo, Route 16 makes its way southeast to Bangor.

Ride 21   The Great North Woods

Distance: *227 miles; requires a minimum of five hours. Be realistic and plan on an all-day ride.*

Highlights: *Small towns and farms, forest, rivers and lakes. Moose if you are lucky and spectacular fall foliage during the autumn. The Old Canada Road, one of the state's four scenic byways; Moosehead Lake.*

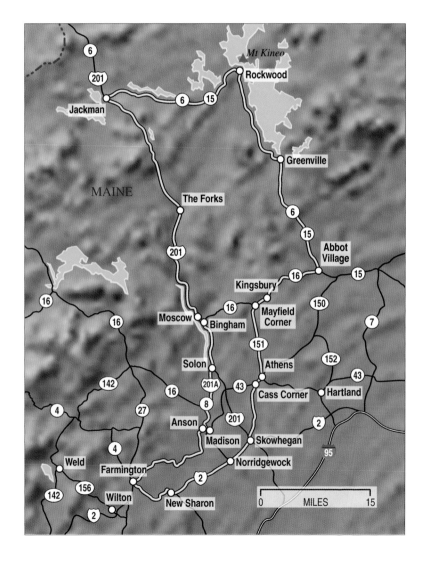

Farmington, a college town of fewer than 8,000 people, is the economic center of the region. The downtown is essentially an extension of the University of Maine campus, with both fast-food and good food options. The Homestead Bakery (207-778-6162; www.homesteadbakery.com) is much more than the name implies, with tempting breakfast, lunch, and dinner menus. Soup For You (207-779-0799) has soups, wraps, and good coffee. I usually pick up a sandwich wrap before heading out for the day. GrantLee's 20th Maine Tavern & Grill (north of downtown on Rte 4/Rte 27; 207-778-0880) has a Civil War theme and hearty fare. Gifford's Ice Cream is also a popular destination, partly because they've twice taken the Grand Champion title at the World Dairy Expo.

Route 43 begins as Perham Street in downtown Farmington and soon becomes a country road that runs through forests and fields. It's called Industry Road, but Industry is the name of a township it passes through, not an indication of miles of industrial parks, as one might assume. There *are* deep ruts

FROM FARMINGTON, MAINE

0	From Farmington at Rte 4/Rte 27 (Main St.), ride east on Rte 43 (Perham St.)
20.5	In Anson, straight onto US 201A/Rte 8
31.9	Right to continue on US Rte 201A/Rte 8
33.0	In Solon, left onto US Rte 201
89.7	In Jackman, right onto Rte 15/Rte 6
137.5	[Pass through Greenville]
159.4	In Abbot Village, right onto Rte 16
173.8	In Mayfield Corner, left onto Rte 151
186.7	In Athens, bear right onto Rte 150/Rte 43
188.7	Straight to stay on Rte 150
198.7	In Skowhegan, right onto US Rte 2 (Water St.)
198.9	Left onto US Rte 2/US Rte 201
199.1	Right onto US Rte 2/US Rte 201A
204.2	In Norridgewock, right to continue on US Rte 2
204.6	In Norridgewock, straight to continue on US Rte 2
217.1	[Pass through New Sharon]
225.9	Right onto Rte 4/Rte 27 into Farmington
226.6	Arrive downtown Farmington at Rte 43 ■

in the pavement, however, since the logging trucks coming from the paper mill on the Kennebec River in Madison aren't subject to weight limits.

Instead of crossing the bridge into Madison, turn left and follow US Route 201A/Route 8 north along the banks of the river. This is not a major highway, but a well-maintained road that cuts through agricultural and pastureland before crossing the river into Solon.

US Route 201 follows the eastern bank of the Kennebec River and from Solon north it is designated as a National Scenic Byway known as the Old

Canada Road, a historic corridor so unspoiled and off the path that it rarely gets any press at all. Running for a mere 78 miles to the border of Canada, the road traces the river trading route of the Abenaki, later used by Benedict Arnold's troops in their unsuccessful 1775 attempt to capture Québec. Later, an influx of French Canadians seeking work in the northern Maine logging camps would leave their distinct influence on the region's food, music, and folk traditions. With almost no human influence to distract, the water will draw your attention on the first half of the Old Canada Road, giving way to deep and untracked forest as you proceed north. I suggest topping off your gas tank in Bingham; you won't see another service station until you reach Jackman.

Damming the river in Moscow created Wyman Lake, and as the road winds along the steep banks of the reservoir you'll be treated to one of the most serene stretches of highway in the Great North Woods. More than you might realize, beavers have played an active role in submerging thousands of acres, creating habitats that benefit other animals, fish, and outdoorsmen. The lake eventually reverts back into a wide river where, depending upon circumstances, you might see a tranquil expanse of smooth rocks covered by a few inches of tea-colored water or a frothing turbulence of boiling spume.

In the homestretch of its 14-state traverse, the Appalachian Trail crosses the road near Caratunk on its way through the 100 Mile Wilderness to its terminus on Mount Katahdin in Baxter State Park. Signs along the highway advertise whitewater rafting trips. The Dead River joins the Kennebec River at The Forks; both offer exceptional Class III to Class V rapids controlled by timed releases of water from upstream reservoirs. The flow of water

It's always exciting to see a moose, but these awkward-looking creatures can move very quickly, so slow down and stop if they are on the side of the highway.

through the Upper Kennebec Gorge is dramatic, while the Dead River is the longest continuous stretch of whitewater in the eastern United States.

After you cross the Kennebec at The Forks, you'll begin to climb into the mountains, where highway signs will warn of the very real dangers of a collision with a moose. Your chances of seeing a moose are higher on this particular ride than any other in New England. These animals can stand about seven feet tall at the shoulder and generally weigh between 900 and 1,400 pounds. They won't move for logging trucks with blaring air horns, so don't get cocky because you've installed deer whistles on your motorcycle. As gawky as they look, with those long legs they

Downtown Farmington is essentially an extension of the University of Maine campus.

can move as fast as a horse—which is faster than you can safely circle around them on the roadside. If you see a moose, stop. Don't approach them— there is a reason wolves won't attack a healthy moose; use your zoom lens if you must, and leave it at that.

North of Palin Pond, but before reaching Jackman, there's a scenic overlook from which Attean Lake is visible. Although I wasn't able to confirm it, the lake was likely named after a Penobscot chief of great political skill who may be best known to history as Henry David Thoreau's backcountry guide on two of his trips to Maine. The land made quite an impression on the poet, and he wrote of an unbroken, "stern and savage" forest, whose virgin growth has since been harvested and regrown, but not yet tamed. When Thoreau died of tuberculosis at the age of 44, his famous last words were "moose" and "Indian."

Jackman is a small village (pop. 500), and the jumping-off place for excursions into the backwoods. I'd suggest you make sure your gas tank is full because the next service station will be in Greenville about 50 miles down the highway. Note that the riot of brilliant incandescence that marks the fall

Backcountry guides and outfitters can take you deeper into Maine's north woods by means of ATVs, boats, or float planes.

foliage tends to arrive to this latitude about two weeks ahead of the more southerly show, often peaking by late September. You'll see signs for outfitters along Route 6/Route 15, but especially near Long Pond and Brassua Lake. There's a vast network of waterways that can be explored by canoe. With regard to paved roads, however, this is the northern boundary of civilization.

Paper companies own most of the land in this part of Maine and clearcut logging is responsible for the patchwork nature of the forest. In a natural growth, the trees will not be as uniform in spacing and size as they are in these tracts. Often only a "beauty strip" is left between the highway and the harvested acreage. Take care as you plan deviations from your route in this remote territory, as many of the roads (such as the Golden Road from Greenville) will be privately owned by said paper companies, who control access and often ban motorcycles outright.

Moosehead Lake is one of the largest bodies of water in New England and it's the least populated. One of the local attractions is the 763-foot cliff on Mount Kineo. The best views will be found just off the highway in the small hamlet of Rockwood. This is also the best place to find rustic accommodations—primarily cabins and campsites—with The Birches (800-825-9453; www.birches.com) being the premier lodging in the region.

From Rockwood the highway follows Moosehead Lake south to Greenville, but don't expect to discover expansive scenic views. Rockwood was your one and only chance for such photo ops. However, this is a beautiful cruise and you'll thoroughly enjoy the ride. Cresting a slight rise on a recent trip, I spotted the largest bull moose I'd ever seen standing in the middle of the road. I stopped, but before I could get my camera out of the tank bag, this huge animal with his massive rack of antlers simply melted silently into the thick scrub.

On the southern end of Moosehead Lake is Greenville, the economic and social services hub for the region. There are numerous restaurants, cafés, a couple of grocery stores, the regional hospital, and gas stations. Most of the cabins, B&B inns, and lodges are located on Lily Bay Road and not Route 6/Route 15.

In January 1963, a B-52 Stratofortress crashed into Elephant Mountain outside of Greenville while practicing low level navigation designed to outwit Soviet radar technology. The two airmen to survive the crash had to weather below-zero temperatures while paper company plows churned 15-foot snowbanks to within a couple of miles of the wounded men, from which rescuers had to snowshoe or snowmobile the rest of the way. Today, the debris of this giant plane is just a short hike off a gravel road (Scammon Road) and the salvaged remains of an engine and ejection seat decorate the clubhouse of the Moosehead Riders Snowmobile Club, whose members sponsor a yearly service with full military honors to commemorate the tragic event.

The Moosehead Marine Museum (207-695-2716; www.katahdincruises.com) focuses on the history of logging and the resort era on the lake. The main exhibit is the SS *Katahdin,* a 110-foot cruise ship originally built by Bath Iron Works in 1914 as a steamship. When the resort era collapsed, the *Katahdin* was used to haul large rafts (booms) of logs, but the last log drive was in 1975. The museum was formed in 1976 with the ship

The scenic overlook of Attean Lake on US Route 201 just south of Jackman.

From the cliffs of Mount Kineo, the panorama of Moosehead Lake stretches to the horizon.

as the main exhibit. In 1995 it was completely restored and during the summer season, they offer three-hour and half-day cruises.

Your route turns onto Route 16 west in Abbot Village, but if you continued on Route 15 you'd get to Bangor. Route 16 east goes to Milo and connects with Ride 20.

Route 16 is a beautiful ride through forests with a few nice curves and some elevation changes. A single house and a place name are all that remain of the small town of Kingsbury. On the west side of Kingsbury Pond, turn onto Route 151 (Athens Road). There will be no major tourist attractions or natural wonders along Route 151 or Route 150, but you'll definitely enjoy the ride.

As with most northern New England towns, Skowhegan's heyday coincided with the flourishing of mills during the first half of the 20th century. Commercial downtown buildings in Skowhegan (pop. 8,000) have a brick elegance that advertised prosperity. In addition, the Margaret Chase Smith Library on Norridgewock Avenue houses an educational center on the life and career of the nation's first U.S. Senator. If you keep experiencing little pangs of déjà vu, it might be because HBO used Skowhegan as a filming location for the movie based on Richard Russo's bestselling novel *Empire Falls*.

Skowhegan is where you'll link up with US Route 2. From here, it will be only 22 miles to Farmington, where you'll have plenty of options for supper.

Ride 22   Rangeley Lakes

Distance: *182 miles that could be covered in four hours, but plan on at least six*
Highlights: *Mountains, lakes, forests, small villages, river valleys, and rolling hills. Wilhelm Reich's estate Orgonon, the Oquossoc Log Church, and miles of wonderful motorcycling roads.*

Departing from Wilton, Route 156 quickly becomes rural and winds into the mountains. There's very little traffic on this road and the forest provides cool shade on hot summer days and spectacular fall foliage at the beginning of October. It'll be a straight shot onto Route 142 in the hamlet of Weld, where the road briefly levels off as it runs between Webb Lake and Mount Blue State Park. There are fewer corners on this highway, but it keeps climbing in elevation while offering sedate cruising through mile after mile of deciduous forest.

Turning onto Route 4, you'll be at 977 feet in elevation, and by the time you reach the shore of Long Pond you will have climbed to 1,800 feet. The peaks of these mountains have been worn smooth and rounded by the advance of great glaciers of the last ice age, which left behind poor, sandy soil as the ice retreated. You might notice a sign for Smith Falls, a very pretty 54-

Route 17, part of the Rangeley Lakes Scenic Byway, is a fantastic touring road along Coos Canyon.

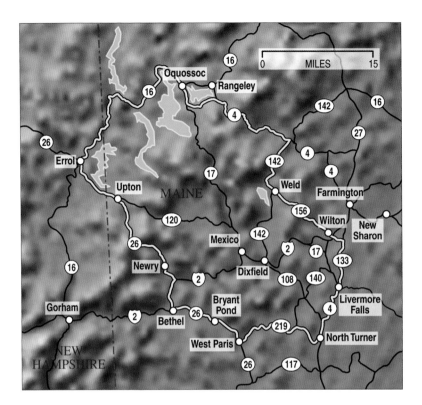

foot cascade that requires a five-minute hike from the parking area. This also marks the beginning of the Rangeley Lakes Scenic Byway, one of four national scenic byways in Maine.

The highway runs along the north shore of Long Pond, then between mountains to reach Rangeley Lake, named for Squire James Rangeley, a Yorkshireman who established a grand English-style estate on 31,000 acres his father had purchased from Massachusetts. The region is a boater's paradise, with more than 200 connected lakes. Unless you dismount and hike beyond the road, however, you won't see more than glimpses of the water. Scenic views have taken a back seat to the necessity of having a buffer zone of trees to prevent the wind from drifting snow from the lake across the road.

The town of Rangeley is an official Appalachian Trail Community, as one of the more memorable sections of that footpath runs along the height of land to the south. Should you need any manner of humble services or accommodations you could likely find them there. It is also the home of the Rangeley Lakes Region Logging Museum (207-864-3939; www.rlrlm.org), with educational exhibits dedicated to preserving and celebrating the heritage of lumbering in western Maine. Located on Route 16 just east of town, the museum also hosts an annual Logging Parade and Festival during the last weekend in July.

After a visit to the museum, I suggest turning left onto South Shore Road past Rangeley Lake State Park. From that point, you'll turn right onto Route 17 to follow the western shore of the lake to Oquossoc. Route 17 is a fantastic touring road over the height of land and along Coos Canyon, and is part of the Rangeley Lakes Scenic Byway on which you began earlier. Although it's not part of this ride, a detour south on Route 17 would reward you with overarching views of Mooselookmeguntic and Rangeley Lakes.

Should you want yet another interesting detour, head east on Route 16 about three miles from Oquossoc to Dodge Pond Road. The Wilhelm Reich Museum (207-864-3443; www.wilhelmreichtrust.org) commemorates the career of a psychiatrist who worked with Sigmund Freud and influenced many famous intellectuals across Europe before escaping Nazi Germany to the United States. He became a controversial figure after claiming to have discovered the cosmic energy that most people call God. Reich built devices to "accumulate" this ethereal force (which he named "orgone") for the purpose of healing and increasing sexual energy. The land he purchased in Rangeley in 1942 became the site of his Orgone Energy Observatory. He eventually ran afoul of the Federal Food and Drug Administration and was jailed for selling orgone accumulators across state lines; tons of his publications were burned by the government in 1956. Although

FROM WILTON, MAINE

0	From Wilton at US Rte 2, northwest on Rte 156 (Depot St.)
14.2	In Weld, straight onto Rte 142
26.3	Left onto Rte 4
43.4	In Rangeley, left onto S. Shore Rd.
50.9	Right onto Rte 17
54.6	Right onto Rte 4
54.9	Left (west) onto Rte 16
81.7	[Enter New Hampshire]
90.5	In Errol, left onto Rte 26 (Upton Rd.)
98.8	[Back into Maine]
120.8	In Hanover, right (west) onto US Rte 2
126.5	Left onto Parkway Rd.
126.8	In Bethel, left onto Rte 26 (Walker's Mills Rd.)
141.8	In West Paris, left onto Rte 219 (N. Paris Rd.)
161.7	In N. Turner, left onto Rte 4
172.5	In Livermore Falls, right onto Rte 17 (after crossing the bridge)
172.6	Left (next left) onto Union St.
172.6	Immediate left onto Church St.
172.7	Straight onto Rte 133
180.2	At Beans Corner, left onto Rte 156
182.0	Arrive at US Rte 2 in Wilton ∎

From the height of land on Route 17 there are sweeping views of Mooselookmeguntic and Upper Richardson Lakes.

Reich died of a heart attack while in prison, he left a trust to maintain his estate and observatory.

The Oquossoc Union Church (c. 1916) is on Route 4 in Oquossoc, between the junctions of Routes 16 and 17. This 32-foot-square log building has been a non-denominational house of local worship since 1915, when it was founded as a Sunday school. From here, the highway loops north along Cupsuptic Lake and around various mountains and lakes following the path of least resistance to Errol, New Hampshire. Route 16 is a fast-paced road and these 35 miles will go by quickly.

Errol is one of the points along Ride 14 and, as on that ride, I suggest

L. L. Cote sells just about anything that is in demand, including motorcycles and snowmobiles.

stopping at L. L. Cote for gas or just about anything else you might need. Route 26 from Errol touches the southern end of Lake Umbagog and the boat launch area offers the only view that is easily accessible. A remote cabin not far from the lake was the setting for Louise Dickinson Rich's humorous and heartwarming memoir *We Took to the Woods,* which recounts her family's life in the backcountry. Less than a mile from the boat launch and you'll be back in Maine and beginning to descend through Grafton Notch, one of my favorite roads. During their geologic history, the sheer cliffs were scraped by glaciers and left exposed to crumble into the talus slopes and boulder fields characteristic of the region.

Route 26 merges with US Route 2 in Newry, along the Androscoggin River. Geologically this region is quite different from anywhere else in the state or in the White Mountains immediately to the west. In the distant past when the White Mountains were formed, molten magma was forced into

Relatively few motorcyclists seem to seek out Route 26 through Grafton Notch, making it one of the most lightly trafficked of touring roads.

large lens-shaped reservoirs that geologists call pegmatite dikes. These are extremely rich in crystalline minerals. Mica was mined for use as stove windows and electrical insulators, feldspar for a wide range of products including household cleaners. These deposits also yield gemstones, most notably beryl and the state gemstone, tourmaline, a fact well-known to mineral collectors and dealers the world over.

In Bethel, the easiest way to reconnect with Route 26 would be to turn onto Parkway Road—which is just a short cross-street. However, if you miss it, take the next left on Cross Street or simply follow the highway signs for the turn onto Route 26. US Route 2 continues west, connecting to Rides 13, 14, 6, 3, 7, 4, 5, and 8 (in that order).

On the shore of Bryant Pond is a village of the same name. This was the last place in the country to have a hand-crank telephone service, which was finally retired in 1983. Next to the post office is a giant candlestick telephone with a crank honoring this historical fact.

At the junction of Route 219 is a famous mineral shop called Perham's of Maine. Although it sells rocks and minerals from around the world, it also provides maps and permission to do a little of your own prospecting at their mine sites.

Your route loops around Bear Pond in North Turner and takes Route 4 to Livermore Falls. However, all of the road in this area, Routes 4, 17, 108, and 140 are thoroughly enjoyable motorcycling roads.

Beyond the asphalt, you might not see the forest through the trees.

Massachusetts

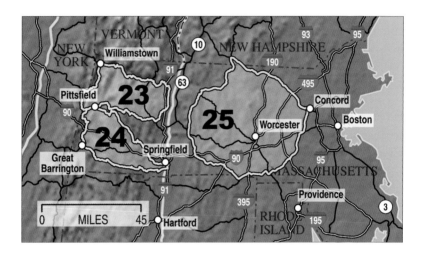

Massachusetts is the 7th smallest state, but has the 3rd highest population density with just over 6.5 million people. Two-thirds of the population live in the Greater Boston Area and the state has 50 cities and 301 towns. There are more than 31,000 miles of highways, but at certain times during particular days it seems like as if most of Massachusetts's registered vehicles herd together on just a few of the most popular ones. In contrast, the rolling hills of the Berkshires can seem like a remote and blissfully forgotten place.

When the great ice sheet that scraped most of New England clean finally melted, the debris that remained formed Cape Cod, Martha's Vineyard, and Nantucket. The rest of Massachusetts seems to be a geological patchwork of mostly left-behind pieces from colliding and retreating continental plates. We do know that dinosaurs roamed in the Connecticut River Valley some 190 million years ago because their footprints were embedded in sandstone.

Massachusetts was settled early, but how early remains an open question. The area was mapped and explored by Samuel de Champlain in 1605, and again in 1614 by Captain John Smith. When the Pilgrims established the second permanent English settlement here in 1620, however, they found prior evidence of an extended European settlement, and there is controversial but widespread lithic evidence to support the idea. In addition, native tribes such as the Wapanogs, Narragansett, Podunk, Mahigan, and Massachusetts had been well established in the region before 90 percent of the indigenous population was wiped out by a smallpox epidemic in the years just prior to the arrival of the Pilgrims.

There's no denying that Massachusetts's influence at pivotal points in America's early history was out of proportion with its physical size—the better-known details of which you may have gotten in school, studying the American Revolution or Civil War. But the ideas that swirled in this hub of activity between conflicts helped to shape the arguments for and against American independence, the Protestant Great Awakening, transcendentalism, temperance, and abolition—movements that all began here. And there are other lesser known and equally influential precedents with which to credit the Bay State, including its legally decreeing in 1647 that every town was responsible for appointing a teacher or establishing a primary school.

With excellent, accessible roads beyond the madding crowds, and first-rate reasons to dismount, motorcycle touring in Massachusetts has a lot to offer.

The roads leading to the summit of Mount Greylock are popular with motorcyclists.

Ride 23   Northern Berkshire Loop

Distance: *131 miles and at least four hours*
Highlights: *Mountains, valleys, villages, and small cities. Hancock Shaker Village, Clark Art Institute, Mount Greylock, Old Deerfield, and the Bridge of Flowers.*

The Berkshires lie between the borders of Vermont and Connecticut, from the Connecticut River to the Taconic Range that straddles the Massachusetts-New York line. Close to my home, the beautiful touring roads that crisscross the Berkshires are familiar territory and choosing where to start and which to recommend in this book was more difficult than you might imagine.

Since Route 7 is the north-south backbone for touring western New England and Williamstown is only 13 miles south of Bennington, Vermont, and 20 miles north of Pittsfield, the same lodging base could be used for Rides 1, 23, and 24. The 1896 House is located on US Route 7/Route 2 south of Williamstown (888-999-1896; www.1896house.com). Most of the rooms are situated on the far side of a bubbling brook, but splurge and

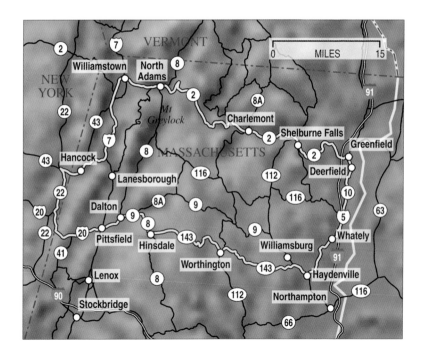

Riders take in the scenic views at a turn-off on the Mohawk Trail.

get one of the period-themed "Barnside" luxury suites attached to the pub, each of which showcases a different historical period; mine was Georgian-themed, with elegantly carved furniture, brass appointments, and seafaring paintings characteristic of the revolutionary era. For the sake of clarity, this ride begins nearby, at the small green in Williamstown where US Route 7 merges with Route 2 and beautiful homes and spacious lawns bespeak old money.

Williamstown is dominated by Williams College, a small liberal arts school with a distinctive pedigree that includes its being one of the rare American colleges whose programs are modeled after the tutorial system common to Oxford and Cambridge Universities. In addition to the art museum at the college itself, Williamstown is home to the Sterling and Francine Clark Art Institute (225 South St.; 413-458-2303; www.clarkart.com), a world-class collection of European and American art from the 15th to 19th centuries. Relying solely on their own taste and judgment, Clark (a former soldier and heir to the Singer Sewing Machine fortune) and his wife amassed an enviable breadth and depth of work. The pantheon of French Impressionists is especially well-represented, as are the works of portrait painter John Singer Sargent, and American modernists Mary Stevenson Cassatt, Frederic Remington, and Winslow Homer—but really, there will be an iconic piece absolutely everywhere you look.

From Williamstown, Route 7 will be a rural two-laner, with an occasional third lane for ascending the grades along the Berkshires. You could simply continue south on US Rte 7 to Pittsfield, but the left onto Brodie Mountain Road has more to offer, since it cuts over the Taconic Mountains to join Route 43 in Hancock before crossing into New York. From there, you'll make a left turn onto Route 22 south to reach US Route 20, and a nice series of sweeping turns will take you back over the Taconic Mountains

FROM WILLIAMSTOWN, MASSACHUSETTS

0	From the green in Williamstown, ride south on US Rte 7/Rte 2
2.2	Straight to continue on US Rte 7
10.8	Bear right onto Brodie Mtn. Rd.
14.1	Left onto Rte 43 (Hancock Rd.)
16.7	Enter New York State
18.3	Hard left onto Rte 22 south
24.0	Left onto Old Rte 20
24.3	Left onto US Rte 20 (east)
25.9	Enter Massachusetts
28.8	Entrance to the Hancock Shaker Village
33.5	In downtown Pittsfield, left onto US Rte 7 (north)
33.7	Bear right when rounding the oval green onto Rte 9
36.9	Bear right onto Rte 9/Rte 8 (Dalton Ave.)
39.3	In Dalton, bear right (straight) onto Rte 8 (Main St.)
42.9	In Hinsdale, left onto Rte 143 (Maple St.)
55.3	In Worthington, left onto Rte 143/Rte 112
56.2	Bear right (straight) to continue on Rte 143 (Williamsburg Rd.)
67.4	Right onto Rte 9 into Williamsburg
69.9	In Haydenville, left onto High St. (becomes Mountain St. (north) and then Haydenville Rd.)
76.5	In Whately, left onto Chestnut Plain Rd.
76.7	Bear right onto Depot Rd./Christian Ln.
77.3	Left onto US Rte 5/Rte 10 (north)
84.1	Left onto Old Main St. into Deerfield
85.3	Left onto US Rte 5/Rte 10 (north)
88.0	In downtown Greenfield, left (west) onto Rte 2A
89.2	Second right on roundabout onto Rte 2 (Mohawk Trail, west)
89.2	In Greenfield, west on Rte 2 (Mohawk Trail) at Exit 26 of I-91
97.6	Left onto S. Maple St. into Shelburne Falls
97.9	Left onto Bridge St.
98.3	[Water St. (right, for parking); Deerfield Ave. (left, for potholes)]
98.4	Right onto State St. (one end of Bridge of Flowers)
99.1	Left onto Rte 2 (Mohawk Trail)
108.7	[Pass Zoar Rd. for the Hoosac Tunnel]
121.6	[Hairpin sweeper]
124.5	[Right for Natural Bridge; EXTREME Caution on this corner]
125.4	[MASS MoCA is on the right (Marshall St.) in downtown North Adams]
126.5	[Notch Rd. is on the left; Mt. Greylock Reservation]
130.7	Arrive Rte 2 at US Rte 7 at the green in Williamstown. Left on South St. for the Clark Art Institute ∎

and into Massachusetts. Note that the junction of US Route 20 and Route 41 at the Hancock Shaker Village (800-817-1137; www.hancockshakervillage. org) is the best place to link into Ride 24 through the southern Berkshires.

Established as the third of nineteen Shaker settlements built in the fifty or so years following the American Revolution, the faithful residents of Hancock lived according to the tenets of equality, simplicity, celibacy, and communal living espoused by their founder, Mother Ann Lee. Known for their dairy and the raising and selling of garden seeds, the early Shakers prospered, their community peaking at around 300 members and 3,000 acres before the influence of western expansion and the Industrial Revolution offered young folks more enticing options.

In spite of their traditional outlook, Shakers embraced such labor-saving modern conveniences as water piped indoors, and dumbwaiters to pass dishes between dining room and kitchen. The two most famous of the many extant buildings on site are beautiful examples of the Shaker's use of

Although the iconic Round Stone Barn at the Hancock Shaker Village made labor more efficient, safe, and clean, the design wouldn't become popular until decades after this one was built in 1826.

space, light, and ventilation, and they showcase the sorts of creature comforts we can appreciate. The great Round Stone Barn built in 1826 consists of four concentric rings that made their labor as efficient, safe, and clean as they could possibly imagine it. The Brick Dwelling once housed more than 100 brothers and sisters, with separate doors and staircases for each so they would not have to pass in close proximity. Whether it is the overall level of workmanship found in the most utilitarian of Shaker items or a fascination with the structure of this communal lifestyle, most will find something of interest here.

Where the traffic comes from is uncertain, but it certainly seems to arrive in Pittsfield, the county seat and largest city in the Berkshires (though it ranks third overall in western Massachusetts, behind Springfield and Chicopee). It is currently undergoing a renaissance of sorts, and has garnered all sorts of national accolades in recent years for such varied attributes as its security, small business climate, green policies, retirement opportunities, and appreciation of the humanities and sciences. And I'll bet there's one more thing you may not know about Pittsfield: a document was found there in 2004, known as the Broken Window By-Law, which in 1791 prohibited the playing of baseball within 80 yards of the meeting house, and which may very well be the earliest known reference to our national pastime.

Route 2 doesn't lack for curves, especially on the descent into North Adams.

The famous Route 2 hairpin on the west side of the Berkshires may be wide, but it can be strewn with loose stone from the restaurant driveway.

Herman Melville and his family lived in Pittsfield from 1850 to 1863 and his former home, Arrowhead (780 Holmes Rd.), is open to the public. The rounded snow-covered hump of Mount Greylock looming daily on the horizon is said to have been Melville's inspiration for the great white whale in *Moby-Dick*. Although this epic novel is now regarded as an American classic, it was very poorly received in its day, earning its author only $556 and failing to sell through its initial printing of 3,000 copies. It took the nascent Modernist movement that followed the cultural upheaval of WWI to appreciate its disparate, kaleidoscopic style and sweeping ambition—and which, in hindsight, may have been Melville's prescient and multi-layered foreshadowing of the American Civil War. The easiest way to reach Arrowhead would be to travel south on US Route 20/US Route 7 about three miles and then turn left onto Holmes Road.

From Pittsfield, take Route 9 to Route 8 to Route 143 and back to Route 9 again. Roads follow the contours of the land—in this case, the glacially sculpted and highly eroded Berkshire Mountains. The highways follow water courses while passing through small villages and past the occasional farm. Although route signs might sometimes cause you to suspect you've been going in a circle, it'll simply be a case of having more than a single option when riding west to east. Your route takes advantage of the great curves and minimal traffic of High Street and Mountain Road to reach US Route 5/Route 10 in Whately.

Ride 25 could be easily reached by following Route 116 east from South Deerfield, but this ride brings you to Old Deerfield Village (www.historic-deerfield.org). Deerfield was a frontier town in the 1600s, and during the French and Indian Wars, a party of about 300 Indians led by French officers raided the settlement at dawn on February 29, 1704. Fifty-six settlers were killed and more than 100 taken prisoner and marched back to Canada. Although forty percent of Deerfield was burned to the ground, the village endured.

The Stebbins House (c. 1799 and open to the public) is one of the few surviving residences designed by Asher Benjamin, a prolific colonial "housewright" whose popular and accessible handbooks of architectural plans would come to define the iconic look of New England villages prior to the Civil War. The First Church of Deerfield (c. 1824) has its original pews, gallery, and pulpit. Other Deerfield homes hold treasures for anyone interested in history or interior design; among other things, you might discover an excellent collection of 19th-century silver and pewter, a textile museum, and the notable Frank L. Boyden Carriage collection.

The most popular motorcycle touring road in the Berkshires—perhaps in all of the state—would be the Mohawk Trail. I happen to prefer riding east to west on this highway, but this is probably due to repetitive conditioning during my formative years. Whether migrating from Ride 2, Ride 9, or Ride 25, you'll pick up Route 2 in Greenfield at Exit 26 of I-91.

The Mohawk Trail crosses the Deerfield River at the junction of Zoar Road.

Dating back to the melting of the glaciers thousands of years ago, potholes were slowly carved into the bedrock by swirling eddies of abrasive sand and gravel.

During the 18th and 19th centuries, waterfalls on the Deerfield River provided the motive power that allowed Shelburne Falls to host industries that flourished for 150 years. The only company from that era to have survived into contemporary times was Lamson & Goodnow, perhaps best known today for their cutlery and tableware. Patriarch Silas Lamson, however, had revolutionized agriculture in 1834 by re-inventing the scythe with a long, curved double-handled shaft, which not only afforded more leverage than a traditional sickle, it also let one work standing upright. Over the years, the company has taken turns in other ventures that have included sewing machines, rifles, and machine tools.

There are two sites of special interest in Shelburne Falls: one is above the river and the other often beneath it. The latter are glacial potholes, perfectly round holes worn into the solid bedrock by powerful swirling eddies of water carrying abrasive sand and stones. Although often attributed to glacial runoff that occurred thousands of years ago, the process is still taking place, albeit at a much slower rate. I played in these potholes as a child, but they have since been blocked off and can only be admired from an observation platform. Perhaps the main tourist attraction in Shelburne Falls is the Bridge of Flowers, an abandoned trolley span that was transformed into a garden in 1929 and has been maintained by the local Women's Club ever since. From April's tulips to October's mums, this lush linear arboretum blooms in fragrant abundance. It may not exactly fit the stereotypical idea of a biker destination, but there are always motorcycles in the parking lot.

Just west of Charlemont at the Deerfield River will be the turn onto Zoar Road, which leads to River Road and the eastern end of the Hoosac Tunnel, a piece of New England history and still the longest active transportation

Mount Greylock Reservation

One of the most popular motorcycle destinations in Massachusetts is the summit of Mount Greylock, from which you can see five states on a clear day. Both access roads, from Route 2 in North Adams or US Route 7 in Lanesborough, wind beneath a forest canopy along miles of narrow, deliciously curvy asphalt. The posted speed limit within the reservation is 25 mph, but the road is still fun even at that speed.

The Mount Greylock State Reservation was created in 1898 as the state's first public land devoted to forest preservation, but it was a popular destination long before that. Henry David Thoreau's solitary overnight excursion on the summit has been credited with inspiring his experiment in self-sufficiency the following year on Walden Pond. A midnight hike of Nathaniel Hawthorne's, in which he observed a burning lime kiln, gave birth to his story, "The Unpardonable Sin." And it was on a summer outing to the peak that Herman Melville first made his acquaintance, later crediting Hawthorne's literary darkness as having had a profound effect in shaping his masterpiece, *Moby-Dick,* whose eponymous cetacean was itself inspired by the pale, saddleback profile of Mount Greylock breaching above the Berkshires.

The glaciation that rounded and wore down the upheaved bulk of Greylock left behind the balanced rock on its west side, known as an "erratic," since its composition is markedly different than the native bedrock on which it has come to rest. The U-shaped valley on the western flank of the mountain, known as The Hopper, is the southernmost glacial cirque in New England.

Man has also strived to leave his lasting mark on this hill. The 93-foot granite lighthouse memorializing the Massachusetts War Veterans was originally intended for a site on the Charles River in Boston. From the observation deck, you'll have a 360-degree panoramic view of the Berkshires, Taconic, and Green Mountain ranges. The rustic Bascom Lodge (413-743-1591; www.bascomlodge.net), constructed by the Civilian Conservation Corps between 1932 and 1938 of local stone and red spruce, is unique enough to require reservations months in advance. For parking, restrooms, and information, seek out the Mount Greylock Information Center on the southern side of the mountain, one and a half miles from Route 7.   ∎

As motorcyclists are discovering, the Bridge of Flowers in Shelburne Falls is a perfect excuse to go for a ride.

tunnel east of the Rocky Mountains. The 25,031-foot Hoosac Tunnel took $21,241,842 and 196 lives to build—earning it the nickname, The Bloody Pit, as well as a reputation for being haunted. Begun in 1851 and finished in 1876, it was only 9/16 of an inch out of alignment when the two excavated halves met in the middle—a major engineering feat. You can learn more about the tunnel at the Western Gateway Heritage State Park (115 State St., Bldg. 4) in North Adams.

After crossing the Deerfield River, the Mohawk Trail climbs over the mountains. The scenic pull-off at the Eastern Summit Gift Shop has an expansive view and a couple of coin-operated binoculars. At this point you'll be directly over the Hoosac Tunnel. Then you'll twist down the western side and unkink the famous hairpin to continue a serpentine descent to the former mill town of North Adams. Few major highways are this fun to ride.

If you plan to visit Natural Bridge State Park (0.5 miles north of Rte 2 on Rte 8, turn right onto McCauley Rd.; 413-663-6392; www.mass.gov/dcr/parks/western/nbdg.htm), slow down before making the hairpin turn onto

The 360-degree view from the observation deck at the summit of Mount Greylock takes in the Berkshire, Green, and Taconic Mountain Ranges.

Route 8—the radically banked corner usually has a bit of sand on it. North America's only naturally formed white marble arch was carved by the runoff from melting glaciers.

With more than 100,000 square feet of exhibition and performance space, Mass MoCA is the largest contemporary art museum in the world. Note the famous hanging trees growing upside-down in the courtyard.

Numerous utilitarian factories lie abandoned in North Adams, but during the last decade or so some have begun to be converted into condominiums and art studios. This staid working-class town is becoming transformed into a rather hip urban oasis. The 13-acre campus for the Massachusetts Museum of Contemporary Art (www.massmoca.org) in downtown North Adams, created from 19th-century mill buildings in 1999, is the largest contemporary art museum in the world with 100,000 square feet of space. Needless to say, there is always a performance or exhibition taking place within those brick walls.

As you leave North Adams heading toward Williamstown, you'll notice a brown-and-white sign for the Mount Greylock State Reservation. Notch Road at the northern entrance leads to the summit of the highest mountain in the Bay State. Located between Mount Fitch to the north and Saddle Ball on the south, the ridgeline that includes the 3,498-foot peak of Mount Greylock is the only place in Massachusetts where you can find a sub-alpine forest of balsam fir and red spruce, while lower slopes sport northern hardwoods, including 555 acres of old growth.

Entering Williamstown, the change in architecture will be striking, revealing a sense of the economic and social differences that have always existed between these two northern Berkshire towns. Going around the tree-filled oval green will put you onto Route 7 south heading back to the 1896 House.

Ride 24 Southern Berkshire Loop

Distance: *At least 136 miles and four hours if you don't stop. Realistically this is an all-day ride.*

Highlights: *Roads are narrow to wide, straight to curvey, and flat to mountainous, through a major urban center and small towns. "Newport of the North" mansions, the studios of Norman Rockwell and Daniel Chester French, Indian motorcycles, antique firearms, Basketball Hall of Fame, and much more.*

The logical places to make your base camp for touring the Berkshires would be downtown Springfield, Great Barrington, or Pittsfield—the latter of which was chosen for this trip. From Pittsfield, all roads lead to Great Barrington, or so it seems. Route 7 is the shortest, quickest, and easiest way to reach that city, but your route takes other roads that are more pleasant and have less traffic.

Begin by taking US Route 20 west from Pittsfield to the Hancock Shaker Village and turning onto Route 41 south, a thoroughly enjoyable touring

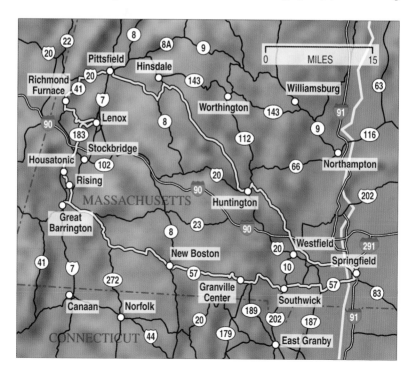

Tanglewood has become the summer home of the Boston Symphony Orchestra and site of the Berkshire Music Festival.

road that runs through West Stockbridge and continues all the way to Great Barrington. However, you are only going to follow it as far as the hamlet of Richmond Furnace, whose name is a reminder that iron was one of the founding industries in the western Berkshires.

When Route 41 crosses the railroad tracks (slow down before the overpass) make an *immediate* left turn onto Lenox Road, which makes a sweeping right corner and then bears right at tiny Fairfield Pond. Don't be alarmed: the rock formation that juts toward the pavement has been painted as a shark head for decades and, so far, no travelers have been attacked. The road will now enter the forest as it climbs the western side of Richmond Mountain, curving delightfully as it crests the ridge and flows downhill.

A few yards to the right on Route 183 will be West Hawthorne Road, which goes past the Tanglewood estate, along the edge of the Stockbridge Bowl—which is a lake—and continues south as Prospect Hill Road into Stockbridge. Bear left onto Route 183 (West Street) and head into downtown Lenox.

Not far from the entrance to Tanglewood is the original site of the family home of Nathaniel Hawthorne, a friend and mentor of Herman Melville who is best known for the two classic novels he wrote while living in Lenox: *The House of Seven Gables* and *The Scarlet Letter.* It was also where Hawthorne finished *A Wonder Book* and *Twice-Told Tales,* and began *Tanglewood Tales.* You'd think he might have been a long-time resident, but he lived here with his family from the spring of 1850 to November 1851, a mere 18 months.

FROM PITTSFIELD, MASSACHUSETTS

0	From US Rte 7 in Pittsfield, west on US Rte 20 (W. Housatonic St.)
4.2	Left (south) onto Rte 41
9.3	Hard left onto Lenox Rd.
11.2	Bear left to continue on Lenox Rd. to Richmond Mtn. Rd.
13.7	Bear left (straight) onto Rte 183 (West St.) into Lenox
15.3	Arrive in downtown Lenox at the monument; south onto Old Stockbridge Rd.
15.6	Bear right onto Hawthorne St.
17.0	Right onto W. Hawthorne Rd.
17.3	[Pass Tanglewood on right]
17.7	Left onto Rte 183
21.7	Straight across Rte 102 [left for downtown Stockbridge]
22.4	[Entrance to the Norman Rockwell Museum is on left]
23.0	[Christian Hill Rd. leads to Chesterwood]
25.5	[Through Housatonic]
25.8	Left at Park St.; through the underpass; over the bridge
27.8	[Division St. (right) leads to the Guthrie Center]
28.7	Right (south) onto US Rte 7 (Stockbridge Rd.)
30.1	[Intersection of Rte 23]
30.6	Arrive at US Rte 7 in Great Barrington

CONTINUING FROM GREAT BARRINGTON

30.6	From US Rte 7 in Great Barrington, east on Rte 23 (State Rd.)
34.7	Bear right onto Rte 57/Rte 183
40.7	Bear left onto Rte 57 (New Marlborough-Sandsfield Ctr. Rd.)
62.4	[Rte 189 is a shortcut to Granby, Connecticut, and Ride 26]
68.9	In Southwick, left onto Rte 57/US Rte 202/Rte 10
69.5	Right to continue on Rte 57
71.6	[N. Longyard Rd. is a shortcut to Leg 3 of this ride]
75.0	Right ramp to continue on Rte 57 (east) to Springfield
80.2	Third right on roundabout onto US Rte 5 north
81.2	First right on roundabout across Memorial Bridge/Connecticut River; proceed straight onto Boland Way; go under I-91
81.7	Right onto Main St. in downtown Springfield
81.9	Left (2nd left) onto State St.
82.2	Left (1st left after crossing Chestnut St.) onto Elliot St.
82.4	Left (no option) onto Edwards St. (one-way)
82.4	Arrive at Springfield Museums in the Quadrangle

(continued)

CONTINUING FROM SPRINGFIELD

82.4	From the Springfield Museums parking lot, left onto Edwards St.
82.5	Right onto Chestnut St. (immediately get in the left lane)
82.5	Left onto Harrison Ave.; it becomes Boland Way; then straight across Memorial Bridge
83.2	First right on roundabout onto ramp for US Rte 5 (north)
84.5	Third right on roundabout onto US Rte 20 (Park St.) (west)
84.7	Right to continue on US Rte 20 (Elm St.)
84.8	Bear left to continue on US Rte 20 (Westfield St.)
89.9	Right onto Union St.
92.2	Left onto US Rte 202/Rte 10 (south)
92.3	Right onto Pochassic St. (don't cross the Westfield River)
92.4	First right on roundabout onto Montgomery St. to Main Rd.
103.8	Left onto Rte 112 into Huntington
105.1	Right onto Basket St.
105.3	Bear left (straight) onto Old Chester Rd. to Cook Hill Rd.
106.7	Bear right (straight) onto Cook Hill Rd. to Skyline Trail
125.4	Hard left onto Rte 8 (Washington Rd.) (south)
127.7	Hard right onto Pittsfield Rd. to Kirchner Rd. to Williams St.
135.0	Bear right onto High St.; immediately bear left onto Appleton Ave.
135.5	Left (2nd left) onto E. Housatonic St.
135.9	Arrive at US Rte 7/US Rte 20 in Pittsfield ■

After turning south onto Route 183 (Interlaken Road), you'll see on top of the hill to your right an expanse of lawn that could double as a golf course. Once Andrew Carnegie's Shadowbrook estate, it is now the Kripalu Center for Yoga & Health, the largest residential center for holistic health in North America.

Farms, rural residences, and patches of forest will make this an easy cruise along a road that was established a couple hundred years ago. After crossing under I-90, it intersects Route 102. You might be tempted to make a left turn to explore Stockbridge, the small village that has always seemed to be the center of the Berkshires, before returning to Route 183.

US Route 7 and Route 102 briefly merge to form Main Street in Stockbridge (pop. 1,947). This village can become absolutely jammed with tourists and traffic during the summer; it's not at all like the laid-back vibe of Lenox. Situated on the intervale between the Berkshires and the Housatonic River, Stockbridge has been famous for different things during different generations. You might want to find a restaurant for lunch, but don't look for Alice's; that's long gone.

Stockbridge was the home of the so-called Stockbridge Indians, members

Lenox

Because of the many grand Gilded Age mansions which still exist in Lenox, the town used to be known as the Inland Newport. To orient yourself, consider beginning your exploration of Lenox at the Museum of the Gilded Age (10 Walker St.; www.gildedage.org) in Ventfort Hall, the Jacobean Revival-style mansion built by Sarah Morgan, sister of J. Pierpont Morgan, in 1891.

The red sandstone and brick mansion may look familiar: it was featured as St. Cloud's Orphanage in the movie *Cider House Rules*. Entering through the portico where Victorian ladies and gentlemen once debarked from horse-drawn carriages, the dark wood and heavy window drapes stand in gloomy contrast to the elegance of the grand hall and dining room, but the imposing style would have helped to keep the summer heat at bay. Modern tastes will find the gracious rear porch, with its canvas awnings, brown wicker furniture, and graceful bronze statues of ballet dancers on the stairway posts much more appealing. Special exhibits upstairs highlight such things as room interpretations and Victorian fashion.

Another mansion open to the public is The Mount (at the junction of Rtes 7 and 7A; 413-551-5111; www.edithwharton.org), the estate owned by Edith Wharton, who became the first woman to receive the Pulitzer Prize for fiction for *The House of Mirth*. The more than 40 titles written by Wharton include *Decoration of Homes* and *Italian Villas and Their Gardens,* so it comes as no surprise that she designed the estate's formal gardens as well as the massive green-shuttered neoclassical house, blending French, Italian, and Georgian influences. Note that there is a quarter-mile walk from the gravel parking lot to reach the house, but it is well worth the effort.

(continued)

Ventfort Hall is home to the Museum of the Gilded Age in Lenox.

Edith Wharton designed the house and gardens at The Mount.

Lenox (continued)

Prestigious luxury can still be found today in Lenox—for a fee. The Winthrop Estate, a historic vacation home, can be rented for as little as $2,600 a night during mid-week of the low season, but could easily set you back ten grand a night during the summer. Rooms at the Blantyre estate, which has been transformed into one of the top-ranked hotels in the country, run $750–$1,400 a night. There are other mansions that remain private, similarly shielded from public view by an indecent amount of forested land, as well as numerous fine inns only somewhat less palatial than the Gilded Age mansions.

Lenox itself (pop. 5,077) feels rather small, its downtown a tranquil place with a smattering of interesting small shops and sculpture placed along the sidewalks. For coffee, pastry, and paninis, try Shots Café (27 Housatonic St. at Church St.; 413-637-1055) or settle in over well-crafted fare to people-watch from the porch of the Church Street Café (65 Church St.; 413-637-2745), where much of the rustic decor has been repurposed. Hardwood flooring shows evidence of its prior life as shipping material for railroad tracks. The seats of the iconic and durable aluminum Emeco chairs, originally designed for the Navy in 1946, were reputed to have been molded from Betty Grable's behind.

From Lenox you could continue south on Route 7 to Stockbridge, but the recommended route follows the more quiet Route 183 by taking Old Stockbridge Road south from the monument downtown, bearing right onto Hawthorne Street, and taking a right onto Hawthorne Road to rejoin Route 183 only two-tenths of a mile south of Richmond Road. ∎

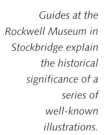

Guides at the Rockwell Museum in Stockbridge explain the historical significance of a series of well-known illustrations.

of the Mahican tribe who allied themselves with the British during the French and Indian Wars and tried adapting to European ways as settlers moved into the area in the 1780s. Despite—or because of—their legal treaties, they were forced to move to central New York and later to Wisconsin. Give pause at the Indian Burial Ground on Main Street to ponder the fact that legal issues between the tribe and the government have yet to be resolved.

Naumkeag (5 Prospect Hill Rd.; 413-298-3239), a 44-room Shingle-style cottage (c. 1885) situated on the edge of downtown Stockbridge, is an especially good early example of this New England style of architecture, with its cross-gables, multi-level eaves, and emphasis on horizontal continuity and visually taut facades, in direct contrast to Victorian ornamentation. Built for Joseph Choate, U.S. Ambassador to England from 1899 to 1905, and his wife, Caroline, who was an artist, Naumkeag's renowned formal gardens were expanded by their daughter Mabel and landscape architect Fletcher Steele. The repeating circular motifs reach their apogee at the Blue Steps, a terraced staircase of fountain pools through a steep birch grove. You could spend hours enjoying those eight blooming acres—don't say I didn't warn you.

Norman Rockwell lived in Stockbridge from 1953 until his death in 1978, and the museum dedicated to his body of work is located on Route 183 just south of Route 102 (9 Glendale Rd./Rte 183; 413-298-4100; www.nrm.org). The easiest way to reach it from downtown Stockbridge would be by following West Main Street, which becomes Glendale Middle Road; turn right (north) and the second right turn will be the driveway into the museum. Knowledgeable tour guides are always ready to explain the relevance and context of the Rockwell paintings and illustrations on exhibit. Just down the hill beyond sight of the museum is the artist's studio, where his brushes, paints, books, easel, and personal effects provide an intimate glimpse into a well-documented creative process that typically used local models and detailed sets and props.

Just south of the Rockwell Museum is Chesterwood (4 Williamsville Rd.; 413-298-3579; chesterwood.org), the primary residence and studio of sculptor Daniel Chester French, who summered among the art and intellectual elite of Augustus Saint-Gaudens's Cornish Colony. Turn right onto Christian Hill Road, directly opposite Glendale Road, and follow the blue-and-white signs.

French was at the forefront of the American Renaissance movement that transformed neo-classical forms into more realistic, natural ones—characteristics that are hallmarks of his work, which include the rumpled-and-ready looking statue *Minute Man* in Concord, Massachusetts, as well as the careworn, gaunt features of his *Abraham Lincoln* gazing down resolutely from his memorial in Washington, D.C., which was a controversial depiction at the time. There is a life-size study of the latter work in French's studio, along with numerous other bas-reliefs, busts, statues, and maquettes that help to illustrate before your eyes the transition from studied Victorianism to that of Art Nouveau. His final and arguably most beautiful work, *Andromeda* (c. 1929), pays tribute to Greek myth but is wholly modern in style. Carved in flawless white Carrara marble, this realistic nude has always had a home at Chesterwood, though it would be a prize for any of the world's major fine art collections. More than 500 other pieces of sculpture can be discovered along the paths, amid cedar trees, and just about everywhere else you'll look.

From Stockbridge, Route 183 will become pretty laid-back as it follows the slow-moving, iron-brown Housatonic River, ducking beneath the railroad tracks in the village of Housatonic and crossing to the other side of the

The general store is the busiest place in the little ol' town of Stockbridge.

Looking up Railroad Street in Great Barrington.

river. A quick forensic glance would pretty much confirm the same story in many a small town in the Berkshires: settlements were initially established on the rivers where water power allowed small industrial mills to develop and, decades later, railroads were built along the banks of these same rivers to more efficiently bring those mill products to distant markets. The arrival of inexpensive electricity would eliminate the need for water power, while the modern roads and motor transport would render trains obsolete. Without the employment offered by these industries, the vitality of the communities has diminished. Just downriver a bit, however, the village of Risingdale was more fortunate.

A slight increase in elevation along the Housatonic River caused this area to be known as Rising. The topography made it ideal for constructing a dam to increase drop (water pressure = power) and create a reservoir (a liquid "battery") for industrial use. The Rising Paper Company, established in

The site of the Thanksgiving Day Massacree (as told by Arlo Guthrie) is now the multi-denominational Guthrie Center.

1876, was less susceptible than other mills to the downsides of electrification, since it also required large volumes of water as part of its production process. Although it evolved successfully to create specialty art and technical papers from recycled materials, this attractive brick factory with its Italian-style towers finally closed its doors for good in 2011.

Once the home of Alice and Ray Brock, the Old Trinity Church in Great Barrington became a place of folk legend when one of Ray's students at the Stockbridge School turned the story of Thanksgiving dinner into a wild spoken monologue strung together with a catchy, repetitive ragtime riff to create the ballad we all have come to know as "Alice's Restaurant Massacree." The old church—turn right onto Division Street by the Taft Farm—is now the Guthrie Center (www.guthriecenter.org), a multi-cultural, non-denominational place of worship.

On the edge of the city of Great Barrington, Route 183 ends at US Route 7, which is the beginning of the second leg of this ride. However, US Route 7/Route 23 (Main Street) continues to the center of Great Barrington, where you'll find an abundance of plebeian lodging and dining, especially north of downtown along Route 7. Worthy of special note for ice cream lovers, though, would be Soco Creamery on Main Street at Railroad Street (www.sococreamery.com), where the ice cream is made in small batches with extraordinary flavors like lavender honey, chai spice, or dirty chocolate. L-shaped Railroad Street is a happening place that's lined with interesting privately-owned boutiques, stores, pubs, restaurants, and even a cinema.

How hip is Great Barrington? Well, they print their own money, which is accepted at almost 400 regional businesses. You can exchange your greenbacks for BerkShares at five different banks at a rate of 95 cents on the dollar, although locals concerned about devaluation have proposed the value of currency be tied to the price of a gallon of maple syrup. Initiated by the New Economic Institute, this highly successful project currently has a few million BerkShares in circulation promoting the local economy.

Great Barrington also has a history it can be proud of. A memorial in front of the town hall commemorates their armed resistance against the British two years prior to the Revolutionary War! Another milestone took place in 1781 when black slave Elizabeth "Mum Bett" Freeman, represented by Tapping Reeve of Litchfield, Connecticut, successfully sued for her freedom in county court. Her legal suit was based on Article 1 of the Massachusetts Constitution which states that, "All men are born free and equal. . ." Also, in 1886 a local mill began generating hydroelectric power to illuminate the lights on Main Street, the first public street in the country to see such amenities.

The next section of this ride follows Route 23 east, then diverges onto Route 183/Route 57. Anyone in a real hurry to reach eastern Massachusetts will be on the Mass Pike (I-90) and truckers absolutely hate the narrow, serpentine track of Route 57 as it cuts across the southern Berkshire Mountains just above the Connecticut state line. Despite the posted speed limits that seem to have been established for slippery winter travel and nervous city drivers, this will be a thoroughly enjoyable motorcycle touring road.

Valleys twist between these low mountains, following the path of least resistance, sometimes going north or south in the course of their eastward journeys. Despite its convoluted path, the road isn't technical and will feel quite benign, when all of a sudden the double yellow line makes a rather tight 90-degree turn to the left. If you're going too fast—what was the speed limit?—your choices will be: 1) to continue straight but overshoot the turn; 2) try to manage an off-road

The bronze plaque commemorating Mum Bett's freedom was missing from the monument in front of city hall during my last visit to GB.

Memorial Bridge over the Connecticut River between Springfield and West Springfield.

excursion through a small hayfield (not advised); or 3) hope that the required lean angle is slightly less than floorboard/peg clearance on your bike.

Along Route 57 there will be some great sweeping corners, elevation changes, narrow ravines, and miles of pavement through forest where there's not a single house to be seen—all interspersed with a few small farms, rural residential homes, and villages so small you could count the number of commercial establishments on one hand, if you needed to.

The highway snakes out of the Berkshires along Granville Gorge to enter the populated Connecticut Valley. As you enter urban Southwick, farmland will be overtaken with strip development. Route 57 finally becomes an expressway in Feeding Hills, leading to US Route 5 and the Connecticut River at Springfield. From this point, a quick glance at a map would reveal many ways to connect this route to a number of adjacent rides in this book.

You can't do everything in Springfield in a day; there are just too many interesting things to see. Springfield is a maze of highways but these directions will show you the quickest and easiest way to reach the Springfield Museums: Exit Route 57 onto US Route 5 north (if you miss this exit, you'll cross the Connecticut River and must take East Columbus Avenue north alongside I-91). Take the first right at the rotary, cross Memorial Bridge, then take your first right onto Main Street (along-

"If you never did, you should. These things are fun and fun is good. —Dr. Seuss

side I-91). The second left will be State Street, which you'll follow through downtown; as you begin to climb the hill, look for Elliot Street—the next left past Chestnut Street—then go past the marble facade of the library. Elliot is not a thru-street so you must turn left onto one-way Edwards Street instead. You will have just ridden around three sides of The Quadrangle.

The Springfield Museums (21 Edwards; 800-625-7738; www. springfieldmuseums.org) are comprised of four buildings on a courtyard that is a memorial to native son Theodor Seuss Geisel—a.k.a. Dr. Seuss. The fifth building is located across the street from the museum parking lot, which is secure—and free. The Smith Art Museum contains plaster casts of Renaissance masterpieces, like *Venus de Milo,* and *Discobolus,* as well as Victorian collections of oddities brought back to their communities by the wealthy and well-traveled for the benefit of those who would never partake of a Grand Tour of Europe, long the fashionable way for those of means to finish their education. The largest collection of Japanese armor outside Japan resides here—encased, but otherwise displayed as originally intended, without interpretation, explanation, or historical context.

The grey granite Art Deco D'Amour Museum of Fine Art exhibits the work of a long list of famous early American and European painters, giving a visitor a rare opportunity in this day of instant virtual artwork to get a feeling for the people and influences that have come to shape our collective visual vocabulary. Reproductions consistently fail to show the subtleties of

The Indian Scout was one of the best models ever produced by the company. Note the drive arrangement on the hill climber in the background.

A rack of rifles in the Springfield Armory, where they manufactured their namesake firearm.

the emotional and atmospheric effects that Claude Monet (whose 1874 painting *Impression, Sunrise* coined the term Impressionism) was attempting to convey in his experimental series *Haystacks,* painted in a field near his home in Giverny, France. Examples in the Smith's permanent collection show the variations of this painter's style at different times in his life. In addition, paintings such as Renoir's 1873 *Monet Painting in His Garden at Argenteuil,* give us a glimpse of the lens through which he viewed his friend.

Of the remaining museums on The Quad, the Lyman & Merrie Wood Museum of Springfield History deserves special note. Springfield has always been at the fore of manufacturing, its armory being among the first to adopt and disseminate the American System for the machine production of precision parts. The first production automobile, the Duryea (c. 1893–95), was also made here, along with the historic Knox car (1900–1914), the last of the Dupont luxury cars (1931–32), and the only Rolls Royces assembled on foreign soil (1921–1931). The second floor of this museum is occupied by what are, by contrast, among the most famous of Springfield's historic industries: Smith & Wesson Firearms and the Indian Motocycle Company— no "r" in the company name.

If you'd ever made the pilgrimage to Springfield to the wonderfully chaotic and overly stuffed Indian Motocycle Museum when it was in its old digs on Hendee Street, you should revisit the machines in their spruced-up, spacious new home. Sequential exhibits will take you step by step through the various eras of this iconic company and its racing history, including some forgotten chapters about Indian's forays into things like outboard motors, aircraft engines, and automobile shock absorbers. Some of the vintage photographs and advertising from Esta Manthos's original collection have made the cut, but sadly missing from the professional presentation are the mountains of toys, tchotchkes, trinkets. and gewgaws—along with the irascible and inimitable hostess herself.

As with art, a little context can make a world of difference in one's understanding and appreciation. For example, the 1917 Model "O"—derisively nicknamed Model Zero for its low power output— had opposed, horizontal cylinders more than a decade before the first BMW, but its potential success was never realized. With the founders long gone, the corporate marketing department, which lacked engineering experience, favored economical bikes like those being manufactured in war-torn Europe. The U.S. market, however, was clamoring for more ponies. Among the more esoterically fascinating machines are a shaft-drive military Model 841 with an opposed horizontal engine, a 1945 Eliason motor toboggan powered by an Indian engine, a 1949 Arrow with retractable skis, and the only known surviving example of an Indian roadster.

As mentioned, Indian shares its exhibition space with part of Smith & Wesson's extensive firearms collection—which is impressive—but only a small sampling of what you are going to find at the Springfield Armory up the hill. Not only was this where they manufactured their eponymous rifles, it was where the American method of manufacturing began to be disseminated, a sharing of technical knowledge and practices that transformed our nation into an industrial player. Before you visit the firearms, note Thomas Blanchard's copy lathe, developed for the making of gunstocks, which was quickly adapted for the mass production of other complicated wooden shapes, such as scythe handles.

If you haven't yet jumped through enough hoops during this visit you might wish to check out the Naismith Memorial Basketball Hall of Fame (877-4-HOOPLA, www.hoophall.com), named for the good doctor who invented the game in Springfield on December 21, 1891. With more than 40,000 square feet of space, the honored inductees currently number 295 individuals and eight teams. There are interactive exhibits and memorabilia, such as celebrity shoes, jerseys, and basketballs. The building is located adjacent to I-91 and is almost impossible to miss.

"Today was good. Today was fun. Tomorrow is another one." –Dr. Seuss

To get back on the road and complete this route, you'll want to pick up US Route 20 heading west. Following Columbus Avenue north beneath I-91, or crossing the Memorial Bridge over the Connecticut River and following US Route 5 north will both take you to US Route 20. The west end of I-291 exits onto either I-91 north or US 20 west. It looks confusing on the map, and traffic won't make it any easier, but if you remember to ride north along the river, the highway signs will guide you.

The Mass Pike (I-90) west to Stockbridge is the quickest and easiest way to return to Pittsfield, though it is a toll road. If you'll be riding after sunset, I'd recommend it, since it would eliminate miles of urban riding. You could resume the section of this route taking Exit 3 from I-90 onto US Route 202/Route 10 south, then making a right onto Pochassic Street to connect with Montgomery Road (turn right at the roundabout). From Westfield, continue to follow Montgomery Road, then Main Road to the village of Huntington and the Skyline Trail. Along the way you'll have the pleasure of elevation changes and corners, a welcome after the pace of city traffic.

No visit to Springfield would be complete without a passing nod to the Naismith Memorial Basketball Hall of Fame.

Turning south onto Route 112, you won't be able to shift into third gear before reaching the Huntington Country Store (413-667-3232; www.huntingtoncountrystore.com), a preferred stop on another popular motorcycle touring road in western Massachusetts. Enjoy some ice cream or coffee and the store's signature pastry, the Wrapple. Originally made using apples and cinnamon sugar, you can now have your choice of fruity filling, but the sugar drizzle across the top comes standard on all models.

The Skyline Trail is one of the lesser-known touring roads, with wildlife that is abundant even during the light of day, so don't do this one at night. Cutting through the mountains, Skyline Trail is somewhat of a secret and that is why you never see mention of it in print. Forest, farms, a few residential houses, and almost no traffic is what you can expect on this local road. It is just one of an entire network that crisscrosses the convoluted topography of the central Berkshires—a good enough reason to keep returning year after year.

Ride 25 **Central Massachusetts**

Distance: *187 miles, but with stops and exploration, this is a one- or two-day trip.*

Highlights: *Forest, fields, towns, and cities. Walden Pond; the site where the first shots of the American Revolution were fired; the grave sites of Emerson, Thoreau, Hawthorne, and Alcott; Old Sturbridge Village; and perhaps Brimfield during one of its antique shows.*

This trip begins near the airport in Orange, Massachusetts, Although far from the capitol of Massachusetts, nearby Quabbin Reservoir is the water supply for Boston, and the largest body of fresh water in the state. An earthen dam a half-mile long and 170 feet high was built between 1936 and 1939, allowing the water from the Swift River to fill the valleys and submerge several towns. There are few access points, and since this area is re-

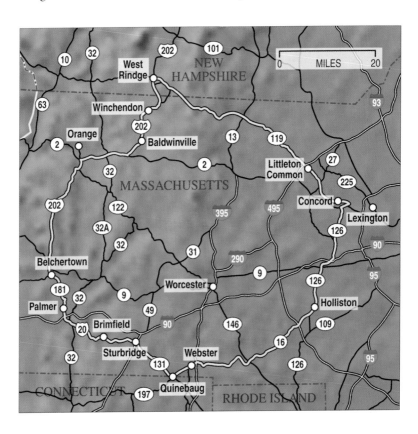

stricted, it now abounds with wildlife—including bald eagles, bear, moose, bobcat, coyotes, and deer—so riding US Route 202 at night requires vigilance.

Once on Route 181 in Belchertown, the nature of the road will change to the rural residences, small farms, and villages typical of central Massachusetts. Your route will join US Route 20 in the village of Palmer. This would be the obvious highway to take if you plan to link Ride 24 to this one, since most of the heavy traffic will be on I-90. Note, however, that there will be three crazy weeks each year when US Route 20 will become absolutely jammed: one of the largest antique shows in the United States takes place in Brimfield during mid-May, mid-July, and early September. These five-day events are actually comprised of some 20 different venues in fields along a single mile of Route 20. It's a heck of an experience, if you are into collectables and such, but not one that I'd seek out on a motorcycle.

When last I rode through this stretch of US Route 20, a tornado had just ripped a giant weed-whacked swath of trashed landscapes and pine trees snapped into kindling—yet there were leaves on the trees just beyond the margins of the destruction. Chippers and chainsaws had already begun to restore some order, and you can note the progress of the recovery on your trip. Fortunately the destruction ended just a few miles before Old Sturbridge Village.

Sturbridge (pop. 9,268) was founded in 1738, but Old Sturbridge Vil-

A bluebird day along the Quabbin Reservoir.

FROM ORANGE, MASSACHUSETTS

0	From Exit 15 of Rte 2 near the Orange Municipal Airport, south on Rte 122
1.5	Straight to continue on US Rte 202
21.2	Continue on US Rte 202 through the intersection of Rte 9
22.2	In Belchertown, straight onto Rte 181
31.5	In Palmer, bear left onto US Rte 20 (N. Main St.)
32.4	Left to stay on US Rte 20
32.5	Right to continue on US Rte 20
40.3	Stay on US Rte 20 through Brimfield, Massachusetts
46.8	Enter Old Sturbridge Village
47.1	In Sturbridge, bear right onto Rte 131
57.2	In Quinebaug, Connecticut, left (east) onto Rte 197
60.8	In Webster, Massachusetts, straight onto Rte 12
62.5	At Exit 2 of I-95, straight onto Rte 16
92.2	Left onto Rte 126 (Concord St.)
110.8	At Walden Pond State Reservation, right onto Rte 2 (Concord Tpke)
112.4	At Minute Man National Historical Park, left onto Rte 2A (Lexington Rd.)
114.6	At the green in Concord, bear left to stay on Rte 2A/Rte 62 (Elm St)
115.3	Bear right on Rte 2A (Elm St.)
117.2	Second right on roundabout onto Rte 2A/Rte 119
123.9	At Littleton Common, straight on Rte 119 near Exit 31 of I-495
153.0	[Enter New Hampshire]
159.6	In W. Rindge, New Hampshire, left (south) onto US Rte 202
163.3	[Enter Massachusetts]
177.2	Ramp left Exit 19 onto US Rte 202/Rte 2 west
187.0	Arrive at Exit 15 onto Rte 122 near the Orange Municipal Airport ■

lage didn't exist prior to 1946. Built on a farm established in the 1790s, it was originally intended as a place to preserve an extensive collection of antiques owned by George Washington Well, the founder of American Optical Company. Some of the buildings on the site are authentic replicas, but many are original structures that were moved here over ensuing years. Old Sturbridge Village (www.osv.org) is a living history museum depicting life in the years 1790–1840, with costumed interpreters who go about their daily chores while answering visitors' questions. The span of years covered in the village is an especially significant time in New England history, as everyday lives were being reshaped by the improvements in manufacturing, agriculture, transportation, immigration, and urbanization. For example,

At Brimfield, the goods come in all sizes and shapes, from world-class treasures to eclectic junk.

the Shoe Shop accurately portrays a cottage industry that took hold in around 1825 and grew to be a sustaining business in central Massachusetts, second only to the manufacturing of textiles. Uppers were jobbed out to women who stitched them at home, while the soles were pegged in small shops like this one, by young men who'd abandoned their farms for the promise of a lucrative trade they could master in a few weeks. A fast worker back then could complete up to four pairs of shoes a day, earning 25 cents a pair. Shopkeepers, who often supplied all the raw materials, would collect the finished product.

Farms and forests are scattered across the central portion of the Bay State, but homes and businesses tend to be concentrated along the old primary roads. As with most of the historic roads in New England, Route 131 follows the course of a river. Architecture along the way tells the history of the area, especially in towns like Southbridge. Mill owners often made fortunes during the late 19th century when this state was an industrial powerhouse. Public buildings and Victorian-styled homes along main streets reflect times of prosperity. Downtown retail spaces for rent are evidence of harder financial times and the ever-changing landscapes of contemporary commerce.

The four corners in the small village of Quinebaug are just south of the state line in Connecticut. Continuing on Route 131 would connect you with Ride 28 in Rhode Island. Turning left onto Route 197—an old turnpike—will rapidly return you to Massachusetts and into the small city of Webster.

Samuel Slater, the "father" of American industrialism, incorporated the town of Webster (named for his friend, Daniel) when he established several mills here that produced textiles and shoes for 125 years (see also Ride 28). Polish immigrants brought to the United States to fill his rank-and-file founded the oldest Polish-American Catholic Church here and their

Tokens at the headstone of Henry David Thoreau.

descendants still make up about a third of the population in this now medium-sized town. Webster is also the Country Music Capitol of New England, with headline acts—not all of them "country"—performing at Indian Ranch throughout the summer (200 Gore Rd.; www.indianranch.com; 508-943-3871).

Once Route 16 passes east of I-395 it will round the northern extent of Lake Chargoggagoggmanchauggagoggchaubunagungamaugg—the longest place name in the United States—and ease into the Douglas State Forest. Some 20 miles farther on, it cuts across I-495, the ring road around the Boston Metropolitan Area, and continues into the city. This ride, however, departs from Route 16 and heads north on Route 126 just after passing through the village of Holliston. Within only the last few decades, the farms and forests that separated the towns and small cities in this portion of eastern Massachusetts have been supplanted by "rural residential," as developers have taken advantage of the network of interstate highways and the willingness of people to commute for a couple of hours—or more—to work each day. Despite this, there remain watershed areas, state reservations, and land trust properties, along with farmers who resist parceling out their land for development. One of these is the Walden Pond State Reservation.

Henry David Thoreau made this small pond famous when he traveled a few miles south of his home in Concord and built a small cabin on a second-growth woodlot owned by his friend Ralph Waldo Emerson. He lived here two years, two months, and two days (1845–1847) and published his reflections on this experiment in simplicity and self-sufficiency. *Walden: Life in the Woods* has received worldwide acclaim and visitors come from far and wide to visit the reconstructed cabin on its original site. Why all the fuss, you may ask? If you've never read Thoreau, you may be surprised at how well his carefully wrought prose has survived time, to say nothing of the accuracy of his big and small observations about society, wilderness, government, and the role he envisions each should have.

In addition, back in the salad days of this country, Thoreau traveled (on foot) all over many of the wilder places detailed in this book, from the mountains of Maine and New Hampshire to the Berkshires. Mostly published after his death, his minutely detailed journal observations of natural history, weather, the yearly seeding of plants—among so many other things—have helped to make his contemporary reputation.

Today, Walden Pond is a popular swimming and hiking destination, but once the parking area on Route 126 reaches maximum capacity, the state lands are closed for the day. If you plan to visit, be sure to arrive early ($5 parking); the Visitor Center is located on Walden Street in downtown Concord (978-369-3254)

Thoreau, Emerson, Hawthorne, and Louisa May Alcott have each written volumes and, in turn, volumes have been written about each of them. They were at the fore of the American Transcendentalist movement, a revolution in thought that decried the corruption of man's inherently true and good nature by such societal and cultural institutions as organized religion and politics—a philosophy first put forth by Thoreau's benefactor, Ralph Waldo Emerson, in his 1836 essay, "Nature," which was written at the Old Manse in Concord. Alas, all stories must have an end, and the earthly epilogues to the lives of these famed American writers and thinkers can be found on Author's Ridge in Sleepy Hollow Cemetery in the village of Concord. Consecrated by Emerson decades before his own planting there, the design, in keeping with their core beliefs, emphasizes the relationship of the living with their natural world, through the use of organic features and native plants.

The cemetery is located on Bedford Street just a block north of Monument Square. Beyond the second gate, follow the signs for Author's Ridge and turn left at the Y, where you should take a moment to check out the Melvin Memorial, a tribute by a Concord Civil War veteran to his three fallen brothers, all members of the First Massachusetts Heavy Artillery. Actually titled *Mourning Victory,* the granite monument was designed by

The first battle of the American Revolution took place at the site of this reconstruction of the North Bridge in Concord.

Daniel Chester French (see also Rides 9 and 24), who is buried not far away. From this point, turn around and bear left, following the granite markers to the stone steps that mount the rise. Don't expect grand headstones: HENRY is all that marks Thoreau's final resting place in his family's plot not far from Hawthorne's and Emerson's.

At first it seems to be of minor historical importance, but the Concord grape was first cultivated at Grapevine Cottage by Ephraim Bull (also resting at Sleepy Hollow). Don't sneer at this fruity jam-quality grape; without the hardy roots of the Concord you couldn't have chardonnay, riesling, pinots, merlot, cabernet sauvignon, or the other vinifera grapes because these European vines must be grafted to Concord and Niagara roots to resist phylloxera ("root lice") and nematodes. So lift your glass to Mr. Bull or make a peanut butter and jelly sandwich in tribute, but if you stop at Grapevine Cottage (491 Lexington Rd.) please respect that this is a private residence.

Paul Revere didn't quite make it to Concord—he was captured outside of Lexington—but by then everyone knew the British were coming. The famous lantern—"one if by land and two if by sea"—which signaled from the Old North Church now resides in the Concord Museum (on Lexington Rd. at Cambridge Tpke; 978-369-9763; www.concordmuseum.org). About 700 British Army regulars marched on Concord to destroy a cache of military supplies that had been kept there. From the North Bridge rang the "shot heard 'round the world," as 500 militiamen defeated three British companies in a pitched battle on open ground, driving them back toward reinforcements in Lexington, from which they staged a tactical withdrawal to Charlestown. Daniel Chester French's iconic *Minute Man* statue stands by the reconstructed North Bridge.

Follow Main Street/Route 62 out of downtown Concord and bear right onto Elm Street, which merges with Route 2A. Continue on Elm Street/Route 2A/Route 119 at the busy rotary on the outskirts of town. Route 119 is just one of many enjoyable touring roads to be found in northern Massachusetts, but this one leads to southern New Hampshire and returns to the beginning of this ride without going through a major city.

The highway briefly runs along the northeastern edge of Nagog Pond, but the right side of the road borders a shopping mall. What once were rural communities are now essentially suburbs intermixed with surviving small farms and patches of woodlands.

After crossing over I-495 near Littleton Common, the farther north and west you ride, the more rural residential the countryside will become. Crossroad centers like Townsend have retained a sense of community, with an economic and social center that "bedroom communities" seem to lack.

The work of sculptor Daniel Chester French, as shown in his rumpled and ready Minute Man *statue, was part of an American movement that transformed neo-classical forms into more realistic, natural ones*

Businesses are strung along Main Street, with more private "mom and pop" stores than chain franchises.

West of Townsend, the highway will meander through the Willard Brook State Forest with its welcome shade on hot summer days. Riding through the Watatic Mountain Wildlife Area you'll see an occasional farm, but for miles you'll be treated to the pleasure of looking into the forest.

Crossing the state line into New Hampshire, the landscape will return to rural residential. Route 119 actually bends around the settlement of Rindge to intersect with US Route 202. At this point you'll have reached part of Ride 9, but of course there are shortcuts if you plan to head south back into Massachusetts. One would be East Monomonac Road along the eastern side of Lake Monomonac, the other would be to take School Street into downtown Rindge and then make a left onto the old Route 202. Both connect Route 119 to US Route 202.

Heading south, you'll pass through the small towns of Winchendon and Baldwinville, Massachusetts, and the relaxing shade of Templeton State Forest before US Route 202 merges with Route 2, the primary east-west highway that will take you back to the beginning of this loop or to Green-field, Massachusetts, farther west.

Connecticut

"Upon the long river" or Quinatucquet, is what the Native American tribes called the region along what we now know as the Connecticut River. A Dutch explorer who sailed upstream in 1614 naturally claimed it for the Netherlands. His countrymen built a fort near Hartford in 1633, but Puritan settlers breaking away from the Massachusetts Colony established a settlement in Hartford in 1636 and another at New Haven in 1638. Overwhelmed by English colonists, the Dutch abandoned their fort in 1654.

Today we think of this small state as being a mostly urban environment that is economically built upon the insurance industry. With only 4,844 square miles of land and just over 3.5 million residents, however, the majority of people live along the Connecticut River corridor and in the southwest corner of the state. Except for those regions, the landscape tends to be rural, with excellent roads for motorcycle touring.

The first copper mine in colonial America was established in 1705 in

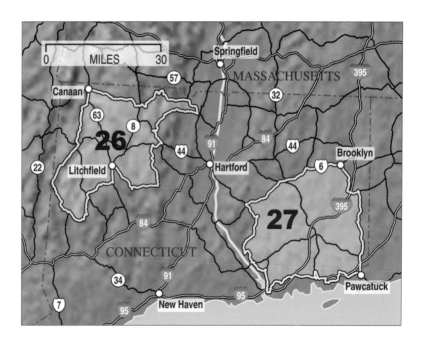

Connecticut. Iron smelting became a major industry in 1762 with the firing of the first blast furnace in Lakeville, a run that lasted until 1925. Quarried limestone was converted to lime to be used as flux, and the hills were denuded of trees for charcoal to fuel the many steps along the way. Streams were dammed to provide power for mills. Connecticut's role as an industrial powerhouse was essential to the revolutionary cause in the late 18th century and the Union Army in the mid-19th. The bucolic countryside you will be enjoying is but a recent incarnation.

The official state animal of Connecticut is the sperm whale, not that any have been seen off its shores in recent years. Sheltered estuaries along the coast, and their proximity to the once-lucrative fishing grounds of Georges Bank, spawned an industry where almost everything was harvested to near extinction. Schooners and square-riggers also maintained a lively trade in goods from around the world.

The legacies of mining, shipping, and manufacturing have been preserved in Connecticut's numerous museums large and small, and though the main trips outlined here avoid the worst of the congestion found around major cities, there is still plenty to be seen and enjoyed from the saddle. Over the years, I've spent extended trips exploring smaller areas even more thoroughly, and would encourage you to do the same, especially on many of the local roads within the circuits of the mapped trips.

Could this be why some roads in Connecticut seem to have exceptionally low posted speed limits?

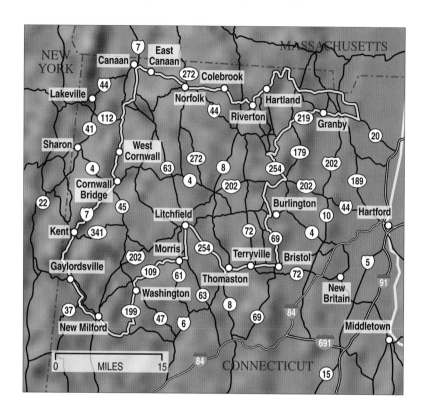

Ride 26 Litchfield Hills

Distance: *160 miles; it can be ridden in just over four hours, but with one or two stops will take all day*
Highlights: *Hilly terrain with river valleys, rural roads with small villages. The American Clock & Watch Museum, Lock Museum of America, New England Air Museum, New-Gate Prison, the Granby Oak, Saville Dam, Connecticut Antique Machinery Museum, Sloane-Stanley Museum, two covered bridges, colonial architecture, and more.*

Northwestern Connecticut offers exceptional touring on local roads, many of which were established during the colonial period. Although highways west of US Route 7 and the Route 37/Route 39 loop between Sherman and New Fairfield aren't described here, these and almost every road within the circular boundary of this ride are thoroughly scenic and enjoyable.

This ride begins in the municipality of Litchfield simply because the

Western Connecticut will be a gentrified series of beautiful farms, rolling fields, stretches of woodland, and nice homes.

majority of roads go through it, but obviously anywhere along this mapped route will be a suitable starting point. You'll begin from the green in this historic village and head toward Thomaston, the city where Seth Thomas established one of the great Connecticut clock manufacturing companies.

Cruising south on Route 254 (Northfield Road), you will get a sense of how "gentrified" western Connecticut has become. Beautiful farms with rolling fields, stretches of wooded areas, and nice residential homes will be the norm. Main Street in Thomaston reveals the first bit of commercialism, but once you cross the river, US Route 6 (Main Street) will become a thread through traditional small towns where things change slowly.

The rise and fall of the clockmaking industry is a signature chapter in Connecticut's history, which begins with the arrival of Englishman Thomas Harland, who set up a prosperous shop in Norwich in 1773 that employed numerous apprentices in the time-consuming hand-crafting and fitting of the pendulum and finicky brass gears of the movement. Twenty years later, after his own apprenticeship, Eli Terry set up a shop and worked at refining a cruder movement of interchangeable gears cut from local hardwoods using water-powered saws, a process that was not only less expensive, it required less skill. His innovations produced a shockingly huge order for 4,000 units, and one of the men he hired was Seth Thomas, who eventually

FROM LITCHFIELD, CONNECTICUT

0	From the green in Litchfield, Connecticut, east on Rte 118 (East St.)
1.0	Right onto Rte 254 (Northfield Rd.)
8.3	In Thomaston, left onto US Rte 6 (S. Main St.)
8.8	Bear right onto US Rte 6; cross the river and go under Rte 8
12.2	[Lock Museum of America in Terryville]
15.8	In Bristol, left (north) onto Rte 69 (Burlington Ave.) [or turn right onto Maple St. for Clock & Watch Museum]
22.8	Right onto Rte 4
23.3	Left onto Covey Rd. in Burlington (the next intersection) to S. East Rd.
27.8	Right onto US Rte 202 (Litchfield Tpke)
31.0	Left onto Rte 179
31.1	Left (north) onto US Rte 44 (Albany Tpke)
35.5	In New Hartford, right onto Rte 219 (Reservoir Rd.)
39.4	[Rte 318 leads to Saville Dam]
42.1	Bear right to stay on Rte 219
47.0	[Day St.—turn left here to visit the Granby Oak (0.8 mi)]
52.2	Left onto Newgate Rd.
54.0	Left onto Copper Hill Rd.
57.5	Continue straight across US Rte 202 onto East St.
59.3	As you cross Rte 189, East St. changes name to Mountain Rd.
63.0	Right onto Rte 20 (Hartland Blvd.)
63.4	In E. Hartland, left, then right to stay on Rte 20
72.0	Right to stay on Rte 20
75.5	In Riverton, right onto Rte 20 (Main St.); cross the bridge
75.6	Straight onto Robertsville Rd.
76.9	Left onto Old Forge Rd.; cross the bridge
77.1	Right onto (another) Robertsville Rd.
77.6	Left onto Rte 8; immediate right onto Deer Hill Rd.
79.1	Right onto Smith Hill Rd.
81.1	At the green in Colebrook, bear left onto Rte 182A (Rockwell Rd.)
82.4	Right (west) onto Rte 182 (Stillman Hill Rd.)
85.2	Right onto US Rte 44
93.8	In Canaan, left onto US Rte 7

(continued)

took his skills to Plymouth Hollow where he was to make his own mark on the industry; clocks made during his lifetime were tagged as manufactured in Plymouth, although the place was renamed Thomaston six years after his death.

From that point on momentum only grew, with a distribution system of peddlers bringing their wares directly to distant farmhouses, where clocks often served more as a modest status symbol than a timepiece. Innovations, intrigue, and opportunity, from the popularization of watches and public clocks, to Mickey Mouse fads, and John Cameron Swayze ads, the rise of clockmaking in the Constitution State was a rollicking ride that was so thoroughly disrupted by World War II that it was never able to regain its pre-war position. To get an even more interesting version of the story, set aside some time to visit the American Clock & Watch Museum in Bristol.

CONTINUING FROM CANAAN

93.8	From Canaan, south on US Rte 7/US Rte 44
106.0	[In W. Cornwall, pass the Cornwall Covered Bridge]
119.4	[In downtown Kent, pass the intersection of Rte 341]
125.9	[Gaylordsville at the bridge]
133.0	Left onto US Rte 202/Rte 67 and cross the bridge into New Milford
133.4	Bear right (straight) onto Rte 67 (Prospect Hill Rd.)
140.8	Left (north) onto Rte 199
144.0	[Left onto Curtis Rd. to visit the Institute for American Indian Studies]
145.4	In Washington, left onto Rte 47
146.5	In Washington Depot, right onto Rte 47/Rte 109 (Bee Brook Rd.)
146.7	Right onto Rte 109 (Blackville Rd.)
155.5	Left onto Rte 63 (Litchfield Rd.)
159.7	Arrive at the green in Litchfield ∎

Terryville wasn't named for Eli Terry, but for his son, Eli Terry Jr., who was also a clockmaker and manufacturing innovator best known for establishing the area as the leading manufacturer of locks in America. The waterwheel (c. 1830) for the mill still exists beside US Route 6 in Terryville (at Benedict Street). Two blocks farther the Lock Museum of America (230 Main St., just past the public library) is across from the site of his original Eagle Lock Company. Eight rooms are covered with a captivating collection of more than 23,000 padlocks, keys, safes, doorknobs, handcuffs, time vaults, escutcheon plates, and ornate hardware. In the Yale room, for locks manufactured by that company between 1860 to 1950, you'll find the original patent model of Linus Yale Jr.'s mortise cylinder pin tumbler lock, which has been called the greatest invention in the history of lockmaking, certainly a wee bit of an overstatement, when you compare it with the 4,000-year-old Egyptian-made pin tumbler lock nearby.

To visit the American Clock and Watch Museum, continue east on US Route 6 into Bristol, and turn right onto Federal Street after the intersection with North Main Street. It's located at the end of Federal Street, but a left-right dog-leg onto Woodland Street is required to enter the parking area for the museum. From the museum, north on Maple Street will lead straight onto Route 69 (Burlington Avenue).

North on Route 69 quickly takes you out of Bristol and into forest. Then Covey Road, a delightful stretch of local pavement, runs through woodlands and past small farms from Burlington to US Route 202. Even on this main highway the terrain is mostly forested.

In the small town of New Hartford, turn right off US Route 44 onto Route 219 (Reservoir Road). This narrow strip of pavement runs along the eastern shore of Lake McDonough and past the Saville Dam.

There's no parking on the Saville Dam Road (Route 318) but there is parking on both sides of the dam. Another option: before you reach Route 318 there will be an entrance road on your left. This goes to and along the base of the dam to a parking area. From this vantage point, the massive concrete wall stretches for 1,950 feet and although it's only 135 feet high, it seems to reach the sky. It's pretty cool, but some people may be uncomfortable having 36 billion gallons of water above their heads.

Route 219 glides along a shallow forest valley to end at Route 20. Day Street is only 0.9 miles east of the junction of Route 20; anyone who appreciates grand, old trees will enjoy a very short side trip up Day Street to see the Granby Oak, a specimen that was growing when European settlers first arrived in the area in 1600. This is a "champion tree," the largest black oak in the country, with limbs spanning 130 feet. Considering that most of this

This medieval-looking turret is actually the water gauge house on Saville Dam.

The Granby Oak was growing before European colonists arrived in the area.

landscape was completely deforested during the 19th century, the survival of this particular tree is amazing. It's only a 1.6-mile roundtrip from Route 20 to where its branches spread across Day Street, making this one of the most readily accessible champion trees in the country.

You can't avoid traffic as Route 20 merges with Route 189 and then intersects US Route 202/Route 10 in Granby. Just 2.7 miles east of this junction, turn left from Route 20 onto Newgate Road.

The first political prison in America, the notorious Old New-Gate, began its otherwise unprofitable existence as a copper mine that provided ore for the minting of America's first coins. Following its conversion in 1773, British loyalists were held in neck chains 70 feet below ground, to sleep on straw mats swarming with vermin and wet with continual seepage. In spite of its reputation for high security, almost as many men escaped as were held in that dismal and forbidding dungeon. They had plenty of incentive to find a way out. Of course, it's now a National Historic Landmark (115 Newgate Rd.; 860-653-3563).

Newgate Road becomes Copper Hill Road as it cuts across a pleasant rural landscape and crosses US Route 202 just a thousand feet south of the state line. Called the Granby Notch, this appears on maps to be a rather odd-looking border intrusion of Massachusetts into Connecticut. On East Street at the junction of Cooley Road, the field on the right looks like a typical hayfield, but it's actually in the state of Massachusetts. Sometimes an odd bit of history is not discernable to the eye. A decades-long colonial dispute by residents who didn't wish to be part of Connecticut was finally settled in 1804 when the Granby Notch was created. The formation of the United States was not as politically smooth as many history books suggest.

Mountain Road ends at Route 20. As you follow Route 20 west, the road

The New England Air Museum

The New England Air Museum (36 Perimeter Rd.; 860-623-3305; www.neam.org) is another great place to visit. Instead of turning onto Newgate Road, continue for another 1.5 miles on Route 20 and take a left (the first left past the intersection of Route 187) onto East Street. Take the second right (Russell Road) and the next left (Perimeter Road) to the museum, which is located on the west side of Bradley International Airport. Several hangars feature exhibits, with a few of the larger planes located outdoors. The museum houses 125 aircraft and more than 200 engines in its collection, including an original Gee-Bee Model A, designed by the Granville Brothers of Springfield, Massachusetts. The original Laird racer (c. 1930) and the Marcoux-Bromberg Special (c. 1934) are also part of the civilian exhibit. I'm fascinated by WWII aircraft, and they have one of the few surviving examples of a B-29 Super Fortress, the plane that carried atomic bombs to Japan. Their Mitchell B-25, Republic P-47 Thunderbolt, and Grumman Hellcat, among others, make for a very impressive collection of WWII-era machines. You'll also find a Lockheed Electra, an aircraft made famous (or infamous) by Amelia Earhart. Another all-time favorite of mine is the Grumman Albatross, an amphibious search-and-rescue plane—but I'm sure you will find a favorite of your own somewhere in this museum. ∎

loops around the north end of Barkhamsted Reservoir. This part of Connecticut is mostly forested and not at all what most people envision the state to be. Smells will change as you ride from pine forest to deciduous and back into pine. The highway is shaded and in places cool, damp air from the reservoir creeps through the forest. Such micro-climatic changes are welcome on hot summer days, but can create unexpected patches of fog in September and October.

The tiny village of Riverton is positioned between the fork of the Farmington and Still Rivers. The way from Riverton through Colebrook follows the contours of the land, passing through tiny hamlets, quaint villages, forests, and small farms. There's always something to see along these tertiary roads. When you reach the town green in Colebrook, turn left at the Colebrook General Store onto Rockwell Road (Route 182A), then go right onto Route 182.

The village of Norfolk has been nicknamed the Connecticut Icebox, because its seasonal temperatures are lower due to its 1,250-foot elevation,

The abandoned copper mines below Old New-Gate Prison held British loyalists in abysmal conditions.

quite high for the topography of this state. It claims a number of interesting buildings, including Infinity Hall on US Route 44. This green-shingled Arts and Crafts-style building (c. 1883) was built as an opera and concert hall and still hosts performances. Of special interest is the very fine restaurant housed there.

Mark Twain used to visit Norfolk during the summers he lived in Hartford. There's a stained glass window in the Episcopal church commemorating his wife, Olivia. One never knows where delicious tidbits of history will be found in small towns such as this one.

In East Canaan you'll find the state's only industrial monument: Beckley Furnace. Turn left by the Congregational Church onto Lower Road for about half a mile. The stack, the old office, and the slag heaps will be visible along the Blackberry River. Built in 1847 and operated until 1919, it was the largest of 43 blast furnaces in the Salisbury Iron District. Today, it's hard to imagine that this beautiful forested landscape was completely denuded of trees to feed the 19th-century maw of industrial progress. You can continue on Lower Road to reach US Route 7.

US Route 44 continues through Canaan, but the second leg of this loop begins in the center of Canaan at US Route 7, a beautiful motorcycle touring road that almost every rider will be happy with. (Another worthy road, even if it has a couple of miles of gravel, would be the Housatonic River

Road. To find it, continue west on US Route 44 from Canaan and take the first left after crossing the river. It will become Dugway Road and end at Route 112 across from Lime Rock Park. Turn left onto Route 112 and in a mile you will re-join this ride at US Route 7.)

US Route 7 runs south from the Canadian border to I-95 in Norwalk, Connecticut. However, the most pleasurable section of this highway for motorcycle cruising lies between Canaan and New Milford, and that's where this route will take you.

Route 7 crosses the Housatonic south of Falls Village, just before the junction of Route 112. Lime Rock Park, the first automotive race course designed and built on scientific principles, is located just a mile west of US Route 7 on Route 112 (860-435-5000; www.limerock.com). Lime Rock hosts Grand Am and NASCAR events, the American Le Mans Northeast Grand Prix, the Ferrari Challenge, and vintage auto racing.

The river is occasionally visible as US Route 7 curves gently through forest shade to West Cornwall along the edge of the rolling hills.

The bridge over the Housatonic River in West Cornwall was built in 1864. Its two spans totaling 172 feet long, the bridge is a Town lattice construction with queenpost trusses that were added in 1887. A concealed steel deck was installed in 1973. It's almost *de rigeur* to show a photo of this bridge in tourism-related publications for Litchfield County. You'll find a small parking area on the west side of the bridge, but the best vantage point for photos will be found on your left immediately after crossing through the bridge.

Forested and with frequent views of the river, the few miles between West Cornwall and the town of Cornwall Bridge are positively bucolic. The southern section of Housatonic Meadows State Park is located in a field about a thousand feet north of where Route 4 merges with US Route 7. It's the only field between West Cornwall and Cornwall Bridge, so there will be no mistaking it. It has a paved turn-off and parking area, with picnic tables overlooking the Housatonic River. A paved road leads down to the riverbank where you'll find a few more tables in the deep shade of the pine forest. It's a

A granite kiln where ore was reduced to pig iron has survived in an area that is still listed on some maps as Kent Furnace.

The Housatonic River Road has a couple miles of gravel, but is a gorgeous ride.

nice place to stop for a short break on a hot summer day. Yes, it even has a basic public toilet.

Crossing the Housatonic, the highway follows the eastern bank of the river, but not within sight of it. When it finally does veer toward the river you probably won't notice, as your eye will inevitably be drawn to the meadow-like expanse of Kent Falls State Park. This is a popular local destination, but you'll have a steep quarter-mile walk from the parking area to view the 250-foot cascade—the highest in the state. There's a $15 non-resident parking fee. Rural residential homes are more numerous south of the state park. As you approach Kent, when US Route 7 hugs the railroad tracks, slow down and prepare to make a right turn onto a gravel driveway that crosses the tracks.

Eric Sloane was an author, illustrator, and collector of Americana. A number of his books, such as *Eric Sloane's America,* are famous, but a couple of them have become classic reference editions: *American Barns and Covered Bridges* and *A Museum of Early American Tools.* The Sloane-Stanley Museum (860-927-3849; www.ericsloane.com) has that collection of tools and his studio. The pioneer cabin next to the museum was built by Sloane, based on descriptions found in the 1805 diary of Noah Blake. Down the hill just below the cabin are the remains of the Kent Iron Furnace that operated from 1826 to 1892—in fact, this area is still listed on some maps as Kent Furnace.

Down the driveway from the Sloane-Stanley Museum is a group of rather unremarkable buildings that house very remarkable collections. Among them is the Connecticut Antique Machinery Association's museum (860-927-0050; www.ctamachinery.com), home to the largest permanent

The covered bridge in West Cornwall is one of the most frequently photographed sights in Litchfield County.

Housatonic Meadows State Park is a great place to pull off the road and take a short break along the river.

collection of operating steam engines in the state. The concrete floor has been custom poured for each engine, with pits for flywheels as large as 14 feet in diameter. There's a double-acting steam engine (c. 1875); a 1910 Laidlaw-Dunn-Gordon cross-compound steam engine made in Cincinnati, Ohio; and a 1939 Skinner Universal Unaflow that generates 200 hp using reciprocating steam technology. The Noble T. Greene engine, built in 1904, delivers 150 hp at 80 rpm at its 12-foot-diameter flywheel, from an 18-inch piston with 36-inch stroke. What a fine engine! Although these antiques are not run every day, when the 200 hp York-Shipley boiler to which they are connected is fired up, it is quite a sight!

Poking among the treasures in a far back corner I make an exciting discovery—so this is where the elusive Hubbard steamcycle ended up! Inspired by an untested design in a two-part article published in *The Model Engineer and Electrician* in 1918, Arthur "Bud" Hubbard of Monroe, Connecticut, cobbled together a prototype between 1963 and 1973 using a 1956 Maico motorcycle chassis. Hubbard's 100cc, two-cylinder, single-acting, 6 hp steam engine operated at 400–700 psi from a triple-coil, superheating flash loop fired by kerosene using a vaporization coil that's preheated by alcohol. (If you're just dying to know what all this means, a visit to CAMA should definitely be on your agenda.) The steamcycle uses less than a gallon of fuel per hour, but the water capacity lasts for only two hours, limiting its potential as an erstwhile touring machine. Before its extensive renovation to its present running condition, it had been stored in a chicken coop.

Out behind the George C. Lay Blacksmith Shop stands a line of rocker pumps for natural gas. Restored stationary gas (not gasoline) engines lie hidden underneath tarps in a garage addition and lean-to. Following the railroad tracks, you'll arrive at another building, one that just barely holds Hawaii No. 5, a completely restored 1925 Baldwin steam locomotive and its tender, which the association runs on its own tracks for special events. The 10,000-square-foot Diebold Agricultural Barn is absolutely crammed with farm tractors, including early steam tractors such as the Russell, a huge mechanical monster. On the catwalks along the wall are curiosities like treadle lathes and saws, a bicycle with an unfamiliar motor conversion, a John Deere tandem bicycle, and the list goes on. It's insane: this association deserves some state funding to build larger exhibition spaces.

The specimens in the Connecticut Museum of Mining and Mineral Science building, which come exclusively from this state, are worth special mention. The extremely large crystals of glimmering blue kyanite are equal to those in any natural science museum, and the fluorescent mineral display

The first motorcycle was made by Connecticut inventor Sylvester Roper in 1867 and it was powered by steam. This modern steamcycle was built a century later by Bud Hubbard of Monroe, Connecticut.

is first class. An alluvial-looking nugget weighing 110 lbs is the largest piece of native copper ever found in Connecticut.

Departing from Kent Furnace, you'll have just enough distance to shift up through the gears before slowing down to enter Kent, a small village that can be crowded on summer weekends. Small boutiques, a couple of galleries, and a few restaurants are all it has to offer, yet there's an undeniable ambience here. The J.P. Gifford Market will be the best place for a deli-style lunch.

Back on US Route 7 south of Kent you'll again approach the river. The large expanse of forest seen on the hillsides is the Schaghticoke Indian Reservation. It's often forgotten that reservation lands still exist in southern New England and that descendants of the Mohican, Potatuck, Podunk, Tunxis, and Weantinock tribes still live on ancestral lands. Established in 1736, this is the oldest Native American reservation in the United States.

Bull's Bridge is the oldest covered bridge in Connecticut and the only one other than the West Cornwall Bridge that is open to vehicular traffic. Once part of a major colonial road, there's been a bridge at this site since 1760. A well-documented incident occurred here during the Revolutionary War. Apparently George Washington's horse, or an important one in his entourage, fell off Bull's Bridge and had to be rescued on March 3, 1781 at a cost of $251. The original structure is long gone, but the one that survives—with a few modern upgrades—was built in 1842. The construction of two dams upstream has reduced the watercourse to a trickle and the creation of a canal to divert water to a hydroelectric generating plant has necessitated a modern bridge just upstream from the historic one. Parking is available between the two bridges and on the west side of Bull's Bridge just 800 yards east of the New York state line.

The road has a nice feel as it continues south. The elevation changes aren't very obvious, but if you stop by the gatehouse or catch a glimpse over the concrete barrier to the hydroelectric plant far below at the river's edge it will become apparent.

Although this ride continues on US Route 7, consider following Riverview Road—which becomes River Road—along the east bank of the Housatonic River. If you do so, you'll come to a T-intersection in a few miles. At the T-intersection, either turn right, cross the river, and continue south on US Route 7 on this mapped ride, or turn left and follow Boardman Road/Housatonic Avenue into New Milford.

Somewhere near the junction of Route 37, you entered the "solar system," but you're still a long way from home. By the time you reach the traffic light for the turn onto US Route 202/Route 67 into New Milford, you will have already arrived within the orbit of Neptune. If you really wanted to get home you'd continue to the inner planets, another 3.7 miles south on US Route 7 at the John J. McCarthy Observatory (860-946-0312; www. mccarthyobservatory.org), where you'll find the Sun—or at least a six-foot representation of it. This solar system model is built to scale and it stretches north for 6.6 miles. Now that you know your place in the universe, or at least our solar system, head back north to the traffic light and cross the bridge into downtown New Milford.

It is only seven miles on Route 67 to reach Route 199. The last miles through rural farmland are pleasant, but the winding road north to Washington will offer deep shade, sweeping turns, and elevation changes. About

Although the displays at the Connecticut Museum of Mining and Mineral Science are a bit of folk art, the collection is first-rate.

Discovering a Buddhist temple set in the colonial landscape of East Morris was a pleasant surprise.

three miles along Route 199 you'll come to Curtis Road on the left. At the end of that narrow, twisting descent through the forest is the Institute for American Indian Studies (860-868-0518; www.iaismuseum.org), an excellent museum and research center with programs that introduce people to Native American culture, especially the history of tribes in Connecticut.

In the village of Washington, make a left turn onto Route 47. Be sure to turn right onto Route 47/Route 109 at Washington Depot—continuing straight would just bring you back to New Milford—then make another right to follow Route 109 up the hill. Rolling across a gentle landscape dotted with farms, Old Litchfield Road represents the antithesis of the cities along the Connecticut River Valley and the coast of Long Island Sound.

Between Morris and East Morris on Route 109 you will be rewarded with the discovery of Buddha Ariyamiett Aram Temple (860-567-0094), a campus with ornate statues, friendly monks, and occasional festivals. You don't even have to be a Buddhist to enjoy it.

Riding past farms and through forest on the way north to Litchfield, it is easy to envision what this region was like during the 18th and 19th centuries. Some places in New England have seen dramatic transformations, with

There are many historic homes along Route 63 in Litchfield.

the advent of railways, factories, and personal vehicles. Litchfield Hills seems to have changed less than most.

Litchfield is a town with a number of original 18th-century buildings and was also among the first to embrace the American Colonial Revival movement. There are many attractive homes to be found along Route 63 (South Street), but of special interest is one originally owned by Tapping Reeve, a lawyer under whom an astounding number of notable Americans studied. He represented "Mum Bett," who sued for her freedom in Great Barrington, Massachusetts, and became the first legally freed slave in the United States. Reeve also established the first law school in the United States at his home in Litchfield.

Ethan Allen was born and grew up in Litchfield. With his brothers and other friends from Connecticut they became involved in land speculation in the New Hampshire Grants where they established the Republic, and later, the State of Vermont. Henry Ward Beecher and Harriet Beecher Stowe *(Uncle Tom's Cabin)* grew up in Litchfield. Oliver Wolcott Sr. was living in Litchfield (across the road from Tapping Reeve) when he signed the Declaration of Independence. His son, Oliver Wolcott Jr., one of Reeve's students, became the U.S. Treasury Secretary (1795–1800) under President George Washington. Many other revolutionary activists came from or spent time in this town. Perhaps there was something in the water.

Lodging will be surprisingly scarce in Litchfield. The Litchfield Inn (432 Bantam Rd./US Rte 202; 860-567-4503; www.litchfieldinnct.com) is nice, and the Tollgate Hill Inn (571 Torrington Rd./US Rte 202; 860-567-1233; www.tollgatehill.com) is a restored 1745 tavern. There are more options in Torrington and Bristol and B&B inns will be scattered across the county. The Litchfield Hills Connecticut tourism office (800-663-1273; www. litchfieldhills.com) can help you find accommodations.

Ride 27 Eastern Connecticut

Distance: *138 miles; with stops it could easily take all day*
Highlights: *Rural roads through forests, interior hills, and coastal cities, Mystic Seaport, USS Nautilus, Chester-Hadlyme ferry, Gillette Castle, Windham Textile Museum.*

This ride starts in Pawcatuck a couple hundred yards from the Connecticut-Rhode Island state line and the city of Westerly. The first half-mile will be along US Route 1, the Boston Post Road. This major thoroughfare continues through the coastal towns and would bring you to Mystic, but your ride leaves US Route 1 and proceeds on Route 234—the Pequot Trail—through forests and farmland.

The village of Old Mystic is located at the head of a long, deep estuary, which provided a safe haven for vessels in the fishing and shipping industries that were so important during the 18th and 19th centuries. Route 27 crosses I-95 at Exit 90, and from this point you will have to be vigilant: distracted vacationing drivers could be an issue for the next couple of miles.

The Mystic Aquarium is a major tourist attraction, but Mystic Seaport (888-973-2767; www.mysticseaport.org) pretty much defines the city.

Mystic is located at the head of a long, deep estuary that provided a safe haven for fishing and shipping vessels during the 18th and 19th centuries.

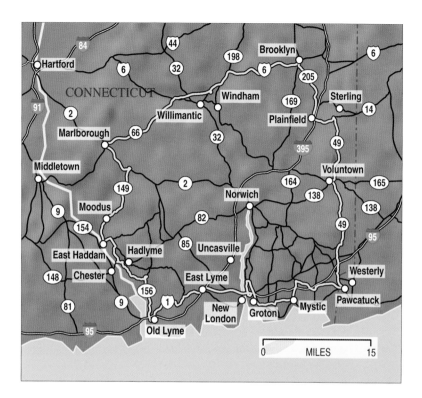

Thirty historic buildings and more than 500 ships from around New England were moved to the site to create a living history museum of a 19th-century fishing village. I'm not sure how a floating ship qualifies as a National Historic Landmark, but four of them lie at Mystic Seaport: the *Charles C. Morgan* (c. 1841), the last surviving New England whaling schooner and last all-wooden whaling ship in the world; the *Sabino* (c. 1908) the oldest surviving coal-fired, steam-powered, wooden passenger ferry in operation in the United States; the *Emma C. Berry* (c. 1866) one of the oldest surviving commercial vessels in America; and the *L.A. Dunton,* a Gloucester fishing schooner designed for working on Georges and Grand Banks. Cruises are offered on the *Sabino* and aboard the beautiful 26-foot wooden motor launch that serviced the America Cup defender *Resolute* for many years. The 111-foot square-rigger *Joseph Conrad* was built in 1882 in Copenhagen as a training ship, and it still serves that purpose as part of the museum's summer educational programs.

The trade of the shipsmith—essentially a blacksmith who specialized in forging ship parts—originated from New Bedford, and the exhibit at Mys-

FROM PAWCATUCK, CONNECTICUT

0	From Pawcatuck, Connecticut, at Liberty St., go west on US Rte 1 (W. Broad St.)
0.5	Bear right (straight) onto Rte 234 (Pequot Trail)
4.0	Left to continue on Rte 234 (Pequot Trail)
7.5	In Old Mystic, left onto Rte 27 (Whitehall Ave.)
9.4	[Mystic Seaport]
9.7	Right onto Holmes St.
10.0	In Mystic, right onto US Rte 1 (W. Main St.)
16.4	In Groton, straight onto Rte 12
18.0	Left onto Crystal Lake Rd. (at the traffic light)
18.4	[Entrance to the Submarine Force Museum]
18.4	[Right (departing museum) onto Military Hwy]
20.2	Left onto Bridge St. (after going beneath the bridge)
20.5	Left onto ramp, stay right onto US Rte 1/I-95 (west)
27.6	Right, Exit 75 onto US Rte 1 (Boston Post Rd.)
35.6	Pass under I-95 and straight onto Lyme St.
37.3	In Old Lyme, right onto Ferry Rd.
37.6	Right (north) onto Rte 156 (Neck Rd.)
43.5	Left onto Joshuatown Rd.
48.4	Left onto Rte 148 (Ferry Rd.)
49.3	[Straight to Chester-Hadlyme Ferry dock]
49.3	Right onto River Rd.
50.0	[Entrance to Gillette Castle State Park]
51.6	Left onto Rte 82 (Town St.)
52.9	Left to continue on Rte 82 (Norwich Rd.) into E. Haddam
54.3	[Straight to swinging bridge and Goodspeed Opera House]
54.3	In E. Haddam, right onto Rte 149 (Main St.)
65.9	Left on-ramp Exit 16 Rte 2 (west)
70.7	Right off-Ramp Exit 13 on Rte 66 (east)
82.5	Straight onto US Rte 6
88.0	Right onto US Rte 6 (Boston Post Rd.)
102.3	In Brooklyn, hard right onto Rte 169 (Canterbury Rd.)
102.3	[Continue on US Rte 6 to join Ride 28]
102.3	[Left onto Rte 169 (north) to join Ride 25]
(continued)	

tic is the only whaling smithy to have survived to the current era. A segment—only 250 feet of what once was a 1,000-foot long building—of the Plymouth Cordage Company's ropewalk was also moved to the museum. Rope needed to be twisted in a straight line, hence the long structure. A ship

CONTINUING FROM BROOKLYN, CONNECTICUT

102.3   From Brooklyn, at US Rte 6, south on Rte 169 (Canterbury Rd.)
102.6   Bear left (straight) onto Rte 205 (Wauregan Rd.)
106.4   In Wauregan, bear right onto Rte 12 (Putnam Rd.)
110.6   Left onto Rte 14A (Academy Hill Rd.)
114.4   Right (south) onto Rte 49 (Ekonk Hill Rd.)
122.6   In Voluntown, right onto Rte 49/Rte 138
123.0   Bear left onto Rte 49/Rte 165
123.1   Left onto Rte 49 (Pendleton Hill Rd.)
132.0   Right to stay on Rte 49 (Pendleton Hill Rd.)
134.1   Straight across Rte 184 to stay on Rte 49
135.0   [On-ramp Exit 92 I-95 (east)]
136.2   Left (south) onto Rte 2 (Liberty St.)
138.2   Arrive at US Rte 1 in Pawcatuck, Connecticut   ■

carver's shop has also been set up for such specialized woodcraft as sculpting the figureheads typically found on traditional vessels. Numerous other shops are centered around the business of building, maintaining, and out-fitting ships, and costumed interpreters explain the work they are doing in the context of the 19th century.

Parking for the museum will be in a large lot across the road. It'd be best to arrive early, since the small workshops of the seaport can become crowded later in the day. Besides, this museum deserves a full day of your time, not a quick run-through.

In the harbor, the masts of another ship may catch your eye. The schooner *Argia* (15 Holmes St.; 860-536-0416; www.argiamystic.com) is a mod-

Four hundred pounds of concrete counterweights means the 85-foot movable span of the Mystic Drawbridge can be raised with the assistance of just two 40 hp electric motors.

ern (c. 1986) replica of a 19th-century vessel. Two-hour cruises on this 81-foot schooner cost $42.

Holmes Street will lead to Main and across the Mystic Drawbridge, a bascule (counter-weighted) bridge designed by the chief engineer of the Otis Elevator Company and built in 1920. The 85-foot movable span of the 218-foot bridge has 400 tons of concrete counterweights and is raised with the assistance of just two 40 hp electric motors. It's a simple but elegant design.

The downtown area by the bridge is usually busy during midday. The bridge is also an excellent vantage point for taking photos of the waterfront portion of the Mystic Seaport Museum—especially if you happen to be carrying a telephoto lens. The Mystic Drawbridge Ice Cream Café (860-572-7978;www.mysticdrawbridgeicecream.com) would be a good choice for deli takeout.

Fortunately, the interstate frees up US Route 1 for local traffic, affording you a more pleasant cruise through the town of Poquonock Bridge. There will be plenty of shade along the highway and not many traffic lights, as US Route 1 leads you directly to Route 12 in Groton. Turn left onto Crystal

The number on the conning tower of the USS Nautilus denotes only that it was the 571st submarine built for the U.S. Navy.

Four mini-subs are positioned outside the Submarine Force Library and Museum.

Lake Road at the traffic light to reach your next stopping point, the Submarine Museum.

The first American submarine was invented in Connecticut in 1775 and was used twice during the Revolutionary War, yet the United States didn't establish its first submarine base until 1916. By 1959 New London had become the largest submarine base in the world. When the first nuclear-powered submarine was built in 1954, it was named *Nautilus,* after the ship in Jules Verne's *Twenty Thousand Leagues Under the Sea.* This is what people come to see.

The Submarine Force Library and Museum (1 Crystal Lake Rd.; 860-694-3174 www.ussnautilus.org; adm. free) is located at the southern perimeter of the Naval Submarine Base at New London. However, the naval base itself is *not* open to the public. Don't be thrown by the title: it's actually located in Groton on the east bank of the Thames River. The first thing you'll notice will be a flat-black conning tower in the river; the second will be the four mini-subs in front of the museum. The Japanese and Italian mini-subs are from WWII, the one used by U.S. Special Ops appears to be of Vietnam vintage, and the fourth is an experimental craft that was discontinued in favor of the nuclear-power naval program. All of these were designed to approach enemy ships, attach explosives, and depart without being detected. The first exhibit in the museum is a replica of the *Turtle,* the submarine built in Connecticut by David Bushnell in 1775, which was designed to do exactly the same thing.

Unless you are very lucky, there will be a line of people waiting to enter the *Nautilus,* threading its way, step by step, through the torpedo room, the wardroom, the attack center, control room, and crew mess in the forward compartments. All the interior rooms—including bathrooms, bunks, captain's cabin, and radio shack—are partitioned behind glass so visitors are confined to the corridors. For a submarine, the *Nautilus* is absolutely spa-

Joshuatown Road to Hadlyme is a wonderful stretch of pavement.

cious and crew accommodations were first class. During the early 1950s, this pioneering sub shattered all speed and distance records, and claimed status as the first ship to reach the North Pole.

When you leave the museum, take a right onto Military Highway, which runs along the river with nice views and little traffic. Slow down after passing beneath the bridge, then turn right and immediately right again. Incongruously located at the turn onto Bridge Street is the National WWII Submarine Memorial-East, and at its center is the top of the USS *Flasher,* which operated in the Pacific fleet during World War II, sinking 21 Japanese vessels totaling 100,000 tons. Surrounding the conning tower are 52 granite stones listing the submarines lost in WWII, as well as how, when, and where they were sunk. In black marble, the Wall of Honor pays tribute to the 3,617 submariners lost during the war.

From Bridge Street, take the ramp onto the Gold Star Memorial Bridge and cross the Thames River between Groton and New London on I-95 to reach US Route 1 in East Lyme.

Old Lyme is a pretty colonial town whose residents deserve kudos for not letting modern development spoil it. However, those who have toured the well-preserved colonial villages in southern Vermont and New Hampshire might find much ado about nothing—except for the Florence Griswold Museum.

It wasn't always a museum; once it was Florence Griswold's boarding house, which became the core of the Lyme Art Colony every summer from 1900 to 1930 as it filled with artists. This became the center of American Impressionism and the bohemian "in" place to be. Woodrow Wilson and his first wife—an artist—summered at the Griswold House in the company of Childe Hassam, Willard Metcalf, William and Elien Noy Chadwick, Frank Vincent DuMond, and dozens of other noted American artists. Some of them actually used the walls, door panels, and such as their canvases. The museum (96 Lyme St.; 860-434-5542; www.flogris.org) has been restored to the 1910 period and many of the paintings that were created here have come home as a permanent collection of American Impressionist art.

Route 156 angles away from the Connecticut River estuary as you head north. There will be an "ah" feeling as you ride through woodlands and past fields on this very pretty road. It will get even better after making the left turn onto Joshuatown Road/River Road. This shortcut to the ferry crossing is a choice motorcycle touring road: narrow, with lots of corners and elevation changes. No lines are painted on the pavement, and the deep shade provided by tree branches arching above the road will provide some welcome relief on hot days. Residential homes line the road and the forest floor looks manicured like a European park.

The Chester-Hadlyme Ferry began commercial service in 1769 and was an important crossing during the Revolutionary War. Two hundred and

The Mohegans

The Last of the Mohicans, a historic novel by James Fenimore Cooper set during the French and Indian War, was the second and best-known book in the pentology of the Leatherstocking Tales. "Mohican" is a misspelling that has been applied to both the Mahicans, who lived in the Hudson Valley and were moved to Stockbridge, Massachusetts, during the American Revolution, and Mohegans, who lived along the Thames River. Their sachem (a.k.a. sagamore or great chief), Uncas—Cooper's hero—was allied with the English colonists in the 1630s. The Mohegans, however, didn't die to the last man, and today the tribe owns the Mohegan Sun, the second-largest casino in the country, which is located—where else?—in Uncasville. To reach the casino and its shops, restaurants, theaters, planetarium, and hotels, simply ride north on Route 12 from the submarine base and cross the river at the first bridge (Route 2A) north of Groton-New London. You can't miss it. To rejoin this ride simply take I-395 south.

■

Access to the state park at Gillette Castle is free and there are motorcycle-only parking spaces.

forty-plus years later, the world is a different place, but the ferry is still here, although it is now driven by diesel engines instead of long poles and muscle power. It operates only during the day (weekdays 7 a.m. to 6:45 p.m.; weekends 10:30 a.m. to 6:45 p.m.; $3 per vehicle, $1 per passenger), so if you are running late and need to cross the river, you will have no choice but to continue upstream to the bridge at East Haddam.

At Hadlyme, steps lead from the ferry to the castle on the bluffs above. Geer Hill Road leads to the castle access road, which you'll probably want to take instead. The turn into the state park and the Gillette Castle (860-526-2336) will be clearly marked; the driveway takes you to the parking area (free).

The view of the river and countryside from the quirky stone mansion is fantastic. This rather bohemian interpretation of a medieval castle built for William Gillette on 184 acres was known as Seventh Sister during WWI (1914–1919). Gillette is best known for establishing the popular image of Sherlock Holmes, with his curved briar pipe and deerstalker hat. It was Gillette, not Doyle, who coined the phrase, "This is elementary, my dear fellow." He was a good playwright whose realistic stage sets, lighting, and sound effects defined modern theater. Gillette was also a bit eccentric—as this house plainly suggests—and his last will stipulated that the estate not be possessed by any "blithering sap-head who has no conception of where he is or with what surrounded." Since such a person could not be found, it fell to the possession of the state in 1943. While access to the state park is free, there's an admission fee to see the interior of the castle.

The next place where you can cross the river will be at East Haddam. The white-clapboard Victorian Goodspeed Opera House (www.goodspeed.org) is famous for premiering *Annie, Shenandoah,* and *Man of La Mancha,* but also has hosted 14 other productions that made it to Broadway and won

William Gillette's castle in Hadlyme is as eccentric and unique as he was.

more than a dozen Tony Awards. The oldest bell in North or South America hangs in the small steeple of St. Stephens Church on Main Street. Cast in the year 815, it made its way from Spain to New York in 1834 as ship ballast. A ship chandler discovered it and sent it to his wife's hometown where it now resides, or so goes one version of the story. However, it is a confirmed fact that the East Haddam Bridge over the Connecticut River has the longest swinging span of any drawbridge in the world. Naturally you'll want to ride across even though you'll have to just turn around and return to continue on the northern part of this loop.

If you plan to go west across the state to reach Ride 26, cross the East Haddam Bridge and follow Route 154 to Route 9A, then get onto Route 9 at Exit 10. Continue north on Route 9 to New Britain where Exit 28 will put you onto Route 72 west to Bristol and Terryville.

Winding through the forest as Route 149 heads to Moodus, any low booming or growling you hear might not be your engine. Strange noises were often heard in this area until modern times. People once believed these sounds coming from the ground were caused by evil gods or Satan, but today they are explained as shallow seismic events.

Small villages, where 19th-century architecture predominates, and gently rolling hills covered with deciduous trees make this portion of the state more similar to eastern Massachusetts than to coastal or western Connecticut. Modern residences are being constructed on what was strictly farmland and forest only a decade or two ago. Still, the tempo will be more that of small towns than suburbs. The highway now avoids the congestion of what were once industrial centers, the foundation of the New England economy up until the post-WWII era.

Willimantic was more than just another New England mill town, it was the archetype. The American Thread Company began as a linen mill in 1854 and grew to be the largest factory in Connecticut and the largest manufacturer of sewing thread in North America. It was established at a place on the river where a 90-foot drop provided massive waterpower. Water gave way to steam, steam to electricity. The company's No. 4 mill was for decades the largest single-story mill in the world and became the prototype for 20th-century factories. It was the first to install electric lights and the first to operate a second shift of workers. Dams for water damaged the aquatic ecosystem, coal smoke from boilers polluted the air, and chemical dyes poisoned streams, *but* this was just the negative side of the coin. The factory provided housing—three workers' villages for this one mill—company stores, credit unions, and much more. Farms were established to feed the workers and many eco-friendly practices were instituted. When the company moved its operations to North Carolina in 1985 (and since to Mexico) the local economy collapsed. To reach the Windham Textile & History Museum simply exit US Route 6 onto Route 66 and follow it east to the historic downtown district.

These 19th-century industrial environments can be as fascinating as colonial sites. I grew up in a New England mill town and know the story only too well. The Windham Textile and History Museum (411 Main St./Rte 66; 860-456-2178; www.millmuseum.org) encapsulates the urban story of New England and why it looks the way it does. North Adams (Ride 23) illustrates the next chapter in the urban history, and Old Sturbridge Village (Ride 25) provides the rural story.

If you make a point to visit railway museums, the Connecticut Eastern Railroad Museum (Rte 32, just a few yards south of Rte 66; 860-456-9999; www.cteastrrmuseum.org) in Willimantic is a stop you should consider. Various railway buildings—a depot, freight house, section house, and sheds—are open to the public. The roundhouse has been recently restored to house various rolling stock, including a rare SPV 2000, a self-propelled commuter car. This is becoming a fine local museum.

You'll find a number of interesting roads east of Willimantic, Route 14 and Route 138 among them. Route 6 is another decent cruising road, despite being a primary highway leading to I-395 and on to Providence, Rhode Island. For you, it'll be a means to the end, which will be reaching Route 49. Turn right onto Route 169 at the green in the center of the small village of Brooklyn, and within 100 yards continue straight onto Route 205 (Wauregan Road). In Wauregan, turn right and go south on Route 12. Rather than maneuvering through Moosup, you'll find it much easier to stay on Route 12 to Plainfield and then take Route 14A (Plainfield Pike Road) east to reach Route 49. It's really quite easy and, except for these small towns, you'll ride through a rural residential countryside—a mix of new homes, farms, and forest.

Touching the various tracts of Pachaug State Forest with only an occasional house or farm to be seen, this western green corridor is as enjoyable to ride as the roads found in northern New England. There's an abundance of wildlife, so I don't recommend it at night. Near Voluntown, Route 138 goes east to the beginning of Ride 28 in Hope Valley, while Route 49 continues south through a bucolic countryside until it passes beneath I-95 and abruptly enters an urban landscape.

If you haven't cut across to Newport, Rhode Island, on Route 138, you'll now have the option of taking I-95 at Exit 92, then Route 78 as a bypass around Westerly to US Route 1 east, or simply calling it a day and finding a place to lay your head for the night somewhere in southwestern Rhode Island.

Looking down at the Chester-Hadlyme Ferry from the Gillette Castle.

Ride 28 The Ocean State

Distance: *123 miles in total, but with stops, two days may not be enough*
Highlights: *Rural small towns, coastal areas, the city of Newport. Grand mansions, historic buildings, and boats, boats, boats.*

It's only 48 miles north to south and 37 miles east to west, but the Ocean State can lay claim to 400 miles of shoreline. Despite its diminutive size, Rhode Island played quite a large role in shaping the ideas that we would eventually embrace as America's destiny. Founder Roger Williams established the first working democracy in 1636 after being banished from the Puritan colony at Plymouth, Massachusetts, for his heretical views on the separation of religion from government, which he believed should include the freedom to worship according to one's own conscience. He founded Providence Plantations on Narragansett Bay on land purchased from the tribe of the same name. A noted linguist, Williams was also a scholar of Native American culture and customs, and settlements attracted by his unprecedented notions of tolerance would follow his lead, at least initially, in their dealings with the local Indians.

As one of the finest natural harbors on the east coast, Narragansett Bay

The motive power of the Blackstone River was harnessed to serve America's industrial ambitions, as seen here in the old mill buildings around Woonsocket.

was ideally positioned to reap the profits of the once-great fishing grounds of Georges Bank, as well as the trade routes established between the Caribbean, New England, and Europe. And while there would be no denying that a great deal of the colony's early prosperity can be traced to its participation in both chattel slavery and its related economies, Rhode Island became the first colony to prohibit the importation of slaves in 1776. Following the securing of our country's liberty from the British Empire, the Rhode Island legislature also passed a bill in 1784 which provided for a gradual emancipation of its state's enslaved population.

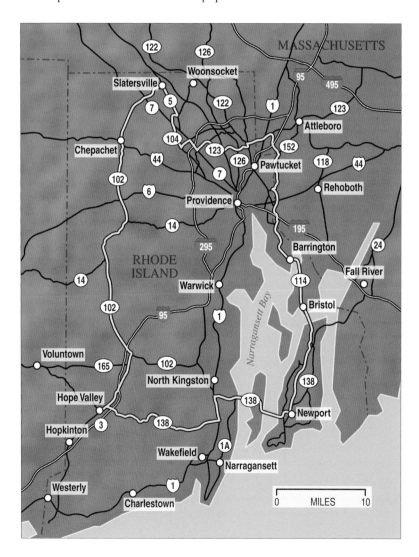

In Providence, a tribute to the man himself, Roger Williams

The location of Narragansett Bay was also of strategic military importance to colonial America, especially in the Age of Sail. (Even today, Newport is a U.S. Navy port and the site of both the U.S. Naval War College and Officer Training Command.) In 1772, the doughty patriots of Rhode Island sunk a British cutter to protest its enforcing of the unpopular revenue laws—and the province renounced its loyalty to George III two full months before everyone else declared their independence. Following America's victory (aided by French troops based in Newport), Rhode Island was the last state to ratify the Constitution, holding out for the assurance of a Bill of Rights to guarantee individual freedoms.

This circumnavigation of the Ocean State begins in the town of Hope Valley, Rhode Island, close to Arcadia State Park, at Exits 2 and 3 just off of I-95, where Route 138 briefly merges with Route 3. Hope Valley is easily accessible from Ride 27 by either taking Route 216 east to Hopkinton and Route 3, or by taking Route 138—a very nice touring road—east from Voluntown, Connecticut. The focus of this loop centers on Newport, however, and your approach to this city may depend more on where you are coming from and whether or not you wish to tackle the main highways through the state's largest urban and industrial areas. Although cities like Providence and Pawtucket have undergone aesthetic revivals during the last decade, this route avoids them in favor of more riding-friendly roads and destinations.

Although the population of Rhode Island totals just a million residents, only Washington, D.C. and New Jersey have a higher population density. This, however, is where bald statistics can be misleading. Rhode Island contains more than just urban, industrial landscapes: potatoes, sweet corn,

FROM HOPE VALLEY, RHODE ISLAND

0	From Hope Valley, north on Rte 3/Rte 138 east
0.9	Straight to continue on Rte 3
6.1	[Junction of Rte 165]
7.4	Left onto Rte 102 (Victory Hwy)
13.8	[Junction of Rte 118 east]
14.9	[Intersection of Rte 117]
18.3	[Merging of Rte 14 (Old Plainfield Pike)]
23.5	Bear left to continue on Rte 102
32.4	In Chepachet, bear right to continue on Rte 102
37.9	[Intersection of Rte 7]
39.4	Right onto Main St.
40.4	Bear right onto Rte 5 south in Slatersville
44.0	Right onto Rte 5/Rte 104
45.3	Merge with Rte 7
45.6	Bear right to continue on Rte 5/Rte 104
48.2	Left onto Rte 116 east
49.4	Right onto Rte 7
50.8	Left onto Rte 123
57.6	Left merge with Rte 114 briefly
57.9	In Cumberland, right to continue on Rte 123 (Dexter St.)
60.0	[Intersection of Rte 1]
60.8	Right onto Read St.
62.5	Right-left dog-leg to continue on Read St.
62.9	Bear right onto Pond St.
63.5	Right onto Rte 152
67.5	Left onto Arcade Ave.
68.9	Straight across US Rte 44 onto Arcade Ave.
69.7	Straight onto Rte 114A (Fall River Ave.)
71.3	Merge onto Rte 6 and get into the right lane
71.4	Bear right onto Rte 114A (Mink St.)
71.9	Straight becomes Rte 114 (Wampanoag Trail)
84.9	[In Portsmouth, pass Boyds Ln.]
93.5	[In Newport, straight onto Rte 138]
94.3	Arrive Rte 138 (Admiral Kalbfus Rd.) at Broadway in Newport
95.6	[Cross the Claiborne Pell Bridge (Rte 138) to Conanicut Island]
100.4	[Cross the Jamestown Bridge (Rte 138) to N. Kingstown]
104.3	Merge with US Rte 1; continue south on Rte 138
107.3	In Kingston, right to stay on Rte 138
122.7	Arrive back in Hope Valley ∎

eggs, dairy products, honey, apples, greenhouse vegetables, and ornamental plants are important agricultural businesses in this state.

The easiest way to reach Newport from Hope Valley is to simply stay on Route 138 east. Even running through small towns and rural residential areas, this road carries very little traffic, and trees line both sides of the highway along most of its length. Rhode Island may be densely populated, but the western side of the state is quite rural. Heading north from the small towns of Hope Valley and Wyoming, it'll be obvious that there's plenty of elbow room left. Route 3 was once the primary road along the backbone of the state; although it is still maintained as a four-lane highway, the heavy traffic is now on I-95.

A stop at the warehouse and showroom of Twisted Throttle (570 Nooseneck Hill Rd./Rte 3; www.twistedthrottle.com) in Exeter will be an absolute must for touring riders and dual sport adventurers. Even if you're not in the market for parts, accessories, or gear, their Twisted Tavern offers an ideal lunch break for individual riders or large tour groups, either in air-conditioned comfort or on the outside patio deck.

Route 102 crosses I-95 at Exit 5, and the truck stop is a good place to tank up 24-7. This road will be a pleasant cruise if you don't get frustrated by posted speed limits that seem unrelated to degree of settlement, road conditions, or traffic density. Tourism obviously isn't a major industry in western Rhode Island, but then again, the big cities are only a few miles away. Almost every numbered highway that intersects this road goes east to a metropolitan area; note, however, that you won't see any gas stations until you reach the village of Chepachet, where US Route 44 briefly merges with Route 102.

The American Industrial Revolution began in 1793 in Pawtucket, where Samuel Slater established the first successful cotton textile factory in the United States. Many other mills were soon built to utilize the flowing waterpower of the Blackstone River. Slater's second factory, as well as the village of Slatersville itself, was designed as a self-contained system of support services that included the church, store, school, and workforce housing for his manufacturing enterprises, and which became a model for the patriarchal "company town" that was to control every aspect of the lives of its employees, many of whom would have emigrated from the Old World in search of opportunity.

The original mill burned and was replaced by the Stone Mill in 1826. More recently, the building has been transformed into condominiums. The village green, Samuel Slater's house, and the church remain original, but sometime in the early 20th century, the workers' houses and stores were remodeled

Slatersville, the first "company town," was designed with a patriarchal system of support services for its workforce, such as a church, store, and housing. The old stone factory mill has since been converted into condos.

to resemble a stereotypical colonial village, and the overall effect is rather lacking in any of the idyllic charm and ambience of the genuine article. Slatersville seems to have lost its sense of historical importance and become merely a bedroom community for the nearby urban economic hubs.

Downtown Providence has been revitalized during the last decade, but this route avoids both the congested city streets of Rhode Island's core cities and the interstate highways by weaving between Pawtucket and Attleboro, Massachusetts, before going south to Aquidneck Island and the city of Newport. The interstate highways are much quicker—except during the weekday rush hours or when there's been a major accident.

From the center of Slatersville, Route 5 leads south to Route 116. The key to avoiding the worst of city traffic will be Route 123, which goes past the North Central State Airport and along the north side of Lincoln Woods State Park. While there's no doubt that this is the scenic route, there's also no way to avoid some degree of traffic, with stretches of stop signs or lights coming one after another, especially between Route 114 and US Route 1 north of Pawtucket and Attleboro. US Route 1 goes to downtown Pawtucket while Route 1A (Newport Avenue) is the main drag through East Providence. To reach Precision Harley-Davidson (269 Armistice Blvd./Rte 15; 401-724-0010; precisionhd.com) follow Route 114 south and Route 15 east. You'll pass the Slater Mill Historic Site, cross over I-95, and the Harley dealership will be at the intersection of the George Bennett Highway. Continue east on Route 15 until it ends at Route 152. Turn right to continue on this loop.

Turning onto Read Street from Route 123 on the west end of Orrs Pond, you'll slip beneath I-95, do a right-left dog-leg, then turn right onto Pond

Battleship Cove in Fall River is home to the USS Massachusetts.

Street to reach Route 152 (Central Avenue). All this maneuvering keeps you on the Massachusetts side of the state border, but here on the very edge of East Providence you'll ride past wood lots and farm fields. In Rumford, turn off Route 152 onto Arcade Avenue by the John Turner Reservoir to stay in Massachusetts, where trees line the streets and traffic is not aggressive.

The objective of your cutting through suburbia will be to reach Route 114, the Wampanoag Trail, and despite the potential of lane confusion when crossing US Route 6, it'll be relatively easy to find. The Wampanoag Trail is a scenic expressway that quickly reverts back to a two-lane highway. Rhode Island is a maze of inlets and peninsulas, so attempting to take short-cuts on local streets is not a good idea; you'll need to know where the bridges are. Stay on Route 114, crossing from Bristol to Aquidneck Island over the Mount Hope Bridge.

At the next intersection, bear right to continue south on Route 114 to Newport or straight on Boyds Lane to Exit 2 of Route 2 and Route 138. Route 24 east goes to Fall River and I-195 is the quickest way to reach New Bedford, Massachusetts, and Cape Cod. Route 138 briefly merges with Route 24 to cross the Sakonnet River Bridge and then goes north through Fall River to Battleship Cove (508-678-1100; www.battleshipcove.com), home of the WWII battleship USS *Massachusetts.* Those coming from Plymouth or Taunton, Massachusetts, can exit onto Boyds Lane or stay on Route 24 until it merges with Route 114 to reach Newport.

There's a plethora of lodging in this city; the easiest way to find a room is by seeking the advice of the Newport Visitor Center. The Best Western Mainstay Inn on Route 138 (151 Admiral Kalbfus Rd.; 401-849-9880; www.bestwestern.com) is a reasonably priced option located directly across from Newport Grand Slots Casino (401-849-5000; www.newportgrand.com). Clean, comfortable, and convenient, it also has a decent restaurant and a view of the parking lot so you can maintain a watchful eye on your bike.

Maps show Newport as a dense maze of streets, but at road level, directional signs are abundant and clear. From the Mainstay Inn, it's a quick and easy ride to the historic downtown center on Route 138A. Staying in the right lane on Route 138A (America's Cup Boulevard), turn right onto Thames Street—riding past the Armory Antiques Marketplace and many tempting restaurants—to bear right onto Wellington Avenue. Continue past King Park and to Harrison Avenue. Turn right onto Harrison Avenue. What looks confusing on a map is actually quite simple and the obvious route around the end of the island is clearly marked because it leads to Fort Adams.

Strategically located Fort Adams (401-841-0707; www.fortadams.org) is the largest coastal fortification in the country. Constructed from 1824 to 1857 and first garrisoned in 1841, it remained a part of the U.S. Army until 1953; the U.S. Navy still uses a portion of the property for housing. However, the historic fort was turned over to the State of Rhode Island in 1965 and is now opened to the public. Naturally it commands great scenic views of the East Passage into Narragansett Bay and Newport Harbor, but the spooky labyrinth of "listening" tunnels beneath the south wall offer a

Strategically located Fort Adams was first garrisoned in 1841, and remained a part of the U.S. Army until 1953.

unique, lesser-known opportunity for a self-guided tour (you need a flashlight, and waterproof boots are recommended). These grounds are where Newport's famous jazz and folk festivals take place and is the venue for the annual Fort Adams Car Show.

Having hosted the first auto show in 1899, one would naturally assume this to be a motor-friendly city, but the first jail sentence for speeding in a car was handed down in Newport in 1904. The offender was driving 15 mph. Since the posted speed limit hasn't increased much during the last hundred years, be careful. Continuing along Harrison and onto Ocean Avenue, you might be surprised to discover farm-like estates, with horses grazing in one pasture, while sheep and llamas roam across another field—all within the bounds of a city which has some of the most expensive residential real estate in the country!

Newport and Conanicut Island started attracting summer visitors in the 1830s, but the boom came during Reconstruction in the decades after the Civil War, when travel by railway and steamship made it easier for well-heeled families to escape the "noxious vapors" and heat of America's rapidly expanding cities. In a time of unbridled growth and invention, the rich got richer with industrialists and financiers—the so-called robber barons—lavishly spending their wealth entertaining during "the season" at their summer "cottages." It was Mark Twain and Charles Dudley Warner who, in 1873, satirically referred to this "golden" time as The Gilded Age—a refer-

The Breakers, the grandest of the Newport mansions, viewed from Cliff Walk.

The Preservation Society of Newport County

The Preservation Society of Newport County (407-847-1000; www. newportmansions.org) was formed in 1945 to purchase, restore, and maintain the colonial Georgian-style Hunter House (c. 1748–54). It has since expanded its holdings to include The Breakers, Chateau-sur-Mer, The Elms, Kingscote, Marble House, the Isaac Bell House, Rosecliff, and Chepstow. This non-profit society maintains these exceptional examples of American architecture as a public trust. Tickets to tour these Newport mansions can be purchased at the properties or the Newport Visitors Center. ■

ence to an extremely thin veneer of quality which masked something very base beneath the surface. The term stuck and has become associated with a carefree period of glamour and opulence epitomized by Newport society during the 1880s and '90s. Vast privately-owned palatial estates and mansions still exist in Newport, but many of the historic estates (www. newportmansions.org), such as The Breakers, The Elms, and Marble House, are now held in public trust by the Preservation Society of Newport County and are open to visitors for a fee. In many ways, The Gilded Age still exists in this summer resort city.

While the fame and focus on Newport's mansions tends to emphasize their opulence rather than their architecture, when money was no object, America's leading designers had the freedom to create monumental residences without the restrictions often imposed on plans for public buildings. Take, for example, the Marble House (c. 1892), designed by Richard Morris Hunt, who was credited with bringing the Beaux-Arts style to the United States, a form that incorporates Greek, Roman, and Renaissance architectural elements. This 48-room home cost 11 million dollars to build, seven million of which was spent on a half-million cubic feet of blazingly white Carrara marble shipped from Italy. Corinthian columns support the portico; the balustrade on the edge of the flat roof, as well as the tall French windows, were inspired by the palace at Versailles; and the fan-shaped windows above the French windows are of Georgian influence. By harmoniously combining these many elements, Hunt was able to reflect America's sense of finally having become the equal of Europe.

A slight detour down Victorian Avenue is required to catch a glimpse of the Italian Renaissance-inspired Breakers (Ochre Point Avenue) behind its imposing iron gates. Designed for a Vanderbilt by the same Richard Morris

Hunt, this 70-room "cottage" was modeled after a 16th-century Genoa palazzo. Considered to be the grandest of the Newport mansions, The Breakers was constructed by a team of the world's finest craftsmen and furnished by the leading interior decorators of the day—and it continues to impress modern visitors. The roofed central courtyard with a mezzanine supported by columns of polished marble can be overpowering from ground level, but much easier to take in from the second-floor balustrades. Bathrooms, bedrooms, and ballroom—every one is simply palatial. Even the mundane aspects—like the kitchen with its custom-built cast-iron coal-fired stoves and an astonishing array of copper pans and skillets hanging from racks above long preparation tables—are first class and of a magnitude not seen even in today's finest hotel resorts.

The Elms is another mansion that's open to the public. Designed after Chateau d'Asnières, a villa outside of Paris, it was completed in 1901 at a cost of 1.4 million dollars (at today's prices, the cost would be 110 million dollars). The grey stone exterior with classically-inspired sculpture positioned on the roof corners leads to an entrance portico with stairs flanked by Art-Deco-styled marble sphinxes upon which sit bronze cherubs—which is positively subdued in comparison to the opulence of the mansion's interior. The grand staircase with its black-streaked white marble support pillars and

Motor yachts come in various ego sizes.

intricate wrought-iron balustrade is the centerpiece of a palatial entry hall from which grand hallways of white marble lead to even more luxurious rooms. One can only imagine what this place looked like when it displayed the original owner's personal collections of Renaissance ceramics, French and Venetian paintings, and Oriental jades.

There are other mansions. Private ones. Immense homes situated behind 20-foot-high steel gates and screened by manicured forests and shrubbery for which no photos or descriptions are available. In fact, most of the mansions in this city are not part of the public trust and one can only wonder what treasures lie within them.

Many of Newport's palatial mansions are strictly private and come complete with imposing gates and very high fences.

Two natural objectives are important to locate in any city: motorcycle parking and public restrooms. The Newport County Visitors Center (23 America's Cup Ave.; 401-845-9123; www.gonewport.com) has public facilities and offers 30 minutes of free parking in the public garage (validation required). Although the signs on the gate clearly state NO MOTORCYCLES, the official word from the attendants is that if your motorcycle is heavy enough to activate the barrier gate, the signs don't apply to you. Go figure. Public parking is clearly marked around the city, but free motorcycle parking is not so obvious. Several spaces can be found at the Seamen's Church Institute at Bowen's Landing (next to the Newport Harbor Hotel) and, although not marked as such, the odd-shaped spaces at the end of metered parking along Thames Street—which is parallel to America's Cup Avenue—are reserved for motorcycles. Public restrooms also can be found at Ann Street Pier in the Armory Antiques Marketplace, Bowen's Wharf, the Harbormaster building, and the Gateway Center.

The best way to experience Newport is on foot. The harbor area from Bowen's Landing to Anne Street Pier is packed with tourist-oriented shops and eateries, one of the most intriguing being the antiques mall in the old armory building. Privately rented booths and display cabinets are filled with tantalizing gifts such as antique and vintage jewelry, porcelain, historical artifacts, and collectibles.

Newport is about boats; this harbor is filled with everything from kayaks to mega-yachts. The Newport Ship Yard and the public pier along the Goat Island Causeway is the place to see some astounding vessels. There are knife-thin, 100-plus-foot sloops with single masts seven stories high and cabin doors that look like submarine bulkheads. A twelve-meter racing yacht could be moored next to a teak masterpiece that hails from a home port halfway around the globe. Numerous cruises are offered aboard motor yachts, wooden schooners, the three-masted "tall ship" *Arabella*, a 1930s replica of a rum-runner's speedboat, and even the Jamestown & Newport Ferry.

Washington Square and Touro Street are part of the historic district. There are reputed to be more restored colonial buildings in Newport than any other city in the United States. The White Horse Tavern (c. 1673) is the oldest tavern in America and a number of homes in this part of town date to the late 1670s. The Great Friends Meeting House (c. 1699), Trinity Episcopal Church (c. 1726), and Touro Synagogue (c. 1759) stand as evidence of Rhode Island's unprecedented religious tolerance, which was embraced by early Quakers and Jews, who were persecuted in the remaining territories. The past and the present seem to co-exist naturally in the 19th-century cedar shake fire station with its ultra-modern second-floor addition of smoked glass at the rear of the building. However, there is one particular piece of architecture that just doesn't seem to fit.

The intended use of the Touro Tower has remained a mystery that still sparks controversy today.

The most enigmatic building in the state is the Newport Tower in Touro Park. Mentioned in 1677 in the last will and testament of the first governor of Rhode Island, the medieval Norse stone silo has numerous proven astronomical alignment points, and has no confirmed use during colonial America. Controversy raged even before Henry Wadsworth Longfellow and Oliver Wendell Holmes promoted the pro-Viking settlement theory in the mid-19th century. It has been traditionally described as the Old Mill, based on its resemblance to a 17th-century windmill in Chesterton, England, not outside the ken of the old governor, who was born in Somerset, but I will maintain that this tower never did duty as a mill—the vibration would have quickly destroyed the support pillars of this structure.

The International Tennis Hall of Fame (194 Bellevue Ave.; 401-849-4777; www.tennisfame.com) is located in the Newport Casino. The street-side facade of exclusive boutiques hides the spectacular

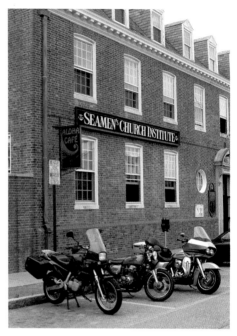

Parking for motorcycles is free at the Seamen's Church Institute.

Directional signs make finding your way around Newport easier than maps would suggest.

The 1,600-foot main span of the Claiborne Pell Bridge is 215 feet above the water and high enough to allow the passage of most ships into Newport Harbor, the entrance of which is marked by the Goat Island Lighthouse.

grass courts of the Hall of Fame Lawn Tennis Club where the first U.S. National Men's Tennis Championship (1881) and the first National Lawn Tennis Championship (1899) took place. The inner courtyard is formed by three sides of the cedar-shingled, green-roof casino joined by an arched veranda to enclose two beautiful grass tennis courts in a formal Victorian setting. The history of the game comes alive with exhibits of trophies from the earliest years up to and including the silver bowls for the current U.S. Open Doubles championships. Photos and endless loop videos of famous matches are positioned in alcoves and hallways along with memorabilia donated or on loan from the great names in the sport.

Newport has always been a city that liked events. Besides the first tennis championships, it also hosted the first U.S. Open [Golf] Championship (1895) and this is where polo was introduced to the U.S. in 1876. The first circus of our young country performed here in 1774 and the first jazz festival in the United States took place in 1954. Most people are familiar with the famous Newport Folk Festival as well as the America's Cup races that made this city synonymous with yachting.

Cliff Walk is the world-famous pedestrian path that follows the edge of

Easton Bay and through the backyards of exclusive properties such as The Breakers, Rosecliff, and Marble House. It runs for 3.5 miles, but a short stroll along the middle section to enjoy the panoramic views of the sea and glimpse the backs of palatial mansions is worth the effort.

By now you should be convinced that a single day in Newport is absolutely insufficient to take in what this city offers. When you are finally ready to depart, the final leg of this ride will consist of Route 138. For the price of the toll, you will be afforded the pleasure of riding over the Claiborne Pell Bridge between Jamestown Island and Newport and for the 11,248-foot crossing of the Eastern Passage of Narragansett Bay. This is almost two miles of bridge! Its height and location offer a sweeping panorama of the bay, but the views are better when riding east into Newport.

If you need a specific part for your bike, make a quick detour north to Razee Motorcycle Center in North Kingston (730 Tower Rd./US Rte 1; 401-295-8837; www.razeemotorcycle.com), an authorized dealer and service center for BMW, Ducati, Honda, Kawasaki, KTM, Moto Guzzi, Yamaha, and Kymco. It's a busy, sprawling place with the parts department located on the second floor. Once you've taken care of business, you can turn around and continue your journey south on US Route 1.

Most people heading to southern Connecticut from Newport would logically choose US Route 1 to Westerly, Rhode Island. Although, supplanted by I-95 as the main artery to Providence, the old divided US Route 1 still remains a busy road, especially in the summer when people are vacationing on Atlantic beaches from Narragansett to Westerly. This also is where most Rhode Island campgrounds are located. While the majority of these cater predominately to RV travelers, some have a small number of tent sites. An exception is Burlingame State Park and Campground (401-322-

The International Tennis Hall of Fame has grass courts, but also an amazing collection of tennis history on display. This is where the U.S. Open Doubles trophies reside and many others are on temporary loan.

Cliff Walk is the pedestrian path that follows the shore along Sheep Point Cove.

7994; www.reserveamerica.com). Located on US Route 1 just west of Charlestown, it has 365 trailer and 365 tent sites, but they're only open from mid-April to the end of October.

Although US Route 1 is generally thought to be the quickest way to reach coastal Connecticut, it doesn't offer a bit of shade and goes through

Side Trip to Conanicut Island

The Claiborne Pell Bridge deposits you onto Conanicut Island, as serene as its more famous neighbor, Newport, is sophisticated. If you go south on East Shore Road, rather than follow Route 138 across the island, you'll arrive in the village of Jamestown. Park in the lot at the harbor and have a cup of award-winning coffee and pastry at East Ferry Market & Deli out on the patio overlooking the bay.

Facing the water from your patio perch, take the road in front of you to the south, following the shoreline to Fort Wetherill State Park, once a shore artillery battery. Picnic tables and the usual day-tripper facilities are available from Memorial Day to Labor Day. The park itself, which remains open all year, is a favorite spot among scuba divers.

Exiting the park, take your first paved left, Hamilton Avenue, which is flanked by some pretty spectacular new homes. At the next intersection, go straight ahead; a small town beach will be on your left. On the right, just at the end of the isthmus, will be the entrance to Fort Getty State Park, a seaside campground on a small knoll, with a magnificent view overlooking the mouth of Narragansett Bay. Although it is usually full during camping season, it's worth a drive-through.

Bear left onto Beavertail Road just after the Fort Getty entrance to get to Beavertail State Park. The lighthouse is the third oldest in the country, built in 1749 after the Boston Light (1716) and the Brant Point Light on Nantucket (1746). The museum inside commemorates the lighthouses of Rhode Island and their keepers.

You can either retrace your trip back to Route 138 or take Southwest Avenue to North Main Street to the bridge. The latter route lets you check out the Jamestown Windmill, which is right beside the road just before you reach Route 138. It's interesting to see anytime, but you can learn how it works when the windmill itself is open to visitors on weekend afternoons during the summer.   ∎

the center of Westerly and past miles of retail development. Making a left turn onto Route 138 (Mooresfield Road) provides a shaded, more leisurely ride through Kingston back to Hope Valley. From there Route 138 continues mostly through forest and past rural residential homes to Voluntown, Connecticut, where it connects to Ride 27, or you could hop onto I-95 south for the fast track to Mystic, Connecticut.

Index